Traditional and Modern Arabic Baby Names

5,000 Authenticated Names for Boys and Girls

Ikram Hawramani

Table of Contents

Introduction

This book is the result of five years of research cataloguing and describing names in use by Muslims, both rare and common. Great care has been taken to ensure the correctness of the meanings provided; all meanings have been validated across various dictionaries and references, such as *Taj al-Lughah wa Sihaah al-Arabiyyah* by Isma'eel bin Hammad al-Jawhari (11th century CE), *Lisaan al-Arab* by Ibn Manzur (14th century), *al-Qamoos al-Muheet* by Fairuzabadi (15th century), and contemporary sources such as the *Loghatnameh* of Dehkhoda, *Qamoos al-Asmaa' al-Arabiyyah* by Shafeeq al-Arna'ut, *Asmaa' al-Banaat wa Ma'aanihaa* by Muhammad Ibraheem Saleem, *Qamoos al-Asmaa' al-Arabiyyah wal Mu'arrabah* by Dr. Hanaa Nasr al-Hatti, and the *Sultan Qaboos Encyclopedia of Arab Names* by a research team at Sultan Qaboos University in Muscat, Oman.

The spellings provided are not meant as perfect transliterations, they are simply the most common. Sometimes "aa" is used to indicate a long "a" (as in the English word "man"), but not always. The variants section can also help you get a better idea of the pronunciation of a name.

A question I often get is "what is the correct English spelling of this Arabic name?" The answer, of course, is that there are no official English spellings. Parents can choose any spelling they prefer or create their own. In this book I have provided common and simple spellings for the names, and more complex variations are sometimes provided in the variants section of the name.

Some sounds that cannot be expressed in English have been merged with their neighbors. For example, there are two types of "t" in Arabic, but in English both would be pronounced "t" without issue, therefore they are treated as the same sound.

Some peculiarities of Arabic are kept. For example, in Arabic "sh" is an independent letter, therefore the names starting with "sh" have their own section. The letters "gh" and "kh" are also kept, since it is possible to express them in English letters.

You will find that some letters seem to be missing, for example "O". The reason is that there is no difference between "O" and "U" in Arabic, therefore in this book we use the letter "U" to express all names starting with the O/U sound. You are free to use "O" in any name that starts with "U". The same is true for the letters "E" and "I".

Certain bilingual names are included where one part of the name is Arabic, such as *Golnisa*, which has a Persian part ("Gol", meaning "flower") and an Arabic part ("nisa", meaning "women", the full meaning being "flower among women", i.e. a superior woman).

It is always a good idea to make sure that the Arabic name you choose does not sound too similar to a funny or embarrasing word in your local language.

Some parents are interested in knowing whether a particular Arabic name is used in the Quran, for this reason if a name is used in the Quran, a note is provided under the name to mention this. Note that this does not mean that the name is used in the Quran as a person's name; for example the name *Aasal*, which means "evenings", is said to be mentioned in the Quran, since the word *Aasal* is used in three places in the Quran to meaning "evenings".

Some names can be used for both boys and girls. These names are provided under both the girls' and the boys' sections.

Ikram Hawramani

Arabic
Names for
Girls

A

Aabida
Devoted to God -
Worshiper
Variants: *Aabidah, Abeda, Abedah, Abida, Abidah*

Aabira
Crossing - Passing By -
Traveling
Variants: *Aabera, Aaberah, Aabirah, Abera, Aberah, Abira, Abirah*

Aadila
Excellent - Fair - Just -
Moderate - Virtuous
Variants: *Aadela, Aadelah, Aadilah, Adela, Adelah, Adila, Adilah*

Aafa
Forgiver - Pardoner
Variants: *Afa, Affa, Affah*

Aafaaq
Horizons
The name Aafaaq is
mentioned in the Quran.
Variants: *Aafaq, Afaaq, Afaq*

Aafira
One Who Waters a Plant
Variants: *Aafirah, Afera, Aferah, Afira, Afirah*

Aafiya
Good Health - Recovery

Aaiza
Replacement - Successor
Variants: *Aaidha, Aayzah, Aezah, Ayza, Ayzah*

Aakifah
Devoted Worshiper of
God
Variants: *Aakefa, Aakefah, Aakifa, Aakifah, Akefa, Akefah, Akifa, Akifah*

Aalam
World
Variants: *Alam*

Aalifa
Amiable - Friendly
Variants: *Aalifah, Alefa, Alefah, Alifa, Alifah*

Aamad
Ages - Eras - Periods of
Time
Variants: *Aamad, Amaad, Amad*

Aameen
Arabic for "Oh Allah,
accept our prayer".
Variants: *Aamin, Ameen*

Aamira
Full of Life - Prosperous
Variants: *Aamera, Aamerah, Amira, Amirah*

Aana
Hours of the Night -
Moments - Ocassions
Variants: *Aanaa, Ana*

Aaneseh
Eloquent - Virtuous

Aaqil
Discerning - Reasonable -
Sensible - Wise
Variants: *Aaqel, Aqel, Aqil*

Aaqilah
Discerning - Reasonable -
Sensible - Wise
Variants: *Aaqleah, Aqela, Aqelah, Aqila*

Aaraf
Heights
Variants: *Aaref, Aref, Arif*

Aaribah
Successful
Variants: *Aareba, Arebah, Ariba*

Aarifa
Knowledgeable - Wise
Variants: *Aarefa, Aarifah, Arefa, Arefah, Arifa, Arifah*

Aarisha
Builder - Maker
Variants: *Aaresha, Aarisha, Aarishah, Aresh, Arishah*

Aasal
Evenings
The name Aasal is
mentioned in the Quran.
Variants: *Aasaal, Asaal, Asal*

Aasira
Captivator - Warrior
Variants: *Aasera, Aaserah,*

Asera, Aserah, Asira, Asirah

Aatifah
Affection - Emotion - Feeling

Aatika
Generous - Pure
Variants: *Aatikah, Atika, Atikah*

Aatiq
Baby Pigeon - Free
Variants: *Aateq, Ateq, Atiq*

Aatiqa
Freed - Liberated
Aatiqa is an Arabic name for girls that means "free".
Variants: *Ateqa, Ateqah, Atiqah*

Aatirah
Fragrant

Aatiya
Bestower - Giver
Variants: *Aatiyah, Atia, Atiya*

Aayizah
Replacement - Restitution

Aayun
Eyes
The name Aayun is mentioned in the Quran.
Variants: *A'yun, Ayon*

Abaal
Rose - Wild Rose
Variants: *Abal*

Abaasa
Lionness
Variants: *Abaasah, Abasa, Abasah*

Aban
Clear - Eloquent - Lucid
Variants: *Abaan*

Abdaar
Full Moons - Moons
Plural of Badir.
Variants: *Abdar, Ebdaar*

Abdiya
Servant of God
Variants: *Abdeya, Abdiah, Abdiyah, Abdiyya, Abdiyyah*

Abeer
Perfume
Variants: *Abeir, Abir*

Abeira
Perfume - Saffron
Variants: *Abeera, Abeerah, Abira, Abirah*

Absaar
Insight - Intellect - Perception - Vision
The name Absaar is used in the Quran.
Variants: *Absar*

Aburah
Fragrance - Perfume

Abyah
Beautiful

Abyan
Clear - Distinct - Eloquent
Variants: *Abyen*

Adaan
Blissful - Happy
Variants: *Adan, Adanne*

Adalah
Fairness - Justice

Adan
Blissful - Happy
Variants: *Eden*

Adaniyyah
From the City of Aden

Adawiyah
Type of Plant
It is unclear what exactly this plant is, Arabic sources only say that it grows in the summer.
Variants: *Adaweyyah, Adawiyya, Adawiyyah*

Adeebah
Excellent - Good-mannered

Adeela
Excellent - Fair - Just - Moderate - Virtuous
Variants: *Adeelah, Adila, Adilah*

Adeen
Obedient - Righteou
Variants: *Adin, Azeen, Azin*

Adeena
Obedient - Righteou
Variants: *Adeenah, Adina, Adinah, Azeena, Azeenah, Azina, Azinah*

Adlaa
Fair - Just

Adlah
Fair - Just

Adlea
Fair - Just
Variants: *Adlia, Adliah, Adliyah, Adliyyah*

Adn
Eden - Place of
Everlasting Bliss
Adn is used in the Quran
in verse 18:31 and others.
Variants: *Edn*

Adnanah
Resident - Settler

Adniyyah
Inhabitant - Resident

Adyan
Creeds - Religions
Variants: *Adiaan, Adian, Adyaan*

Aeni
Pure - True
Variants: *Ainee, Ainy, Aynee, Ayni*

Afaf
Chaste - Modest -
Virtuous
Variants: *Afaaf, Affaf*

Afana
Modest - Virtuous
Variants: *Afaana, Afaanah, Afanah*

Afeen
Forgiver - Pardoner
Variants: *Afin*

Afeera
Gazelle
Modern-day variant of
Ufairah.
Variants: *Afeerah, Afira, Afirah*

Afifa
Chaste - Modest -
Righteous
Variants: *Afeefa, Afeefah, Afefa, Afefah, Afifah*

Afiyat
Health - Recovery
Turkish pronunciation of
Afiyah.
Variants: *Aafiyat, Afiat, Afyat*

Afkar
Ideas - Thoughts

Afnan
Spreading Branches of
Trees
The name Afnan is
mentioned in the Quran.
Variants: *Afnaan*

Afra
Maple
(Also used in Persian)
Variants: *Afraa*

Afraa
Blonde - Fair-skinned -
White

Afrah
Delight - Happiness
Variants: *Afraah, Efrah*

Afsah
Eloquent - Expressive -
Fluent
The name Afsah is
mentioned in the Quran.
Variants: *Efseh*

Aghla
Precious - Valuable
Variants: *Aghlaa*

Ahbab
Beloved Ones
Variants: *Ahbaab*

Ahd
Covenant - Promise
The name Ahd is
mentioned in the Quran.

Ahdaf
Goals - Objectives -
Targets

Ahdia
Faithful - Sincere - True
Variants: *Ahdeyah, Ahdiya, Ahdiyyah*

11

Aheedah
Ally - Confederate

Ahida
Caretaker - Promiser
Variants: *Aaheda,
Aahedah, Aahida, Aahidah,
Aheda, Ahedah, Ahidah*

Ahina
Ascetic - Firm -
Unshakable
Variants: *Aahinah, Ahena,
Ahenah, Ahina*

Ahlam
Dreams
The name Ahlaam is
mentioned in the Quran.
Variants: *Ahlaam*

Ahmaraan
Gold - Saffron
Variants: *Ahmaran*

Ahnaf
Upright - Worshiper of
God
Variants: *Ehnef*

Ahram
Pyramids
Variants: *Ahraam*

Ahyas
Brave
Variants: *Ahias*

Aida
Returner - Visitor
Variants: *Aidah, Ayda,
Aydah*

Aidan
Tall Palm Tree
Variants: *Aidaan, Aydan,
Eidan, Eydan*

Aidana
Tall Palm Tree
Variants: *Aidanah, Aydana*

Ain
Fountain - Spring
The name Ain is
mentioned in the Quran,
such as in verse 88:12.
Variants: *Aene, Aine, Ayn,
Ayne, Eiyn*

Aisha
Alive - Living-well -
Thriving
Variants: *Aaisha, Aaishah,
Aayesha, Aayeshah,
Aayisha, Aayishah, Aaysha,
Aayshah, Aishah, Ayesha,
Ayeshah, Ayisha, Ayishah,
Aysha, Ayshah*

Ajaar
Rewards
Variants: *Ajar*

Ajab
Amazement - Wonder
The name Ajab is
mentioned in the Quran.

Ajam
Date Seed - Foreign -
Persian

Ajaweed
Acts of Kindness -
Generosity

Ajeeb
Amazing - Wondorous
The name Ajeeb is
mentioned in the Quran.

Ajwa
Type of Date
Ajwa is a type of date (the
fruit of palm trees) that
grows in al-Madinah.
Variants: *Ajua, Ajuaa,
Ajwaa*

Akwan
Cosmos - Universes
Variants: *Akuaan, Akuan,
Akwaan*

Ala
Favors - Wonders
The name Ala is
mentioned in the Quran.
Variants: *Aala, Alaa*

Alamafruz
Enlightener of the World
(Also used in Persian)
Variants: *Alamafrooz*

Alamara
Beautifier of the World
Variants: *Alamaara*

Alaya
Glory - Greatness
Variants: *Alaaia, Alaaya,
Alaayaa, Alaia, Alayaa*

Aleefa
Amiable - Friendly - Kind
Variants: *Aleefah, Alifa,
Alifah*

Aleema
Intellectual -
Knowledgeable - Learned
Variants: *Aleemah, Alima,
Alimah*

Aleena
Gentleness - Softness
Variants: *Aleeina, Aleina,
Alena, Alenaa, Alinaa,
Alyena, Alyina*

Aliaa
Highest - Uppermost
Variants: *Alea, Alia, Alya,
Alyaa, Alyaa'*

Alima
Knowledgeable - Scholar
Variants: *Alimah*

Aliyah
Exalted - High Status -
Sublime and Superb
The name Alia is
mentioned in the Quran
in verse 69:22.

Aliyya
Exalted - Great - High -
Sublime
Variants: *Aleyya, Aliah,
Aliya, Aliyyah, Eliye*

Allamah
Extremely Wise -
Knowledgeable

Alnoor
Light
The name Alnoor is
mentioned in the Quran.
Variants: *Eleanor, Elinor,*

*Elinour, Elnoor, Elnour,
Elnur, Ileanor, Ilinor*

Altaaf
Gentleness - Kindness
Variants: *Altaf*

Aludra
Virgin
Variants: *Alodra, Aluza,
Aluzraa*

Alwan
Colors
The name Alwan is
mentioned in the Quran.
Variants: *Aluan*

Alyaanah
Great - High in Status

Amaal
Expectations - Hopes
Variants: *Aamaal, Aamal*

Amad
Age - Era - Period of Time

Amal
Expectation - Hope
The name *Amal* is
mentioned in the Quran.
Variants: *Amel, Amele,
Amell, Emal, Emel, Emele,
Emell, Emelle*

Amala
Hope - Wish
Variants: *Amalah*

Aman
Peace of Mind - Safety -

Security
Variants: *Amaan*

Amana
Devotion - Faith -
Guardianship

Amanaat
Amanat
The name Amanaat is
mentioned in the Quran.
Variants: *Amanat*

Amanah
Devotion - Guardianship -
Loyalty - Trust
The name Amanah is
mentioned in the Quran.
Variants: *Amaanah,
Amana*

Amanat
Devotion - Guardianship -
Trust
Turkish pronunciation of
Amanah. (Also used in
Persian, Turkish, Urdu)

Amanatullah
God's Consignment

Amani
Hope
The name Amani is
mentioned in the Quran
in verse 4:123.
Variants: *Amaani, Amanee,
Amany*

Amanullah
God's Peace - God's
Protection

Amara
Fleet - Tribe
Variants: *Amaara,*
Amaarah, Amarah

Amatul Aakhir
Servant of God

Amatul Aala
Servant of God

Amatul Afuw
Servant of God

Amatul Ahad
Servant of God

Amatul Akram
Servant of God

Amatul Aleem
Servant of God

Amatul Awwal
Servant of God

Amatul Azim
Servant of God

Amatul Aziz
Servant of God

Amatul Baatin
Servant of God

Amatul Baseer
Servant of God

Amatul Basit
Servant of God

Amatul Birr
Servant of God

Amatul Elah
Servant of God

Amatul Fattah
Servant of God

Amatul Ghaffar
Servant of God

Amatul Ghafoor
Servant of God

Amatul Ghani
Servant of God

Amatul Haafiz
Servant of God

Amatul Hadi
Servant of God

Amatul Hafeez
Servant of God

Amatul Hai
Servant of God

Amatul Hakam
Servant of God

Amatul Hakeem
Servant of God

Amatul Haleem
Servant of God

Amatul Hameed
Servant of God

Amatul Haq
Servant of God

Amatul Haseeb
Servant of God

Amatul Jabar
Servant of God

Amatul Jaleel
Servant of God

Amatul Jameel
Servant of God

Amatul Kabir
Servant of God

Amatul Kareem
Servant of God

Amatul Khabir
Servant of God

Amatul Khaliq
Servant of God

Amatul Khallaq
Servant of God

Amatul Latif
Servant of God

Amatul Maalik
Servant of God

Amatul Majeed
Servant of God

Amatul Maleek
Servant of God

Amatul Manaan
Servant of God

Amatul Mateen
Servant of God

Amatul Mawla
Servant of God

Amatul Mubeen
Servant of God

Amatul Muhaimin
Servant of God

Amatul Muheet
Servant of God

Amatul Mujeeb
Servant of God

Amatul Muqaddim
Servant of God

Amatul Muqit
Servant of God

Amatul Muqtadir
Servant of God
Variants: *Amatul Muqtader*

Amatul Musawwir
Servant of God
Variants: *Amatul Musawir*

Amatul Mutaal
Servant of God
Variants: *Amatul Mutal*

Amatul Mutaali
Servant of God
Variants: *Amatul Mutali*

Amatul Naseer
Servant of God
Variants: *Amatul Nasir*

Amatul Qadeer
Servant of God
Variants: *Amatul Qadir*

Amatul Qadir
Servant of God

Amatul Qahir
Servant of God
Variants: *Amatul Qaher*

Amatul Qareeb
Servant of God
Variants: *Amatul Qarib*

Amatul Qawee
Servant of God
Variants: *Amatul Qawi*

Amatul Qayyum
Servant of God
Variants: *Amatul Qayum*

Amatul Quddus
Servant of God
Variants: *Amatul Qudus*

Amatul Shaheed
Servant of God
Variants: *Amatul Shahid*

Amatul Shakoor
Servant of God
Variants: *Amatul Shakur*

Amatul Tawwab
Servant of God
Variants: *Amatul Tawab*

Amatul Wadud
Servant of God
Variants: *Amatul Wadood*

Amatul Wahaab
Servant of God
Variants: *Amatul Wahhab*

Amatul Wahid
Servant of God
Variants: *Amatul Waheed*

Amatul Waleei
Servant of God
Variants: *Amatul Wai*

Amatul Waris
Servant of God
Variants: *Amatul Waaris*

Amatullah
Servant of God
Variants: *Amat Ullah,*
Amatollah

Amatur Rab
Servant of God
Variants: *Amatul Rab*

Amatur Raheem
Servant of God
Variants: *Amatul Raheem*

Amatur Rahman
Servant of God
Variants: *Amatul Rahman*

Amatur Raqeeb
Servant of God
Variants: *Amatul Raqeeb*

Amatur Razzaq
Servant of God
Variants: *Amatul Razzaq*

Amatus Salam
Servant of God
Variants: *Amatul Salam*

Amatus Samad
Servant of God
Variants: *Amatul Samad*

Amatus Samee
Servant of God
Variants: *Amatul Samee*

Amatuz Zaahir
Servant of God
Variants: *Amatul Zahir*

Amber
Amber - Ambergris
(Also used in Persian)
Variants: *Ambar*

Ameena
Loyal - Trustworthy
Variants: *Ameeina,*
Ameeinah, Ameeineh,
Ameenah, Ameene,
Ameeneh, Ameeyna,
Ameeynah, Ameeyneh,
Ameina, Ameinah,
Ameineh, Ameyna,
Ameynah, Ameyne,
Amiena, Amienah, Amiene,
Amieneh, Amina, Aminah,
Amineh, Amiyna,
Amiynah, Amiyne,
Amiyneh, Amyna, Amynah,
Amyneh, Emeeyna,
Emeina, Emeinah, Emeine,
Emeineh, Emeynah,
Emeyneh, Emiena, Emina,

Eminah, Emine, Emineh,
Emyna, Emyne

Amial
Lighthouses
Variants: *Amyaal, Amyal*

Amila
Hoper - Striver - Worker
Variants: *Aamila, Aamilah,*
Amela, Amelah, Amilah

Amina
Safe
The name *Amina* is
mentioned in the Quran.
Variants: *Aamena,*
Aamenah, Aameneh,
Aamina, Aaminah,
Aamine, Aamineh, Amena,
Aminah, Amna, Amnah

Aminan
Calm - Unafraid
Variants: *Ameenan*

Aminat
Faithful Ones -
Trustworthy Ones
Variants: *Ameenaat*

Amira
Chief - Commander -
Leader - Ruler
Variants: *Amirah*

Amiraa
Chief - Leader
Variants: *Amira*

Amlaas
Plains - Steppes

Amlahan
Dew

Amlas
Delicate - Smooth - Soft

Amman
Citizen - Resident
Also name of the capital of
Jordan.
Variants: *Amaan, Aman*

Ammatun Naafe
Servant of God
Variants: *Amatul Nafi,*
Ammatunnafi

Ammuna
Faithful - Trustworthy
Variants: *Amoona,*
Amoonah, Amuna

Ammuni
Away From Harm - Safe
Variants: *Amuni*

Ammura
Beautiful - Captivating -
Lovable

Ammuri
Beautiful - Captivating -
Lovable

Amnan
Safe - Secure
Variants: *Amnaan*

Amnati
My Hope - My Wish
Variants: *Amnaty*

Amnian
Safe - Secure
Variants: *Amniyan*

Amras
Mountains
Variants: *Amraas*

Amsal
Best - Exemplary -
Optimal
The name Amsal is
mentioned in the Quran.
Variants: *Amthal*

Amyali
Ambitious - Desirous
Variants: *Amialy*

Anaa
Full Potential - Maturity
Variants: *Ana*

Anaat
Patience - Vritue
Variants: *Anat, Enaaat,*
Enat

Anan
Clouds
Variants: *Anaan*

Anar
Glowing - Radiant
Variants: *Anaar*

Anarat
Beauty - Clarity -
Radiance

Anasa
Comfort - Tranquility
Variants: *Anasah*

Anasat
Comfort - Tranquility
Turkish pronunciation of
Anasa.
Variants: *Anaasat*

Anasi
Consoler - Goo Friend
Variants: *Anasee*

Anasiya
Consoler - Good Friend
Variants: *Anasia,*
Anasiyyah

Anat
Calmness - Composure -
Forbearance - Poise
Variants: *Anatte*

Anaya
Care - Diligence -
Protection
Variants: *Anaaya,*
Anaayah, Anaia, Anaiah,
Anayah

Andaleeb
Nightingale
(Also used in Urdu)
Variants: *Andalib*

Andalus
Andalusia

Andalusi
From Andalusia
Variants: *Andaloosi*

Aneesa
Close Friend - Comforter
Variants: *Aneesah, Anesa,*

Anessa, Anisa, Anisah,
Anissa, Anissah

Anfa
Dignity - Self-respect
Variants: *Anfah*

Anfani
Dignified

Anfas
Breaths - Souls - Spirits
Variants: *Anfaas*

Anghum
Melodies - Tunes
Variants: *Anghom*

Anhar
Rivers
Variants: *Anhaar*

Anifa
Dignified
Variants: *Aneefah*

Aniq
Attractive - Elegant -
Graceful - Stylish
Variants: *Aneek, Aneeq,*
Aneiq, Anik

Aniqah
Elegant - Stylish
Variants: *Aneeqa, Aneeqah,*
Aniqa

Aniyah
Affectionate - Caring -
Consoler
Variants: *Aaniya, Aaniyah,*
Aneya, Aneyah

17

Aniza
Staff - Sword
Variants: *Aneeza, Aneezah, Anizah*

Anjam
Star
Variants: *Anjaam*

Anjud
Heights - Plateaus
Variants: *Anjod*

Anjum
Stars
Variants: *Anjom, Anjoum*

Anmar
Tigers
Variants: *Anmaar*

Ann
Occassion - Time
The name Ann is
mentioned in the Quran.
Variants: *Aan, Aann*

Anoud
Loved - Popular - Strong-
willed

Ansab
Better - Worthier

Ansam
Breezes
Variants: *Ansaam*

Ansharah
Cheer - Relaxation -
Relief
Non-standard

pronunciation of Inshirah.
Variants: *Ansharaah*

Antarah
Brave

Anum
God's Blessings - God's
Favors
The name Anum is
mentioned in the Quran.
Variants: *Anom, Anoum*

Anumullah
God's Blessings - God's
Favors

Anush
Beautiful - Handsome

Anwaar
Lights - Radiant
Variants: *Anwar*

Anwara
Glow - Light - Radiance
Variants: *Anuaara, Anwaarah*

Anzar
Eyesight - Vision
Variants: *Andhar*

Aqeelah
Discerning - Reasonable -
Sensible - Wise
Variants: *Aqeela, Aqila, Aqilah, Aquilleah*

Aqiba
Consequence - Result
The name Aqiba is
mentioned in the Quran.

Variants: *Aaqibah, Aqeba, Aqebah, Aqibah*

Aqidah
Creed - Faith - Tenet
Variants: *Aqeeda, Aqeedah, Aqida*

Aqiq
Agate
(Also used in Persian)
Variants: *Aqeeq*

Aqrab
Scorpion
Variants: *Akrab*

Aqsaa
Farthest
Name of the third holiest
site in Islam: Masjid al-
Aqsa (al-Aqsa Mosque) in
Palestine.
Variants: *Aksa, Aqsa*

Araa
Opinions - Perspectives
Variants: *Ara, Ara'*

Araarah
Greatness - Might -
Strength

Arar
Lent Lily - Wild Daffodil
A type of flower.

Arbab
Chiefs - Masters
The name Arbab is used in
the Quran.
Variants: *Arbaab*

Areebah
Intelligent - Wise
Variants: *Areiba, Areyba, Ariba, Aribah*

Areefa
Knowledgeable - Learned - Wise
Variants: *Areefah, Arifa, Arifah*

Areej
Fragrance
Variants: *Arij*

Areeqa
Deep-rooted - High-born - Noble
Variants: *Areeqah, Ariqa, Ariqah*

Areesha
Howdah
Variants: *Areeshah, Arisha, Arishah*

Arf
Fragrance - Scent

Arfa
Elevated - Exalted - Great
Variants: *Arfa', Arfaa*

Arfaana
Spiritual Knowledge - Wisdom
Non-standard variant of the name Irfana.
Variants: *Arfaanah, Arfana, Arfanah*

Arhaa
Calm - Serene
Variants: *Arhaa*

Arham
Compassionate - Kind - Merciful
The name Arham is mentioned in the Quran in verse 12:64.

Arinah
Lion's Den

Ariqaat
High-born - Noble

Aroob
Cheerful - Happy - One Who Loves Her Husband
Variants: *Aroub, Arub*

Arooba
Cheerful - Happy - One Who Loves Her Husband
Variants: *Aroobah, Aruba, Arubah*

Aroofa
Knowledgeable - Patient - Wise
Variants: *Aroofah, Arufa, Arufah*

Aroos
Beautiful - Bride
n
Variants: *Arous, Arus*

Aroosa
Beautiful - Bride
Variants: *Aroosah, Arusa, Arusah*

Arsh
Power - Throne
The name Arsh is mentioned in the Quran.

Arshan
Thrones
Variants: *Arshaan*

Arshi
Royal
Literally meaning "worthy of a throne".
Variants: *Arshee, Arshy*

Arubiyyah
Elouent - Fluent

Arwaa
Agile - Beautiful - Ibex
Variants: *Arwa*

Arz
Breadth - Mountain - Width

Asaalat
Greatness - Nobleness - Originality
Turkish pronunciation of Asalah.
Variants: *Asalat*

Asadah
Lionness
Variants: *Asadeh*

Asah
Correct - Healthy - Proper
Variants: *Aseh*

Asal
Honey
The name Asal is
mentioned in the Quran.
Variants: *Esel*

Asalah
Greatness - Nobleness -
Originality
Variants: *Asaala, Asaalah,
Asala*

Asali
Honey-like - Sweet
Variants: *Asalee, Asaly*

Asareer
Good Features of the Face
Variants: *Asarir*

Asbah
Beautiful
Variants: *Esbeh*

Asdaf
Seashells
Variants: *Asdaaf*

Aseel
Creative - Deep-rooted -
Evening Time - High-born
- Nighttime - Original
The name Aseel is
mentioned in the Quran.
Variants: *Asil, Assil*

Aseela
Creative - Deep-rooted -
High-born - Original
Variants: *Aseelah, Asila,
Asilah*

Asfa
Pure - Purest
Variants: *Asfaa*

Asfiya
Pure Ones
Variants: *Asfiaa, Asfiyaa*

Asfour
Bird
Variant of Arabic Osfur.
(Also used in Urdu)
Variants: *Asfoor, Asfur*

Asheeqa
Beloved - In Love
Variants: *Asheeqah,
Ashiqa, Ashiqah*

Ashiqah
In Love - Obsessed

Ashwaq
Longing - Yearning
Variants: *Ashuaq, Ashwaaq*

Asifah
Hurricane - Storm
The name Asifah is used
in the Quran.
Variants: *Aaasifah, Aasifa,
Asefa, Asefah*

Asima
Chaste - Guardian -
Protector - Virtuous
Variants: *Aasema,
Aasemah, Aasima, Asema,
Asemah, Asimah*

Asiya
Melancholic - Pensive -

Wishful
Variants: *Asya*

Asiyeh
Melancholic - Wistful
(Also used in Persian)
Variants: *Aseya, Aseyah,
Asiah, Asiya, Asiyah*

Asma
Elevated - Exalted - Great
- High
Variants: *Asma', Asmaa,
Asmaa'*

Asmar
Brown - Tan
Describes a person whose
skin color is not too dark
and not too light.

Asna
Brilliant - Radiant
Variants: *Asnaa, Esna,
Esnaa*

Asrar
Mysteries - Secrets
Variants: *Asraar*

Atafah
Affectionate -
Compassionate

Ataya
Gifts - Gifts from God
Variants: *Ataaya, Atayaa*

Atayat
Gifts

Ateebah
Gentle - Soft

Ateef
Affectionate -
Compassionate

Ateefah
Affectionate -
Compassionate

Ateeqa
Ancient - Freed -
Liberated - Noble
Variants: Ateeqah, Atiqa,
Atiqah

Ateera
Fragrant
Variants: Ateerah, Atera,
Atira, Atiraa, Atirah

Atefeh
Affection - Emotion -
Instinct
Persian variant of Atifa.

Atfah
Affection - Compassion

Atfat
Affection - Compassion

Atheel
Deep-rooted - High-born
- Noble
Variants: Aseel, Asil

Atifa
Affection - Emotion -
Instinct
Variants: Atefa Atefah,
Atifah

Atiyaa
Gift

Atiyya
Gift - Gift from God
Variants: Atea, Ateya,
Ateyya, Ateyyah, Atia,
Atiah, Atiyah, Atiyyah,
Atya, Etiye, Etiyye

Atiyyaat
Gifts

Atiyyatullah
Gift from God

Atqaa
Good - Honorable -
Virtuous

Attarah
Perfume-maker

Attawah
Generous - Philanthropist

Atubah
Delicate - Gentle - Soft

Atyaaf
Images in the Mind -
Thoughts
Variants: Atiaf

Auraq
Dust-colored - Sand-
colored
Variants: Awraaq

Ausa
Gift - Help - Support
Variants: Awsa

Ausaq
Loads
Variants: Authaq, Awthaq

Awafita
Shepherdesses
Variants: Awafetah,
Awafitah

Awaidia
Consoler - Visitor of the
Sick
Variants: Awayidiyyah

Awaisha
Alive - Prospering

Awaiza
Consoler

Awamila
Active - Industrious
Variants: Awamilah

Awamira
Long-lived

Awarif
Intelligent - Wise

Awatif
Emotions - Instincts -
Passions
Variants: Awaatef,
Awaatif, Awatef

Awayeda
Guide - Visitor of the Sick
Variants: Awayidah

Awb
Repentance
Variants: Aub

Awbi
Repentant
Variants: Awby

21

Awbia
Repentant
Variants: *Awbiyyah*

Awdaq
Friendly – Genial –
Intimate
Variants: *Audaq*

Awdiya
Valleys
Variants: *Audia*

Awfa
Faithful – True
The name Awfa is
mentioned in the Quran.
Variants: *Aufa, Awfaa*

Awisa
Beautiful – Dimpled

Awja
Pinnacle – Top
Variants: *Auja, Awjah*

Awla
Worthier
Variants: *Aulaa*

Awlya
Close Friends –
Supporters
Variants: *Auliya*

Awqa
Guarding – Protective
Variants: *Auqaa*

Awsal
Becoming Closer to God
Variants: *Ausaal*

Awsam
Badges of Honor
Variants: *Awsaam*

Awsima
Badges of Honor
Variants: *Ausima,
Awsimah*

Awwalan
Advanced Ones – First
Ones
Variants: *Awalaan*

Awwazah
Restitutioner

Ayaat
Proofs – Signs – Verses of
Scripture
The name Ayaat is
mentioned in the Quran.
Variants: *Aayaat, Aayat,
Ayat*

Ayah
Proofs – Signs – Verses of
Scripture
The name Ayah is
mentioned in the Quran.
Variants: *Aaya, Aayah, Aya*

Ayamin
Blessed Ones – Fortunate
Ones
Variants: *Ayaamin,
Ayamen*

Ayan
Era – Time
The name Ayan is
mentioned in the Quran
in verse 51:12.
Variants: *Ayaan, Ayyan*

Ayana
Beautiful – Perceptive
Literally means "one who
has large beautiful eyes".
Variants: *Ayaana,
Ayaanah, Ayanah,
Ayyanah*

Ayasha
Alive – Prosperous
Variants: *Ayyashah*

Ayat
Proof – Sign of God's
Greatness – Verse of the
Quran
Ayat is the Turkish
pronunciation of Ayah.
Variants: *Ayet*

Ayd
Power – Strength
Variants: *Aid, Eyd*

Aydania
Slender – Tall
Variants: *Aidaniyyah,
Aydaniyyah*

Aydi
Hands – Power – Strength
The name Aydi is
mentioned in the Quran.
Variants: *Aidi, Aidy, Aydee*

Ayeh
Proof of God's Greatness
– Verse of the Quran
Ayeh is the Persian
variant of the Arabic girl
name Ayah
Variants: *Aayeh*

Ayna
Beautiful-eyed
Variants: *Aina, Ainaa, Aynaa, Eina*

Aynoor
Moonlight
(Also used in Turkish)
Variants: *Ainoor, Ainur, Aynur*

Ayoosh
Alive - Long-lived
Variants: *Ayush, Ayyoosh, Ayyush*

Ayse
Alive - Prosperous
Ayse, also written as Ayşe, is the Turkish variant of the Arabic girl name Aisha.
Variants: *Ayşe*

Ayusha
Alive - Prosperous

Ayyam
Days
Variants: *Aiam, Ayaam*

Azal
Eternity - Perpetuity
(Also used in Persian)

Azalia
Eternal - Perpertual
Variants: *Azaalia, Azalea, Azalea, Azaleah, Azaliaa, Azaliah, Azaliya, Azaliyah, Azaliyya, Azaliyyah*

Azalia
Dahlia

Azari
Maidens - Virgins
(Also used in Persian)

Azayiz
Mighty - Powerful

Azbah
Fresh Water

Azeebah
Fresh Water

Azeema
Determined - Resolved
Variants: *Azeemah, Azimah*

Azila
Guardian - Protector
Variants: *Aazelah, Aazila, Aazilah, Azela*

Aziza
Beloved - Dear - Exalted - Great - Noble
Variants: *Azeeza, Azeezah, Azizah*

Azmia
Brave - Determined - Resolute
Variants: *Azmeah, Azmeea, Azmeeah, Azmeya, Azmiah, Azmiya, Azmiyah*

Azra
Virgin
Variants: *Adhra, Adra, Adraa, Azraa, Ezra*

Azrah
Help - Support

Azyan
Adornments - Decorations - Virtues
Variants: *Azian*

Azza
Gazelle - Young Gazelle
Variants: *Aza, Azah, Azzah*

Azzaa
Gazelle

Azzat
Gazelle
Turkish pronunciation of Azzah. (Also used in Turkish)

B

Baan
Slender - Tall

Baanah
Slender - Tall
Variants: *Bana*

Baaqa
Bouquet

Badaa
Energy - Goal - Strength

Badawiya
Bedouin

Badaya
Beginnings - Genesis

Badeea
Creative - Innovative

Badeeda
Example - Sample -
Specimen

Badeela
Replacement

Badhaa
Initiation - Start

Badiha
Creative - Intuitive -
Witty
Variants: *Badeeha,
Badeehah, Badihah*

Badiha
Improvisation - Instinct -
Intuition

Badir
Full Moon - Moon
Variants: *Baader, Baadir,
Bader*

Badira
Full Moon - Moon
Variants: *Baadera,
Baaderah, Baadira,
Baadirah, Badera,
Baderah, Badirah*

Badra
Ahead - Early - Quick
Variants: *Baadra*

Badra
Early - On Time

Badrah
Full Moon
Variants: *Badra*

Badran
Beautiful - Radiant
Literally "like the full
moon".

Badri
Autumn Rain - Fullness of
the Moon
In Islamic history this
word means "one who
took part in the Battle of
Badr".
Variants: *Badry*

Badriya
Beautiful - Moon-like
Literally "like the full
moon".
Variants: *Badriah,
Badriyah, Badriyyah*

Baduah
Creative - Innovative

Baghisha
Light Rain

Bahayah
Beauty - Radiance

Baheeja
Beautiful - Radiant
Variants: *Baheeja,
Baheejah, Baheja, Bahija,
Bahijah*

Baheela
Beautiful

Baheenah
Beautiful

Baheerah
Beautiful - Radiant -
Talented

Bahira
Brilliant - Lucid -
Renowned
Variants: *Baahera,
Baahira, Baahirah, Bahera,
Bahirah*

Bahiri
Brilliant - Renowned

Bahiriya
Brilliant - Renowned

Bahisa
Researcher - Seeker

Bahiyyah
Beautiful - Radiant
Variants: *Bahia, Bahiah,*
Bahiya, Bahiyah, Bahiyya

Bahr
Ocean - Sea
The name Bahr is
mentioned in the Quran.

Bahraa
Brilliant - Lucid -
Renowned
Variants: *Bahra*

Bakheeta
Fortunate - Lucky

Bakhta
Good Fortunate - Luck

Bakhtia
Fortunate - Lucky

Bakira
Virgin
Variants: *Bakirah*

Balaghah
Eloquence

Baleegha
Eloquent - Far-reaching
Variants: *Baleeghah,*
Balighah

Baljah
First Light of Dawn

Balooja
Radiant

Balqees
Variant of Bilqees.

Banan
Fingertips
The name Banan is
mentioned in the Quran.
Variants: *Banaan*

Baqaa
Eternity - Perpetuity
Variants: *Baqa*

Baqat
Bouquet
Variants: *Baqaat*

Baqiya
Enduring - Everlasting
The name Baqiya is
mentioned in the Quran.
Variants: *Baqia, Baqiah,*
Baqiyah

Baraa
Blameless - Healed -
Innocent
The name
Baraa mentioned in the
Quran.
Variants: *Bara*

Baraaem
Fresh - Innocent -
Unopened Flower Bud -
Young
Variants: *Bara'im*

Baraha
Fair-skinned

Baraka
Blessings
Variants: *Baraca, Barakah,*
Barakeh, Barekah, Bereka,
Berekah, Bereke

Barayek
Blessed

Bareea
Blameless - Innocent
Variants: *Baree'a, Bareeah,*
Bareeia, Bareeya,
Bareeyah, Bareya, Baria

Barhamah
Flower Bud

Barikaa
Persevering - Striving

Barikah
Continuous Rain - Striver
Variants: *Bareka*

Bariyya
The Creation
Variants: *Bareeya,*
Bareeyah, Bariya,
Bariyyah

Barizah
Prominent - Visible
The name Barizah is
mentioned in the Quran.
Variants: *Barizeh*

Barizia
Prominent - Visible
Variants: *Bariziyyah*

Barjaa
Beautiful-eyed
Variants: *Barja*

Barjees
Planet Jupiter
Urdu variant of Birjis.
(Also used in Urdu)
Variants: *Barjis*

Barqah
Flash of Light - Flash of
Lightning

Basaair
Clear Proofs - Clear Signs
The name Basaair is
mentioned in the Quran.
Variants: *Basaaer, Basaer*

Basalah
Boldness - Bravery

Basama
Happy - Smiling
Variants: *Basaama,*
Basamah

Baseemaa
Cheerful - Smiling

Baseemah
Cheerful - Smiling

Baseera
Insight - Proof - Wisdom
The name Baseera is
mentioned in the Quran.
Variants: *Baseerah, Basira*

Bashara
Good News - Good
Tidings

Variants: *Bashaara,*
Bashaarah, Basharah

Basheera
Bringer of Good News -
Bringer of Good Tidings
Variants: *Basheerah,*
Bashira, Bashirah

Basheesha
Cheerful - Optimistic

Bashrah
Good Tidings

Bashurah
Cheerful - Glad -
Optimistic

Bashush
Cheerful - Optimistic
Variants: *Bashoosh*

Bashusha
Cheerful - Happy

Basila
Brave
Variants: *Basela, Baselah,*
Basilah

Basima
Happy - Smiling
Variants: *Baasimah,*
Basema, Basemah,
Basimah

Basimia
Happy - Smiling
Variants: *Basmiyyah*

Basiqa
Lofty - Outstanding -

Superior - Tall
Variants: *Baaseqa,*
Baasiqa, Baasiqah, Baseqa,
Baseqah, Basiqah

Basiraa
Perceptive
Variants: *Baseeraa*

Basita
Generous - Gracious

Basma
Cheerful - Happy -
Smiling
Variants: *Baasma*

Basmaa
Cheerful - Smiling

Basmat
Smile
Turkish pronunciation of
Basmah.
Variants: *Besmet*

Basmin
Cheerful Ones - Happy
Ones - Smiling Ones
Variants: *Basmeen*

Basoomah
Cheerful - Smiling

Bathna
Beautiful - Delicate
Variants: *Basna, Basnah,*
Bathnah

Batia
Slender - Tall

Batlaa
Resolute - Resolved
Variants: *Batla*

Batlah
Independent

Batool
Ascetic - Virgin -
Virtuous
Variants: *Batol, Batul*

Batula
Ascetic - Virgin
Variants: *Batoola, Batoolah*

Bawasim
Cheerful - Smiling

Bayan
Declaration - Elucidation
- Exposition - Illustration
Variants: *Baian, Bayaan*

Baydaa
Great Desert
Name of a place between
Mecca and Medina.

Bayyina
Clear Proof - Clear Sign
The name Bayyina is
mentioned in the Quran.
Variants: *Bayena,
Bayenah, Bayina, Bayinah,
Bayyena, Bayyenah,
Bayyinah*

Bayyinat
Clear Proofs - Clear Signs
The name Bayyinat is
mentioned in the Quran.
Variants: *Bainaat,*

*Bayenaat, Bayinaat,
Bayyinaat*

Bayzaa
Moonlit Night - Pure -
White
The name Bayzaa is
mentioned in the Quran.
Variants: *Baiza, Baizaa*

Baza
Northern Goshawk
A type of bird of prey.
Variants: *Bazah*

Bazigha
Radiant - Shining
The name Bazigha is
mentioned in the Quran.
Variants: *Bazegha,
Bazighah*

Bazija
Adorner - Beautifier
Variants: *Bazeja, Bazijah*

Bazira
Sower
One who plants seeds.
Variants: *Baazirah, Bazera*

Baziriya
Sower of Seeds

Besharat
Good News - Good
Tidings
Turkish pronunciation of
Basharah.
Variants: *Beshaarat,
Bisharat*

Bidar
Earliness - Punctuality

Bidayah
Beginning - Genesis -
Inception

Bidayat
Beginning - Genesis -
Inception
Turkish pronunciation of
Bidayah.

Billah
Provision

Bilqees
Arabic name for the
Queen of Sheba. The
meaning of the name is
not known.

Birjees
Planet Jupiter

Birjis
Planet Jupiter
Variants: *Berjees, Berjis,
Birjees*

Bisharah
Good Tidings

Bishra
Good Tidings

Bishry
Cheerful - Glad -
Optimistic

Bizrah
Seed

Bokhur
Incense

Boshry
Gladness - Happiness

Budaida
Example - Sample -
Specimen

Budaira
Full Moon

Buddah
Fortunte - Share

Budur
Full Moons
Variants: *Bodoor*

Buduriya
Beautiful - Radiant
Literally "like the full
moon".

Buhairah
Lake
Variants: *Bohaira,*
Buhayra

Buhur
Oceans - Seas
Variants: *Bohoor, Buhoor*

Bujud
Residence - Stay
Variants: *Bojud*

Bukrah
Dawn
The name Bukrah is
mentioned in the Quran.

Bulainah
Little Pigeon

Bulbul
Nightingale
Variants: *Bolbol*

Bullah
Beauty of Youth

Bulooj
Radiance

Buraikaat
Blessings

Burhanah
Clue - Demonstration -
Proof

Busain
Beautiful - Delicate -
Tender

Busaina
Beautiful - Delicate
Variants: *Busainah,*
Busaynah, Buthaina,
Buthainah

Bushra
Glad Tidings - Good
Tidings
The name Bushra is
mentioned in the Quran.
Variants: *Boshra, Bushraa*

Busraq
Yellow Sapphire
Variants: *Busraaq*

Butaila
Devoted to God - Pious -
Virtuous

Buthainaa
Beautiful - Delicate - Soft
Variants: *Busainaa*

Buzur
Seeds

29

D

Daaemiyyah
Constant - Perpetual

Dafqah
Burst - Gush - Surge

Dahiah
Intelligent - Wise

Dahiyyah
Intelligent - Wise

Dalia
Dahlia
(Also used in Kurdish, Persian)
Variants: *Daliaa, Dalya*

Dalilah
Guide - Leader

Dalkah
Sunset

Dalmaa
Extremely Dakr

Dalmah
Darkness

Dalu
Well Bucket
The name Dalu is mentioned in the Quran.

Dalwah
Well Bucket

Damaa
Ocean - Sea

Variants: *Da'maa, Daama, Dama*

Dania
Close - Near
The name Dania is mentioned in the Quran.
Variants: *Daaneya, Daaneyah, Daania, Daaniah, Daaniya, Daaniyah, Daniah, Daniya, Daniyah*

Dariya
Good-mannered - Intelligent - Lady-like - Perceptive
Variants: *Daaria, Daariyah, Darea, Daria, Dariyah*

Daulah
Power - State
Variants: *Daula, Dawla, Dawlah*

Daulat
Power - State
Turkish pronunciation of Daulah.
Variants: *Dawlat*

Daumaa
Ocean - Sea
Variants: *Dauma, Dawma*

Dawmah
Hypaene thebaica
A type of palm tree.

Dawmat
Hypaene thebaica
A type of palm tree.

Dawub
Conscientious - Diligent
Variants: *Da'ub, Daoob, Daub, Dawood*

Dibaaj
Silk Cloth
A type of silk cloth.

Dilalah
Guidance - Instruction

Dimah
Silent Rain

Dinar
Gold Coin
The name Dinar is mentioned in the Quran.
Variants: *Deenar*

Dinarah
Gold Coin

Diyanat
Creed - Religion

Dordaneh
Pearl - Precious
Variants: *Dordana, Dordanah*

Doreen
Pearl-like
Variants: *Dorrin, Durin, Durrin*

Dornaz
Pearl-like
Variants: *Durnaz*

Dorsa
Pearl-like
Variants: *Dursa*

Dua
Call - Prayer -
Supplication
The name Dua is
mentioned in the Quran.
Variants: *Doa, Doaa, Doua,*
Douaa, Dowa, Dowaa,
Du`a, Du`aa', Duaa, Duwa,
Duwaa

Duhat
Intelligent - Sensible

Dunaa
Worlds

Dunya
Worldly Life
The name Dunya is
mentioned in the Quran.
Variants: *Donyaa, Dunya,*
Dunyaa

Durar
Pearls
Variants: *Dorar*

Duriya
Brilliant - Dazzling -
Radiant
Variants: *Duriyah,*
Duriyya, Durriyya,
Durriyyah

Durrah
Large Pearl

Duryab
Finder of Pearls
Variants: *Doryab, Duryaab*

E

Eeda
Commitment -
Consignment
Variants: *Idaa'*

Eesha
Life - Way of Life
The name Eesha is
mentioned in the Quran
in verse 69:21.
Variants: *Eisha, Esha,
Eysha, Isha*

Eezah
Clarification - Elucidation
Variants: *Izaah*

Efah
Chastity - Modesty -
Virtue
Variants: *Efa, Effa, Effah,
Ifah, Iffa, Iffah*

Eftikhar
Beauty - Magnificence -
Stateliness
Variants: *Iftikhar*

Ehsaneh
Doer of Good Deeds -
Virtuous
(Also used in Persian)
Variants: *Ehsana, Ihsaneh*

Eifa
Faithfulness - Loyalty
Variants: *Eefaa, Ifaa*

Eihaa
Inspiration - Non-verbal

Communication
Variants: *Ihaa*

Eiham
Fantasy - Illusion
Variants: *Eyham, Iham*

Eima
Gesture - Insignia - Mark
Variants: *Eema, Imaa*

Einas
Comfort - Consolation -
Peace of Mind
Variants: *Eenas*

Eira
Kindling - Starting a Fire
Variants: *Eera, Eiraa,
Eyra, Ira*

Eithar
Love - Preferring Another
Person to Yourself
Variants: *Isaar, Isar*

Eiwa
Guardianship - Protection
Variants: *Eewaa, Eiwaa,
Eywa, Eywaa, Iwa, Iwaa,
Iywa*

Elaf
Safety - Security Promise
The name Elaf is used in
the Quran.
Variants: *Elaaf, Ilaaf, Ilaf*

Eshaal
Excitation - Kindling
Variants: *Eshal, Ish'al,
Ishaal, Ishal*

Etemad
Reliance - Trust
Variants: *I'timad, Itimad*

Etimad
Dependence - Reliance
Variants: *Ettimad, Itimad*

F

Faahima
Intelligent -
Understanding
Variants: *Fahema,
Fahemah, Fahimah*

Faaria
Long-haired - Slim - Tall
Variants: *Faari'ah,
Faariah, Fari'a, Fariah,
Fariyah*

Faariqah
Differentiator - Judge

Fadia
Heroic - Self-sacrificing
Variants: *Fadiah, Fadiya,
Fadiyah*

Fadwaa
Heroism - Self-sacrifice
Variants: *Faduaa, Fadwa*

Fadwah
Heroism - Self-sacrifice
Variants: *Fadua, Faduah,
Fadwa*

Faghira
Hercules' Club
A type of plant.
Variants: *Faghirah*

Fahadah
Leopard-trainer

Fahama
Intelligent -

Understanding
Variants: *Fahhama*

Fahdah
Leopard

Faheema
Intelligent - Keen -
Perceptive -
Understanding
Variants: *Faheemah,
Fahema, Fahemah,
Fahima, Fahimah, Fehime*

Fahimat
Comprehending -
Intelligent

Fahisa
Investigator - Tester
Variants: *Fahesa, Fahesah,
Fahisah*

Fahmat
Comprehension -
Understanding

Faiha
Vast Landscape - Vista
Variants: *Faihaa, Fayhaa*

Faihah
Scenic View

Faiqa
Excellent - Extraordinary
- Superb
Variants: *Faaeqa, Faaiqah,
Faeqa, Faiqah, Fayeka*

Fairuz
Successful - Victor
(Also used in Kurdish,

Persian, Urdu)
Variants: *Fairooz, Fayrooz,
Fayruz*

Fairuza
Turquoise
From Persian Firuzeh.
Variants: *Fairooza,
Fairoozah, Fairuzah,
Feeroza, Firoza*

Faitahah
Right Guidance

Faiza
Successful - Winner
Variants: *Faaeza, Faaezah,
Faaiza, Faaizah, Faeza,
Faezah, Faizah, Fayeza,
Fayezah, Fayiza, Fayizah*

Faizee
Abundance - Gracious -
Virtuous
Variants: *Faidhi, Faizy*

Faizunnisa
Victor - Winner
Literally meaning "winner
among women".

Fajr
Dawn - Daybreak
The name Fajr is
mentioned in the Quran.

Fakhira
High Quality - Luxurious
Variants: *Faakhira,
Fakhera, Fakhirah*

Fakhr
Glory - Honor - Pride
Variants: *Fekhr*

Fakhri
Cause for Pride - Glorious
Variants: *Fakhry*

Fakhrjahan
Pride of the World

Fakiha
Fruit
The name Fakiha is
mentioned in the Quran.
Variants: *Fakeha, Fakehah, Fakihah*

Falak
Cosmos - Orbit - Ship -
Space
The name Falak is used in
the Quran.
Variants: *Felek*

Falak Ara
Beautifier of the World
Variants: *Falakara*

Falaq
Dawn - Daybreak
The name Falaq is used in
the Quran.

Faleehah
Successful

Falih
Prosperous - Successful
Variants: *Faaleh, Faalih, Faleh*

Faliha
Prosperous - Successful
Variants: *Faaliha, Faalihah, Falehah, Falihah*

Fannana
Artist
Variants: *Fannanah*

Faqeeha
Expert - Knowledgeable -
Learned - Scholar
Variants: *Faqeehah, Faqiha, Faqihah*

Faraaid
Independent-minded -
Unique

Farah
Cheer - Happiness - Joy

Farahdokht
Happy

Farahnaz
Beautiful - Happy
(Also used in Persian)

Farahnoush
Eternal Happiness
Variants: *Farahnush*

Farahrouz
Blessed - Fortunate
Variants: *Faharooz*

Farahzad
Bringer of Happiness

Farashah
Butterfly

Fardan
Unique
Variants: *Fardaan*

Fardanah
Intelligent - Unique -
Wise

Fareea
Long-haired - Slim - Tall
Fareea is the name of a
number of Sahabiyaat.
Variants: *Faree'ah, Fareeah, Fareeyah*

Fareeda
Matchless - Unique
Variants: *Fareedah, Farida, Faridah*

Fareeha
Fareehah - Fareha -
Farehah - Fariha - Farihah

Farha
Happiness - Happy
Occasion
Variants: *Farhah*

Farhaa
Beautiful

Farhana
Happy - Joyful
Variants: *Farhanah*

Farhatah
Happiness - Joy

Farheen
Happy - Joyous
(Also used in Urdu)
Variants: *Farhin*

Faridaa
Unique

(Also used in Persian)
Variants: *Fareedaa*

Farihat
Happy

Farradah
Independent-minded -
Jeweler - Original

Farrahah
Happy

Farrajah
Happy

Farwa
Crown - Wealth
Variants: *Farua, Faruah,*
Farwah

Fatat
Young Man

Fateem
Weaned Off Breast Milk

Fateemah
Weaned Off Breast Milk

Fateemat
Weaned Off Breast Milk

Fathiyyah
Conqueror - Guide

Fatihah
Conqueror - Initiator

Fatima
Weaned Off Breast Milk
Name of the daughter of
Prophet Muhammad

PBUH.
Variants: *Fatema,*
Fatemah, Fatimah

Fatin
Intelligent - Perceptive
Variants: *Faatin, Faten*

Fatina
Intelligent - Perceptive
Variants: *Faatina, Fatena,*
Fatenah, Fatinah

Fatiriyyah
Gentle - Relaxed - Soft -
Tranquil

Fatoom
Weaned Off Breast Milk

Fattahah
Conqueror - Victor

Fattuhah
Conquest - Guidance

Fattumah
Weaned Off Breast Milk

Fauz
Victory - Win
The name Fauz is
mentioned in the Quran.
Variants: *Fawz, Fouz, Fowz*

Fawwazaa
Successful - Winner

Fawzah
Success - Win

Fawziyyaa
Successful - Winner

Fawziyyah
Successful - Winner

Fayyah
Repentance

Fazar
Leopard

Fazeelah
Excellence - Merit -
Virtue

Fazeelat
Excellence - Merit -
Virtue

Fazila
Excellent - Generous -
Praiseworth
Variants: *Faazila, Fadhila,*
Fadhilah, Fazela, Fazelah

Fida
Bail - Bailout
Variants: *Feda, Fidaa*

Fikr
Concept - Intellect -
Thought

Fikraat
Concepts - Ideas -
Thoughts

Fikrat
Concept - Idea -
Thoughts
Turkish pronunciation of
Fikrah.

Fikri
Conceptual - Perceptive - Thoughtful

Fikriyaa
Conceptual - Perceptive - Thoughtful

Fikriyyah
Intelligent - Thoughtful

Firtan
Cool Fresh Water

Firzah
Rare - Unique

Fitrah
Innate Nature - Instinct - Natural Disposition
The name Fitrah is mentioned in the Quran.

Fizzah
Silver
The name Fizzah is mentioned in the Quran.

Fizzi
Silvery

Fizziyah
Silvery

Fuadah
Heart - Spirit

Fuhaidaa
Little Leopard

Fuhaidah
Little Leopard

Fukairaa
Intelligent - Thoughtful

Fulailah
Jasmine

Fullah
Jasmine

Furaihaat
Happy

Furaihah
Happy

Furaihat
Happy

Furat
Cool Fresh Water
The name Furat is mentioned in the Quran.

Furjah
Relief - Rescue

Fursah
Chance - Opportunity

Fursat
Opportunity - Right Time
(Also used in Turkish)

Futaihah
Beginning - Conquest - Guidance

Futaimah
Weaned Off Breast Milk

Fuzailah
Excellence - Merit - Virtue

Gh

Ghaaniyah
Beautiful

Ghadah
Gentle - Soft

Ghaddaa
Early Riser

Ghadinah
Gentle - Soft

Ghadiya
Early Morning Rain - Early Riser

Ghaffara
Forgiving
Variants: *Ghaffarah*

Ghafira
Forgiving
Variants: *Ghafirah*

Ghaidaa
Delicate - Gentle

Ghaisat
Rain

Ghalia
Dear - Respected - Valuable

Ghaliaa
Precious - Valuable

Ghaliba
Victor

Ghaniyyah
Needless - Rich - Self-sufficient
Variants: *Ghaneya, Ghaneyah, Ghania, Ghaniah, Ghaniya, Ghaniyah, Ghaniyya*

Gharam
Devotion - Infatuation - Love
The name Gharam is mentioned in the Quran.

Ghareezat
Instincts - Intuitions

Gharidah
Chanter - Singer

Gharisah
Newly Planted Tree - Newly Sown Seed

Gharizah
Instinct - Intution

Ghasina
Beautiful
Variants: *Ghasena, Ghasinah*

Ghawani
Beautiful - Needless

Ghaya
Ultimate Goal

Ghayat
Aim - End Goal

Ghaysah
Rain

Ghazaal
Gazelle - Young Gazelle
Variants: *Gazaal, Gazal, Ghazal, Ghazalle, Ghezal*

Ghazal
Love Poem - Song
Variants: *Gezel*

Ghazalaat
Gazelles

Ghazalah
Gazelle

Ghazia
Warrior

Ghaziyyah
Enduring - Patient

Ghaziyyat
Enduring - Patient

Ghazulah
Spindle

Ghizlan
Gazelles

Ghudwah
Early Morning

Ghufrah
Baby Mountain Goat

Ghufran
Forgiveness - Pardon
The name Ghufran is mentioned in the Quran.

Ghuraibah
Gold - Silver

Ghuraisah
Newly Planted Tree –
Newly Sown Seed

Ghurrah
Chief – Leader – Moonrise

Ghusna
Tree Branch
Variants: *Ghosna,*
Ghusnah

Ghuwaidah
Gentle – Soft

Ghuzail
Beautiful
(Also used in Turkish)

G

Golnisa
Flower Among Women
The *Gol* part is from
Persian and means
"flower", while *nisa* is the
Arabic word for "women".

The "g" sound is not
native to Standard Arabic,
therefore there are no
native Standard Arabic
names that start with this
sound.

H

Haalah
Halo
Variants: *Haala, Hala,*
Halah

Hababah
Affectionate – Loving
Variants: *Habbaba*

Habaq
Basil - Ocimum
A type of plant.

Habibah
Beloved
Variants: *Habeeba*

Habibiyyah
Beloved

Habiyyah
Little Girl

Habriyah
Blessed - Scholar -
Virtuous
Variants: *Habriyyah*

Hadahid
Hoopoes

Hadal
Mistletoe
A type of plant.

Hadees
Hadeeth - Hadis - Hadith
- Hedis
The name Hadees is
mentioned in the Quran.

Hadfah
Aim - Target

Hadiqah
Garden
Variants: *Hadeeqa*

Hadiya
Guide
Variants: *Hadiyah, Hadye,*
Hadyeh

Haelah
Beautiful - Exceptional

Hafifah
Rustle - Swish
Variants: *Hafeefah*

Hafizah
Protector
Variants: *Hafeedha,*
Hafeezah

Haibaa
Greatness - Majesty

Haibah
Greatness - Majesty

Hajirah
Midday Heat
Variants: *Haajera,*
Haajerah, Haajira,
Haajirah, Hajera, Hajerah,
Hajira

Hajraa
Independent - Needless –
Self-sufficient
Variants: *Hajra*

Hakeema
Decisive - Wise
Variants: *Hakeeima,*
Hakeemah, Hakeima,
Hakema, Hakemah,
Hakiema, Hakima,
Hakimah, Hakimeh,
Hakymah, Hekeema,
Hekeeyma, Hekeima,
Hekeimah, Hekeimeh,
Hekiema, Hekima,
Hekimah, Hekime,
Hekimeh, Hekiyma,
Hekyma, Hekymah,
Hekyme, Hekymeh

Halaa
Sweet

Halaat
Sword Gems

Halawah
Sweetness

Haliyah
Adorned

Hallamah
Enduring - Forbearing -
Lenient

Hallumah
Forbearing - Lenient -
Patient

Halul
Pouring - Torrential

Hamamah
Dove - Pigeon

Hamasah
Ardency - Eagerness -
Zeal

Hamda
Noble - Praiseworthy
Variants: *Hamda',*
Hamdaa, Hemda, Hemdaa

Hamdanah
Praise - Praiser

Hamdat
Praise
Turkish pronunciation of
Hamdah. (Also used in
Turkish)

Hamdiya
Admirable - Noble -
Praiseworthy
Variants: *Hamdeya,*
Hamdia, Hamdiah,
Hamdiyah, Hamdiyya,
Hamdiyyah, Hemdye

Hameda
Praiser of God - Thankful
Variants: *Haameda,*
Haamedah, Hamedah,
Hamida, Hamidah

Hameeda
Praiser of God - Thankful
Variants: *Hameedah,*
Hamida, Hamidah

Hamidat
Praiseworthy
Turkish pronunciation of
Hamidah.

Hamim
Close Friend

The name Hamim is
mentioned in the Quran.
Variants: *Hameem*

Hamimah
Devoted - Loyal

Hammadah
Praiser
Variants: *Hamada*

Hammadiyyah
Praiseworthy

Hammatah
Extremely Sweet

Hammudah
Praiseworthy

Hammuzah
Lion

Hamraa
Fair-skinned

Hamyaa
Defender - Protector

Hamziyyah
Brave

Hanaa
Happiness - Peace
Variants: *Hana, Hanaa'*

Hanan
Love - Sympathy
The name Hanan is
mentioned in the Quran.
Variants: *Hanaan*

Haneen
Desire - Longing - Love -
Nostalgia
Variants: *Hanin*

Hanifaa
Devout Believer -
Monotheist
Variants: *Haneefaa*

Hanifah
Devout Believer -
Monotheist
Variants: *Haneefa, Hanifa*

Hanifiyyah
Monotheism
Variants: *Haneefiyah*

Haniya
Happy - Joyful - Peaceful
Variants: *Haneya,*
Haneyah, Hania, Haniah,
Haniyah, Hanya, Hanyah

Haniyya
Delighted - Happy - Joyful
Variants: *Hanea, Haneeah,*
Haneeia, Haneeya, Hania,
Haniyah, Haniyya,
Haniyyah, Heneea, Heneia,
Heniye, Henyye

Hannah
Kind - Loving -
Sympathetic
Variants: *Hana, Hanah,*
Hanna

Hannanah
Affectionate - Caring -
Sympathetic

Hannufah
Devout Believer -
Monotheist

Hanoon
Affectionate -
Sympathetic
Variants: *Hanoun, Hanun*

Hansaa
Brave Warrior

Hanunah
Affectionate - Tender

Hanwa
Xeranthemum
A type of flowering plant.

Haqqaat
Privileges - Rights -
Truths

Harayir
Free - Generous - Pure
Variants: *Haraayer*

Hareem
Sanctuary - Sanctum
Variants: *Harim*

Haritha
Cultivator - Farmer - Lion
Variants: *Haaretha,
Haarethah, Haaritha,
Haarithah, Haresah,
Haretha, Harethah,
Harithah*

Haroona
Mountain
Haroona is the Arabic
feminine form of Harun.

Harun is not an Arabic
word, some Arabic
sources say it means
"mountain".
Variants: *Haroonah,
Haruna, Harunah*

Harz
Guardianship - Protection

Harzanah
Guardian - Protector
Variants: *Harzana*

Hasana
Good Deed
The name Hasana is
mentioned in the Quran.
Variants: *Hasanah*

Hasanaa
Beautiful

Haseemah
Assiduous - Diligent -
Persevering
Variants: *Haseema*

Haseena
Beautiful - Good
Variants: *Haseenah,
Hasina, Hasinah*

Hashimah
Modest - Reserved -
Virtuous
Variants: *Hasheema*

Hasinah
Beautiful

Hasisah
Inspired - Rapid - Swift
Variants: *Haseesa*

Hasnaa
Beautiful
Variants: *Hasna, Hasnaa',
Hesna, Hesnaa*

Hasnaat
Beautiful

Hasnah
Beautiful
Variants: *Hasna*

Hasnaw
Beautiful

Hassunah
Beautiful
Variants: *Hassoona*

Hatima
Decisive - Wise
Variants: *Haatima,
Haatimah, Hatema,
Hatemah, Hatimah,
Hatyma*

Hattabah
Woodcutter

Hattal
Heavy Rain

Hawa
Tree With Dark Leaves
Variants: *Hawaa*

Hawraa
Fair-skinned - White

Variants: *Haura, Hauraa, Hawra*

Hayaa
Chastity - Modesty - Virtue
Variants: *Haia, Haya*

Hayat
Life
The name Hayat is mentioned in the Quran.
Variants: *Hayaat*

Haydaraa
Lioness
Variants: *Haidara*

Haydarah
Lioness
Variants: *Haidara*

Hayiyyah
Bashful - Modest

Hayyin
Facilitated - Lenient
The name Hayyin is mentioned in the Quran.

Hazarah
Civilization - Culture
Variants: *Hadaara, Hadharah*

Hazeem
Continuous Rain - Thunder

Hazeemah
Intelligent - Wise
Variants: *Hazima*

Haziqa
Brilliant - Excellent - Sagacious - Skillful
Variants: *Haazeqa, Haaziqa, Hazeqah, Haziqah*

Hazmiyah
Determined - Resolute
Variants: *Hazmiyyah*

Heba
Bestowal - Blessing - Gift - Gift from God
Variants: *Hebah, Heiba, Hiba, Hibah, Hybah*

Hend
Group of 100 to 200 Camels - India - Indian

Hiddah
Activity - Swiftness
Variants: *Hidda*

Hijra
Asceticism - Avoidance of Sin - Migration
Variants: *Hejra, Hejrah, Hijrah*

Hikma
Wisdom
The name Hikma is mentioned in the Quran.
Variants: *Hekma, Hekmah, Hikmah*

Hikmat
Wisdom
Variants: *Hekmat, Hikmet*

Hilf
Alliance - Treaty

Hillah
Downpour - Show of Rain

Hilyah
Adornment - Jewelry - Virtues

Himaa
Harbor - Haven - Hideaway

Himayah
Care - Guardianship - Safekeeping

Himayat
Care - Defense - Protection - Safekeeping
Turkish pronunciation of Himayah. (Also used in Turkish)

Hishmah
Modesty - Virtue
Variants: *Hishma*

Hishmat
Modesty - Virtue
(Also used in Turkish)
Variants: *Heshmat*

Hobb
Affectionate - Love
The name Hobb is mentioned in the Quran.

Hoor
Beautiful - Beautiful-eyed - Companion of Paradise
The name Hoor is

mentioned in the Quran.
Variants: *Hour, Hur*

Hoori
Beautiful - Beautiful-eyed
- Companion of Paradise
Variants: *Hoory, Houri,
Huri, Huriy*

Hooriyah
Beautiful - Beautiful-eyed
- Companion of Paradise
Variants: *Hooria, Hooriah,
Hooriya, Huriya, Huriyah*

Hubab
Beloved

Hubabah
Beloved

Hubaibah
Beloved

Hubbah
Loving

Huda
Guidance
The name Huda is
mentioned in the Quran.
Variants: *Hoda, Hodaa,
Hudaa*

Hufaizah
Protector
Variants: *Hofaidhah*

Hulaa
Jewelry
Variants: *Holaa*

Hullah
Costume - Dress

Hulou
Sweet
Variants: *Hulu*

Hulwah
Sweet

Hulwi
Sweet

Huma
Guardian - Protectors
Huma is the plural of the
boy name Hamee.
Variants: *Homa, Homaa,
Homaat, Houma, Houmaa,
Howma, Howmaa, Humaa,
Humaat, Huwma,
Huwmaa*

Humaira
Healthy - Red-colored -
Rosy
Variants: *Homairaa,
Humairaa, Humayra,
Humayraa*

Hunaifah
Devout Believer -
Monotheist
Variants: *Honaifa*

Hunain
Hunain is the name of a
valley between at-Taif
and Mecca in which a
battle took place. The
literal meaning of the
word is not known.
Variants: *Honain, Honayn,
Hunayn*

Hunoon
5th Month of the Islamic
Calendar
Synonym for Jamad al-
Ula.
Variants: *Honoon, Hunoun*

Huraira
Cat - Kitten
Variants: *Horaira,
Horairah, Hurairah,
Hurayrah*

Hurvash
Beautiful
Variants: *Hoorvash*

Husaimah
Assiduous - Diligent -
Persevering
Variants: *Hosaima*

Husainah
Beautiful
Variants: *Hosaina*

Husamah
Sharp Sword - Sword
Blade
Variants: *Husama*

Hushaimah
Modesty - Virtue
Variants: *Hoshaima*

Husna
Best - Most Beautiful
The name Husna is
mentioned in the Quran.
Variants: *Hosnaa, Husnaa*

Husniyyah
Beautiful

Huwainaa
Composure - Leniency –
Serenity

I

Iba
Dignity - Reserve - Self-respect
Variants: *Eba, Ebaa, Eibaa, Iba', Ibaa*

Ibadaat
Acts of Worship

Ibadah
Worship
The name Ibadah is mentioned in the Quran.

Ibhar
Breadth - Graciousness
Variants: *Ebhar, Ibhaar*

Ibrah
Interpretation - Lesson - Wisdom
The name Ibrah is mentioned in the Quran.
Variants: *Ebrah, Ibra*

Ibrat
Interpretation - Lesson - Wisdom
Ibrat is the Turkish pronunciation of the Arabic name Ibrah.
Variants: *Ebrat*

Ibreez
Gold
Variants: *Ebreez, Ebriz, Ibriz*

Ibtihal
Humble Prayer -
Supplication
Variants: *Ebtehal*

Ibtisam
Smile
Variants: *Ebetesam, Ebtesaam, Ibtesam, Ibtisaam*

Ibtisama
Smile
Variants: *Ebtesama, Ebtisama, IBtisamah, Ibtesama*

Idrak
Maturation - Perception - Understanding
Variants: *Edraak, Edrak, Idraak*

Iffat
Chastity - Modesty
Turkish pronunciation of Iffah.

Ifra
Enjoining of Good
Variants: *Efra, Efraa, Ifraa*

Ifrah
Gladdening - Heartening - To Make Someone Happy - Uplifting
Variants: *Efraah, Efrah, Ifraah*

Ihdaf
Closeness - Proximity
Variants: *Ihdaaf*

Ihkam
Decisiveness - Mastery
Variants: *Ehkaam, Ehkam, Ihkaam*

Ihlal
Clarity - Radiance
Variants: *Ehlal*

Ihram
Prohibition
The word ihram is used to refer to a pilgrim's entering into a state of prohibition once he starts his pilgrimage, in which many things are prohibited to him, such as hunting or wearing perfume.

Ihsan
Generosity - Good Deeds - Graciousness - Kindness
The name Ihsan is mentioned in the Quran.
Variants: *Ehsaan, Ehsan, Ihsaan, Ihsan*

Ihtiram
Consideration - Esteem - Regard
Variants: *Ehteram, Ehtiram, Ihteram*

Ihtisham
Modesty - Virtue
Variants: *Ehtisham, Ihtesham, Ihtishaam*

Ijada
Excellence - Proficiency - Skill
Variants: *Ejada, Ejadah, Ijaada, Ijaadah, Ijadah*

Ijlal
Greatness - Majesty
Variants: *Ejlaal, Ejlal, Ijlaal*

Ikha
Brotherhood - Friendship
Variants: *Ekha, Ekhaa, Ikhaa, Ikhaa'*

Ikhlas
Faithfulness - Loyalty - Sincerity
Variants: *Ekhlaas, Ekhlas, Ikhlaas*

Ikleel
Crown
Variants: *Iklil*

Ilan
Announcement - Proclamation
Variants: *Elaan, Ilaan*

Ilana
Gentleness - Softness
Variants: *Elaana, Elana, Ilaana, Ilanah*

Ilham
Inspiration - Muse
Variants: *Elhaan, Elham, Ilhaam*

Ilhan
Eloquence
Variants: *Elhaan, Elhan, Ilhaan*

Iliya
Great - High in Status - Noble

Variants: *Eliyah, Eliyyah, Iliyah, Iliyya, Iliyyah*

Illiyeen
Best Place in Paradise - Highest of Rank - Paradise - Sublime
The name Illiyeen is mentioned in the Quran in verse 83:18.
Variants: *Elienne, Eliyeen, Eliyin, Elliyeen, Elyeanne, Elyinne, Iliyeen, Illiyin, Ilyeen*

Ilm
Knowledge - Science
The name Ilm is mentioned in the Quran.

Ilya
Great - High in Status - Noble
Variants: *Elia, Eliah, Ilia, Iliah, Ilyah*

Ilyana
Gentleness - Leniency - Softness
Non-standard derivation from Liyana and Ilan.
Variants: *Eliana, Elyaanah, Elyana, Ilyaana, Ilyaanah*

Imama
Command - Leadership
Variants: *Imamah*

Iman
Faith
The name Iman is mentioned in the Quran.
Variants: *Eemaan,*

Eimaan, Eiman, Emaan, Eman, Imaan

Imani
Faithful
Variants: *Imaani, Imaany, Imany*

Imhal
Forbearance - Leniency
Variants: *Emhal, Imhaal*

Imtisal
Adoration - Imitation - To Follow
Variants: *Emtisal*

Inab
Grape
The name Inab is mentioned in the Quran.

Inabah
Grape Seed - Vine

Inam
Blessings - God's Favors
Variants: *Enaam, In'am, Inaam*

Inan
Grade - Level - Rank - Status
Variants: *Enan, Inaan*

Inara
Enllightenment - Illumination
Variants: *Einara, Enara, Enarah, Eynara, Inaara, Inaarah, Inarah*

Inaya
Care - Diligence -
Protection
Variants: *Enaaya, Enaya,
Enayah, Inaaya, Inayah*

Inayaat
Care - Consideration -
Protection

Inayatullah
God's Care and Protection

Inbihaj
Cheerfulness - Delight -
Mirth
Variants: *Enbihaj, Inbehaaj*

Inbisat
Cheerfulness - Joyfulness
- Relaxation
Variants: *Enbisat, Inbesaat*

Infisal
Distance - Divergence -
Separation
Variants: *Infesal*

Inhal
Pouring of Rain
Variants: *Enhal*

Injah
Success
Variants: *Injaah*

Injeel
Messenger - The Gospels
The name Injeel is
mentioned in the Quran.
Variants: *Enjil*

Injeela
Messenger
Variants: *Enjila, Injila*

Inji
Pearl
(Also used in Turkish)

Insaf
Fairness - Justice
Variants: *Insaaf*

Insha
Creation - Expression
Variants: *Ensha*

Inshad
Chanting - Singing
Variants: *Enshad, Inshaad*

Inshiraf
Glory - Greatness -
Honor
Variants: *Insheraaf*

Inshirah
Cheer - Relaxation -
Relief
Variants: *Ensherah,
Insheraah, Insherah,
Inshiraah*

Insijam
Harmony - Symmetry
Variants: *Ensejam,
Insejam*

Intibah
Alertness - Attention -
Care - Vigilance
Variants: *Entebah,
Entibah, Intibaah*

Intiha
Completion - Conclusion
- End
Variants: *Intehaa*

Intisar
Triumph - Victory
Variants: *Entisar, Intesaar*

Intishal
Healing - Recovery
Variants: *Entishal,
Intishaal*

Intizar
Anticipation - Expectation
- Wait
Variants: *Intezaar*

Iqra
Read - Recite
The name Iqra is
mentioned in the Quran
in verse 96:1. The name is
in the form of a command
(to read or recite).
Variants: *Eqra, Iqraa*

Irfa
Knowledge - Recognition
- Wisdom
Variants: *Erfa, Erfah, Irfah*

Irfana
Knowledge - Wisdom
Variants: *Erfaana,
Erfaanah, Erfana, Erfanah,
Irfaana, Irfaanah, Irfanah*

Irhaa
Calm - Serene
Variants: *Erhaa, Irha,
Irhaa*

Irtiqa
Ascension - Ascent -
Improvement - Promotion
Variants: *Ertiqa, Ertiqaa,
Irteka, Irteqa, Irtika,
Irtiqaa*

Isam
Bond - Connection -
Promise
Variants: *Esaam, Esam,
Isaam*

Ishrah
Companionship -
Fellowship

Ishraq
Daybreak - Emergence -
Illumination - Sunrise -
Vividness
The name Ishraq is
mentioned in the Quran.
Variants: *Eshraaq, Eshraq,
Ishraaq*

Ismat
Majesty - Purity - Virtue
Variants: *Esmat, Ismet*

Israa
Night Journey
Variants: *Esra*

Israr
Determination -
Insistence - Resolve

Istiqlal
Independence -
Sovereignty
Variants: *Esteqlal, Estiqlal,
Istiqlaal*

Itaa
Growth - Maturing - Yield
Variants: *Eta, Etaa, Ita*

Ithath
Plenty - Splendor
Variants: *Esaas, Esas,
Ethaat, Ethath, Isaas, Isas,
Ithaath*

Itqan
Mastery - Proficiency -
Skill
Variants: *Etqaan, Etqan,
Itqaan, Itqan*

Iyan
Era - Time
The name Iyan is
mentioned in the Quran.
It is an alternate reading
of the word Ayyan used in
verse 27:65.
Variants: *Eyaan, Eyan,
Eyyan, Iyaan, Iyyan*

Izaan
Acceptance - Obedience -
Submission
Variants: *Ezaan, Iz'an*

Izdihar
Blossoming - Flourishing
Variants: *Ezdihar*

Izma
Greatness - Importance -
Might
Variants: *Ezma, Ezmah,
Izmah*

Izmat
Greatness - Importance -

Might
Variants: *Ezmat*

Izzaa
Greatness - Might -
Power

Izzat
Greatness - Majesty -
Might

Izzi
Mighty - Powerful -
Strong

J

Jabaa
Slender - Slim

Jabbadah
Attractive - Charming

Jabeehah
Beautiful

Jabira
Fixer - Improver -
Mender
Variants: *Jaabera,
Jaaberah, Jaabira,
Jaabirah, Jabera, Jaberah,
Jabirah*

Jablah
Power - Strength

Jabraa
Mender

Jabrah
Brave

Jadirah
Deserving - Essence -
Nature

Jafeerah
River

Jafurah
River

Jahdaa
Striver

Jahidah
Striver

Jahizah
Prepared - Ready

Jahudah
Striver

Jamalah
Beauty

Jamila
Beautiful - Radiant
Variants: *Gamilah,
Jameela, Jameelah,
Jameeleh, Jameila,
Jameilah, Jameileh,
Jameyleh, Jamilah, Jamyla,
Jemeela, Jemeelah, Jemeila,
Jemeilah, Jemila, Jemilah,
Jemile, Jemileh, Jemylah,
Jemyleh*

Jamilaa
Beautiful

Jamlaa
Beautiful
Variants: *Gemla*

Jamlah
Beautiful

Janina
Garden - Silk Chador
Variants: *Janeena,
Janeenah, Janinah*

Jannaat
Gardens - Paradise
The name Jannaat is
mentioned in the Quran.

Variants: *Janaat, Janat,
Jannat, Jennat*

Jannah
Garden - Paradise
The name Jannah is
mentioned in the Quran.
Variants: *Jana, Janah,
Janna, Jena, Jenah, Jenna,
Jennah*

Jasimah
Hulking - Muscular -
Strong
Variants: *Jasemah, Jasima*

Jawahar
Jewels - Precious Stones
Alternative form of
Jawahir.
Variants: *Jawaahar,
Joaahar, Joahar, Jowahar*

Jawahir
Jewelry - Jewels -
Precious Stones
Plural of Jawharah.
Variants: *Jawaaher,
Jawaahir, Jawaher,
Jowaher, Jowahir*

Jawd
Torrential Rain

Jawdah
Goodness - Virtue

Jawdat
Goodness - Virtue

Jawhar
Essence - Jewel -
Precious Stone

53

Variants: *Johar, Jouhar,*
Jowhar

Jawhara
Essence - Jewel -
Precious Stone
Variants: *Jawharah,*
Johara, Joharah

Jayidah
Good - Gracious

Jazaa
Recompense - Reward
The name Jazaa is
mentioned in the Quran.
Variants: *Jaza, Jaza', Jeza,*
Jezaa

Jazal
Delight - Happiness

Jazilaa
Great - Tremendous

Jazilah
Great - Majestic

Jibal
Mountains
The name Jibal is
mentioned in the Quran.
Variants: *Jebaal, Jebal,*
Jibaal

Jibalah
Mountains

Jidah
Generosity -
Graciousness

Jihadah
Strife - Struggle

Jinan
Gardens - Paradises

Jinani
Heavenly

Jodd
Beach - Coast - Fortunate
- Side

Johd
Strife - Struggle

Joud
Generosity -
Graciousness

Joudah
Generosity -
Graciousness

Jubaihah
Face

Jublah
Essence - Nature

Judiyah
Generous - Selfless

Judy
The name *Judy* is
mentioned in the Quran.
Variants: *Joodi, Joody,*
Joudi, Judi

Juhainah
Young Woman

Jumalaa
Beautiful

Jumanah
Pearl

Jumlanah
Nightingale

Junaina
Garden
Variants: *Jonaina,*
Jonainah, Junainah,
Junayna, Junaynah

Juwayriya
Damask Rose - Rose -
Young Woman
Variants: *Jouaria,*
Jowairiah, Juairia,
Juairiyah, Juwayriyyah,
Jwairiyyah

K

Kaarima
Excellent - Generous -
Gracious - Noble
Variants: *Kaarema,
Kaaremah, Kaarimah,
Karema, Karemah,
Karima, Karimah*

Kabira
Chief - Great - Powerful
The name Kabira is
mentioned in the Quran.
Variants: *Kabeera,
Kabeerah, Kabirah*

Kafiyah
Sufficient

Kahal
One Who Has Beautiful
Dark Eyelids

Kahhalah
Kohl-wearer

Kahlaa
One Who Has Beautiful
Black Eyes

Kaina
Being - Event - Existing -
Happening
Variants: *Caena, Caina,
Cainah, Cayena, Ka'ina,
Kaena, Kainah*

Kainaat
The Creation
Variants: *Kaenat, Kainat*

Kalifah
Adorer - Lover

Kalima
Word
The name Kalima is
mentioned in the Quran.
Variants: *Kalema,
Kalemah, Kalimah*

Kalsum
Beautiful
Lterally "one who has full,
healthy cheeks". Variant
of Kulsum.

Kalsumah
Beautiful
Variant of Kulsumah.

Kamalah
Completeness -
Perfection - Wholeness

Kamaliyyah
Complete - Perfect -
Whole

Kamayilah
Complete - Perfect -
Whole

Kamilaa
Complete - Whole

Kamilah
Complete - Flawless -
Perfect - Whole
The name Kamilah is
mentioned in the Quran
in verse 2:196.
Variants: *Camilla,
Kaamila, Kaamilah,
Kamela, Kamelah, Kamella,*

*Kamellah, Kamila, Kamilla,
Kamillah*

Kamilat
Complete - Perfect -
Whole

Kamillaa
Complete - Perfect -
Whole

Kandus
Magpie
A type of bird.

Kanza
Treasure
Variants: *Kanzah, Kenza,
Kenzah, Kinza*

Karam
Generosity -
Graciousness

Karamah
Graciousness - Honor

Karawan
Curlew
A type of bird.

Kareema
Excellent - Generous -
Gracious - Noble
Variants: *Kareemah,
Karima, Karimah*

Kashaaf
Discoverer - Finder
Variants: *Kashaaf,
Kashshaf, Keshaf*

Kateebah
Battalion - Regiment

Katibah
Writer

Kattamah
Keeper of Secrets

Kawkab
Star
The name Kawkab is
mentioned in the Quran
in verse 6:76.
Variants: *Kaukab, Kokab*

Kawkabah
Planet - Star - Venus
Variants: *Kaukabah,
Kawkabah, Kokaba,
Kowkaba*

Kawnaa
Existing - Hapening

Kawnah
Existing - Hapening

Kawnain
Beings - Existences -
Universes

Kayaneh
Queen-like - Royal
(Also used in Persian)
Variants: *Kaianeh,
Kayaaneh*

Kazimah
One Who Controls His
Own Anger

Kifah
Strife - Struggle
Variants: *Kefaah, Kefah,
Kifaah*

Kifahah
Strife - Struggle

Kifayah
Adequacy - Contentment
- Satisfaction

Kifayatullah
God's Contentment
Contentment that is
bestowed by God.

Kinanah
Quiver
A container that holds
arrows.

Kindiyyah
Mountain-dweller

Kiram
Gracious Ones -
Honorable Ones
The name Kiram is
mentioned in the Quran.

Kiswa
Clothing - Garment
Refers to the black silk
cloth that covers the
Kaaba in Mecca, Saudi
Arabia.
Variants: *Keswa, Keswah,
Kiswah*

Kohl
Kohl

Kufah
Mound of Sand

Kulaisim
Beautiful - Full-cheeked

Kulbahar
Flower of Spring
From Persian Gulbahar.

Kulfah
Burden - Charge - Tan
Color

Kulfat
Burden - Charge - Tan
Color

Kulsoom
Beautiful - Full-cheeked

Kulsumah
Beautiful - Full-cheeked

Kumailah
Complete - Perfect -
Whole

Kumailiyah
Complete - Perfect -
Whole

Kunaizah
Little Treasure

Kundas
Magpie
A type of bird.

Kuram
Gracious Ones -
Honorable Ones

Kh

Kh is pronounced the same way the "ch" is pronounced by Scots in the word "Loch Ness", and the way native Germans pronounce the "ch" in the name of the famous composer Bach. You can easily find videos on YouTube by Scots explaining the proper pronunciation of "Loch Ness".

Khabirah
Experienced - Expert

Khadijah
Born Preterm
Variants: *Hadija, Hedije, Kadija, Khadeeja, Khadeejah, Khadija*

Khadujah
Preterm Giver of Birth
Pet form of Khadijah.

Khafifah
Nimble - Sprightly
Variants: *Khafeefa*

Khaira
Beautiful - Virtuous
Variants: *Caira, Cairah, Caire, Caireh, Hairah, Kaireh, Kayra, Kayrah, Kayre, Kayreh, Keira, Keirah, Keire, Keireh, Kerah, Keyrah, Keyre, Keyreh, Khairah, Khaireh,* *Khayrah, Kheirah, Kheireh, Khera, Kheyra, Kheyrah, Kheyre, Kheyreh*

Khairaat
Beauty - Goodness
The name Khairaat is mentioned in the Quran in verse 55:70.
Variants: *Khairat, Khayraat, Khayrat, Kheirat*

Khaldaa
Immortal

Khaleedah
Immortal

Khaleef
Leader - Successor
Variants: *Kaleef, Khaleif, Khalif*

Khaleefa
Leader - Successor
The name Khaleefa is mentioned in the Quran.
Variants: *Kalifa, Kalifah, Khaleefah, Khalifa, Khalifah*

Khaleela
Companion - Friend
Variants: *Helile, Kaleela, Kalila, Kalilah, Kalyla, Khaleelah, Khalilah, Khalyla, Khelile*

Khalidah
Immortal
Variants: *Khaleda, Khalida*

Khalisah
Pure
The name Khalisah is mentioned in the Quran.
Variants: *Khalesa*

Khaliyah
Bygone - Solitary
The name Khaliyah is mentioned in the Quran.

Khalsat
Purity - Safety

Khalulah
Nimble - Sprightly

Khamrah
Fragrance

Khasabah
Blessed
Variants: *Khasaaba*

Khasibah
Blessed - Fertile - Productive

Khatibah
Orator - Speaker

Khatrah
Idea - Notion - Occurrence

Khawatir
Ideas - Notions - Thoughts

Khawdan
Delicate - Good-mannered

Khawlah
Gazelle

Khayal
Fantasy - Imagination -
Vision

Khayriyyah
Charitable - Good
Variants: *Kahyriyya,*
Khayrea, Khayria,
Khayriah, Khayriya,
Khayriyah

Khayyira
Beautiful - Virtuous
Variants: *Cayyera,*
Cayyira, Hayyire, Kayera,
Kayerah, Kayyerah,
Khaiyrah, Khayera,
Khayerah, Khayirah,
Khayyera, Khayyerah,
Khayyirah

Khazraa
Green - Green-colroed

Khazrat
Green - Softness

Khazzarah
Green - Soft

Kheer
Generosity - Honor -
Virtue

Khibrah
Deep Knowledge -
Expertise

Khilal
Companionship -

Friendship
The name Khilal is
mentioned in the Quran
in verse 14:31.
Variants: *Kelal, Khelaal,*
Khelal, Khilaal, Khylal,
Kilal

Khilfah
Successor

Khilfat
Successor

Khimar
Cover - Scarf - Veil

Khimrah
Fragrance - Scarf - Veil

Khiraa
Purification - Selection

Khisbah
Blessed

Khulaifah
Successor

Khulaisah
Pristine - Wholesome

Khullah
Friendship - Love

Khulud
Immortality
Variants: *Kholood, Kholud,*
Khulood

Khusaibah
Blessed - Fruitful -
Productive

Khuta
Steps

Khuwaid
Delicate - Good-
mannered - Tender

Khuwairah
Good - Virtuous

Khuzaimah
Gabal Elba Dragon Tree
A type of tree.

Khuzarah
Ocean - Sea

Khuzrah
Green - Softness

L

Laaiqah
Eligible - Qualified -
Suitable

Labeebaa
Intelligent

Labeebah
Intelligent - Sagacious

Labisah
Wearer

Ladeenaa
Gentle

Ladeenah
Gentle - Good-mannered

Lahjah
Dialect

Lahzah
Blink of an Eye - Instance
- Moment
Variants: *Lahza, Lahzeh*

Lail
Night
The name Lail is
mentioned in the Quran.
Variants: *Layl, Leil, Leyl*

Laila
Ecstasy - Intoxication
Name of a Sahabiyyah.
Variants: *Lailaa, Layla,
Laylaa, Leila, Leyla*

Lailah
Night
The name Lailah is used in
the Quran.
Variants: *Laila, Layla,
Laylah*

Lailan
Two Nights

Lailat
Nights

Laily
Belonging to the Night -
Nightly

Laithaa
Lioness

Laithah
Lioness

Lalaa
Glimmer - Shine

Lalee
Pearls
Variants: *La'aali, La'ali,
Laalee, Laalei, Laali, Laaly,
Lalei, Lali, Laly*

Lamaah
Glimmer - Shine

Lamaan
Glimmer - Shine

Lamihah
One Who Glances

Lana
Gentle - Lenient - Soft
Variants: *Laana*

Lasiniyyah
Eloquent - Fluent

Lasnaa
Eloquent - Fluent

Latafat
Gentleness - Kindness

Latayif
Gentle - Kind

Lateefa
Gentle - Kind
Variants: *Lateefah, Latifa,
Latifah*

Lawahiz
Eyes - One Who Glances

Laweeh
Apparent - Manifest -
Visible

Layaal
Nights
The name Layaal is
mentioned in the Quran.

Layan
Gentleness - Softness
Variants: *Laean, Laian,
Laiane, Layaan, Layane,
Layanne*

Layliyyah
Belonging to the Night -
Nightly

Layyanah
Affable - Friendly - Gentle

Layyasah
Brave

Layyin
Delicate - Soft - Tender
The name *Layyin* is
mentioned in the Quran.
Variants: *Layen, Layene,
Layinne, Layyen, Layyene,
Layyine, Leine, Leyin,
Leyinne, Leyyin*

Layyina
Delicate - Soft - Tender
Variants: *Layena, Layenah,
Layene, Layeneh, Layineh,
Layyena, Layyenah,
Layyinah, Layyineh,
Leinah, Leyina, Leyyina*

Lazimah
Desired - Wished For

Leanne
Delicate - Gentle - Soft
Variants: *Leane, Leyanne,
Lian, Liyan, Liyane,
Liyanne, Lyan*

Leen
Delicate - Gentle - Soft -
Tender
Variants: *Leein, Leene,
Leeyn, Lein, Leine, Leine,
Lene, Leyn, Leyne, Liene,
Lin, Liyne, Lyn, Lyne*

Leena
Delicate - Gentle - Soft -
Tender
The name Leena is

mentioned in the Quran
in verse 59:5.
Variants: *Leeinah, Leenah,
Leina, Leinah, Leinah,
Leineh, Lenah, Liena, Lina,
Linah, Liynah, Lyna,
Lynah, Lyneh*

Leeniyyah
Friendly - Gentle

Liqa
Meeting
The name Liqa is
mentioned in the Quran.
Variants: *Leqa, Liqaa*

Liwaa
Banner - Ensign - Flag

Liyana
Gentleness - Softness -
Tenderness
Variants: *Leana, Leeanah,
Liana, Lianna, Liannah,
Liyanah*

Lubabaa
Affluence - Pure

Lubabah
Pure

Lubaibah
Pure

Lughah
Language

Luha
Amount - Measure

Luham
Great

Lujain
Silver

Luluah
Bead of Pearl - Pearl

Lumaihah
Glance
Lumaihah is an Arabic
name for girls that means
"glance".

Lutaifah
Gentle - Kind

Lutfah
Gentleness - Kindness -
Leniency

Luwaihah
Painting Canvas

M

Maab
Place of Return
The name Maab is mentioned in the Quran in verse 13:29. The Quran uses this name to refer to Paradise.
Variants: *Ma'aab, Ma'ab, Mab*

Maadah
Recurrence - Return

Maadulah
Balanced - Rectified - Tuned

Maanah
Easy

Maarib
Destiny - Goal
The name Maarib is mentioned in the Quran in verse 20:18.
Variants: *Ma'aareb, Ma'arib, Maareb, Mareb, Mareyb, Mareybe, Marib*

Maarifah
Awareness - Knowledge - Wisdom

Maarifatuddin
Knowledge of the Faith

Maarij
Ascents - Routes of Ascent - Stairs

The name Maarij is mentioned in the Quran.

Maash
Livelihood - Sustenance
The name Maash is mentioned in the Quran.

Maawa
Refuge - Sanctuary
The name Maawa is mentioned in the Quran.
Variants: *Ma'wa, Maawaa, Mawaa*

Maazah
Affection - Honor - Love - Respect
Variants: *Maaza, Maazza, Mazzah*

Maazuzah
Powerful - Strong

Mabrukah
Blessed

Madeehaa
Praise

Madeehah
Praise

Madihah
Praiser

Madina
City
Madina is the name of the city of the Prophet (pbuh) in Arabia.
Variants: *Madeenah,*

Madeina, Madinah, Madyna, Medina, Medyna

Madinaa
City
Variant of Madinah.

Maeen
Fountain - Spring - Water Stream
The name Maeen is mentioned in the Quran.
Variants: *Maein, Main*

Maeena
Helper - Supporter
Variants: *Maeeneh, Maeyna, Maiena, Maina, Mayina, Mayna*

Mafaz
Salvation - Success
The name Mafaz is mentioned in the Quran.
Variants: *Mafaaz, Maphaz, Mefaz*

Mafazah
Salvation - Success
The name Mafazah is mentioned in the Quran.
Variants: *Mafaaza, Mafaza, Mefaaza, Mefaza, Mefaze, Mephaze*

Maftooh
Free - Open
Variants: *Maftuh*

Mafzalah
Graciousness

Maghdah
Gentle - Soft

Maghfira
Forgiveness - Pardon
The name Maghfira is
mentioned in the Quran.
Variants: *Magfira,*
Maghfera, Maghferah,
Maghfirah

Mahaada
Comforter - Facilitator
Variants: *Mahaadah,*
Mahada, Mahadah

Mahabbat
Affections

Mahara
Expertise - Skill - Talent
Variants: *Mahaara,*
Mahaarah

Mahasen
Beauty - Good Qualities -
Virtues
Variants: *Mahaasen,*
Mahaasin, Mahasin

Mahasti
Moon Lady
(Also used in Persian)
Variants: *Mahastee*

Mahbub
Adored - Loved

Mahbubah
Adored - Loved

Mahd
Cradle - Place of Comfort
- Starting Point
The name Mahd is
mentioned in the Quran.
Variants: *Mehd*

Mahdah
Flat Land - Plain

Mahdia
Rightly-guided - Well-
guided
Variants: *Madiah,*
Mahdeya, Mahdiya,
Mahdiyah

Mahfuzah
Guarded - Protected

Mahia
Life - Lifetime
The name Mahia is
mentioned in the Quran
in verse 6:162 and others.
Variants: *Mahiaa, Mahya,*
Mahyaa

Mahida
Comforter - Facilitator
Variants: *Maaheda,*
Maahedah, Maahida,
Maahidah, Maheda,
Mahedah, Mahidah

Mahirah
Adept - Proficient -
Skilled

Mahjabeen
Moon-like

Mahlaa
Forbearing - Lenient

Mahmudah
Praiseworthy

Mahmunir
Radiant Moon
(Also used in Persian)

Mahnisa
Moon Among Women

Mahnoor
Moonlight
(Also used in Persian)
Variants: *Maahnoor,*
Maahnur, Mahanoor,
Mahenoor, Mahinoor,
Mahnur, Mehnor, Mehnur

Mahrusah
Guarded - Protected

Mahsima
Moon-like
Variants: *Maahsimaa*

Mahsumah
Decided - Determined -
Resolved

Mahsunah
Beautified - Improved

Mahulah
Beautiful

Maidan
Arena - Plaza

Maira
Nimble - Swift
Variants: *Ma'irah, Maaera,*
Maaerah, Maaira,
Maairah, Maera, Maerah,
Mairah

Maisarah
Affluence
The name Maisarah is
mentioned in the Quran.

Maithah
Flat Land
Variants: *Maisah*

Maiza
Distinguisher
Variants: *Maaeza,
Maaezah, Maaiza,
Maaizah, Maeza*

Majal
Chance - Elbowroom -
Opportunity - Space

Majd
Distinction - Glory -
Honor
Variants: *Mejd*

Majdah
Glorious - Praiseworthy

Majdiyah
Laudable - Praiseworthy
Majdiyah is an Arabic
name for boys that means
"praiseworthy",
"commendable",
"glorious".

Majeedah
Glorious - Laudable -
Praiseworthy

Majidaa
Praiseworthy

Majidah
Praiseworthy

Makaana
Greatness - Highness of
Status

Makeen
Deep-rooted - Firmly
Established - Honored -
Powerful
The name Makeen is
mentioned in the Quran.
Variants: *Mackein,
Macken, Mackene,
Mackeyne, Makeene,
Makein, Makeine, Makene,
Makin, Mekeen, Mekein,
Mekeine, Mekene, Mekin,
Mekyn, Mekyne*

Makeenah
Influential - Powerful

Makkiyah
Meccan

Makramah
Generosity -
Graciousness - Honor

Makrumah
Generous - Good Deeds -
Gracious

Malahah
Beauty - Good Looks

Maleekah
Lady - Owner - Queen

Maleknaz
Queen of Beauty - Queen
of Charm

Maliha
Beautiful - Eloquent -
Happy
Variants: *Maleeha,
Maleehah, Malihah*

Malikaat
Queen

Malikah
Queen

Malkah
Queen
Hebrew for "queen". It can
also be a colloquial Arabic
pronunciation of the
name Malikah, which also
means "queen". (Also used
in Jewish)

Mamduhah
Praiseworthy

Manal
Achievement -
Attainment - Success
Variants: *Manaal, Menaal,
Menal, Menale, Menall*

Manaliaa
Achievement -
Attainment

Manar
Illuminating - Radiant
Variants: *Manaar, Menaar,
Menar*

Manara
Illuminating - Lighthouse
- Radiant
Variants: *Manaara,
Manaareh, Manarah,
Manare, Manareh,
Menaara, Menara,
Menarah, Menareh*

Manari
Radiant

Maneehah
Gift from God

Manhal
Fountain - Spring - Water
Well

Manhiyyah
Generous - Giving

Manja
Place of Safety

Mansurah
Backed - Supported -
Victor

Manusriyyah
Vicor

Manzurah
Anticipated - Foreseen -
Seen - Visible

Maqbulah
Accepted - Approved

Maqsurah
Affluent

Marab
Destiny - Goal
Variants: *Ma'rab,
Maarabb, Maarabbe,
Maarabe, Maareb,
Maarebb, Maarebbe,
Maarebe, Marab, Marabb,
Marabbe, Marabe, Mareb,
Mareb, Marebb, Marebbe,
Marebe, Merab, Merabb,
Merabbe, Merabe, Mereb,
Merebb, Merebbe, Merebe*

Marah
Activity - Fun - Joy
The name Marah is
mentioned in the Quran.

Maram
Goal - Intention
Variants: *Maraam*

Maranat
Gentleness - Softness
(Also used in Turkish)

Mareekh
Lead Monoxide
A chemical used in
Medieval times in
alchemy and medicine.

Mareerah
Resolved - Strong

Marghaa
Garden - Meadow

Marghah
Garden - Meadow

Marhaa
Exuberant - Lively

Mariam
Wished for Child
The name *Mariam* is
mentioned in the Quran.
Variants: *Maream,
Mariem, Mariemme,
Marium, Mariyam,
Mariyem, Maryam,
Maryem, Maryeme,
Maryum, Meream,
Meriam, Meriem,
Meriemme, Merium,
Meriyam, Meriyem,
Merryum, Meryame,
Meryamm, Meryamme,
Meryem, Meryemme*

Marihaat
Exuberant - Lively

Mariwah
Type of Plant
Known as Maerua
scientifically.

Marjan
Pearl - Red Coral
The name *Marjan* is
mentioned in the Quran.
Variants: *Marjanne,
Merjaan, Merjan*

Marjana
Pearl - Red Coral
Variants: *Marjaana,
Marjaanah, Merjaanah,
Merjana*

Marjani
Coral-like - Pearl-like

Marjia
Desirable - Desired -
Wished For

Variants: *Margiyah,*
Marjeya, Marjeyah,
Marjiah

Marjina
Pearl - Red Coral
Marjina is a non-standard
modification of the name
Marjana.
Variants: *Marjeena,*
Marjinah

Marjuwwah
Desired

Marmaraa
Heavy Rain - Marble

Marmari
Heavy Rain - Marble-like

Marmuri
Marble-like

Marwa
The name *Marwa* is
mentioned in the Quran.
Variants: *Maruah, Marva,*
Marvah, Marve, Marveh,
Marwa, Marwah, Marweh,
Merua, Meruah, Merva,
Mervah, Merve, Merveh,
Merwa, Merwah, Merweh

Marwanah
Quartz

Marzia
Content - Pleasing to God
The name Marzia is
mentioned in the Quran
in verse 89:28.
Variants: *Mardeyah,*
Mardheyya, Mardhiyyah,

Mardia, Mardiah,
Mardiyah, Mardiyeh,
Mardya, Marzea, Marzeya,
Marziah, Marziyah,
Marziyeh, Marziyyah,
Merziah, Merziyah,
Merziyeh

Marzuqah
Blessed by God - Given
Provision

Masakin
Habitation - Residence
The name Masakin is
mentioned in the Quran.

Masar
Path - Road
Variants: *Masaar, Mesaar,*
Mesar

Masarra
Delight - Good Tidings -
Joy
Variants: *Masara,*
Masarrah, Mesarrah

Masarrat
Gladness - Happiness -
Joy

Masbubah
Poured

Mashaa
Willpower

Mashael
Lanterns - Lights -
Torches
Variants: *Masha'il,*
Mashaael, Mashaail,
Mashail

Mashahirah
Famous - Popular

Mashal
Lantern - Light
Variants: *Mash'al, Mashaal*

Mashar
Honeycomb Cell

Mashara
Honeycomb Cell

Mashariqah
Eastern - Oriental

Mashiyat
Will - Willpower
Variants: *Masheat,*
Masheeat, Mashi'at,
Mashiat, Mashiyyat

Mashta
Winter Resort

Mashurah
Long-hiared
Variants: *Mash'ura*

Masla
Comfort - Consolation

Maslamah
Peace - Safety

Masrur
Glad - Happy
The name Masrur is
mentioned in the Quran.

Massat
Contact - Touch

Mastoor
Covered - Hidden -
Modest
The name Mastoor is
mentioned in the Quran.

Mastoorah
Covered - Hidden -
Modest

Masudah
Glad - Happy

Masudiyyah
Glad - Happy

Masus
Unripe Date

Masyunah
Guarded - Protected

Mataf
Place of Tawaf - Place of
Visitation
Variants: *Mataaf*

Matahir
Cleansers - Purifiers

Mataraa
Rain

Matarah
Bout of Rain - Rain

Mateerah
Rainy

Matheelah
Exemplary - Ideal - Model

Mathlaa
Exemplary - Ideal - Model

Mathnawi
Binary - Couplet
Usually refers to a type of
poetry.

Mathwa
Abode - Home
The name Mathwa is
mentioned in the Quran.

Matia
Excellent - Superb
Variants: *Maateah,
Maatia, Maatiah, Matea,
Mati'a, Mati'ah, Matiah*

Matlubah
Desired - Sought

Mawaadah
Affection - Love

Mawadda
Affection - Love
Mawadda is mentioned in
the Quran.
Variants: *Mauada,
Mawada, Mawadah,
Mawadda, Mawaddah*

Mawfaa
Faithful - Loyal

Mawiyyah
Fair-skinned White-
skinned

Mawiza
Admonition - Guidance -
Word of Encouragement

The name Mawiza is
mentioned in the Quran.
Variants: *Maweza,
Mawezah, Mawizah*

Mawjudah
Accessible - Existing -
Obtainable

Mawmah
Great Success

Mawoudah
Appointed - Determined -
Promisee

Mawsim
Festival Day - Season -
Time

Maymun
Blessed - Prosperous
Variants: *Maimoon,
Maimun, Maymoon*

Maymuna
Blessed - Prosperous
Variants: *Maimoona,
Maimoonah, Maimuna,
Maimunah, Maymoona,
Maymoonah, Maymunah*

Maysura
Needless - Prosperous
Variants: *Maysurah,
Meisoura, Meisura,
Meysora, Meysura*

Maziyyah
Complete - Good Quality
- Perfect - Virtue - Whole

Mazna
Beautiful - Rain-Bearing
Cloud
Variants: *Maazina,
Maazinah, Maazna,
Maaznah, Mazena,
Mazenah, Mazina,
Mazinah, Maznah*

Mazyunah
Adorned - Beautified

Mehrnesa
Beautiful Among Women
Variants: *Mehrnisa,
Mihrnisaa*

Mibkar
Drivenn - Motivated

Midhah
Poem of Praise

Midhat
Poem of Praise
(Also used in Turkish)

Miesha
Life - Livelihood
The name
Miesha mentioned in the
Quran in verse 28:58.
Variants: *Ma'ishah,
Maisha, Mayeesah,
Mayeesha, Maysha,
Myesha, Myiesha, Mysha*

Mietaa
Generous

Mifrah
Happy - Joyous

Variants: *Mefraah, Mefrh,
Mifraah*

Miftah
Guide - Key

Miftahah
Guide

Mihad
Cradle - Place of Comfort
- Plain
The name Mihad is
mentioned in the Quran.
Variants: *Mehaad, Mehad,
Mihaad*

Milhaan
Pure White Color
Variants: *Melhaan,
Melhan, Milhan*

Minbarah
Dais - Platform - Pulpit -
Stage

Minhaj
Clear Path - Clear Way -
Curriculum - Method
The name Minhaj is
mentioned in the Quran.

Minhal
Generous - Honorable

Minna
Charity - Gift from God
Variants: *Menna, Mennah,
Mina, Minah, Minnah*

Minnatullah
God's Blessings - God's
Bounty

Mirsalah
Message-bearer -
Messenger

Mirwaa
Beautiful

Misam
Beautiful
Variants: *Meesam,
Meysam, Miesam, Mysam*

Misaq
Covenant
The name Misaq is
mentioned in the Quran.
Variants: *Meesaq,
Meethaq, Misaaq, Mithaaq,
Mithaq*

Misbah
Lamp - Lantern - Light -
Oil Lamp
The name Misbah is
mentioned in the Quran.
Variants: *Mesbaah,
Mesbah, Misbaah*

Misbahah
Lamp

Mishaali
Kindler - Lighter

Mishal
Lantern - Light
Variants: *Mesh'al, Meshaal,
Meshal, Mish'al, Mishaal*

Mishkat
Niche
The name Mishkat is
mentioned in the Quran.

Variants: *Meshkaat,*
Meshkat, Mishkaat

Miskah
Musk

Miskiyyah
Musk-like

Mislafah
Advanced - Ahead

Misriyyah
Egyptian

Mizn
Rain-Bearing Cloud -
White Cloud

Mizna
Rain-Bearing Cloud -
White Cloud
Variants: *Mezna, Meznah,*
Miznah

Mizyan
Beautiful

Moeza
One Who Honors Others
- One Who Values Others
Variants: *Moeizah, Muizza,*
Muizzah

Mona
Desired - Wanted

Moonam
Given Blessings
Variants: *Mounam,*
Mun'am, Munam

Moujabah
Amazed - Impressed -
Pleased

Moujibah
Amazing - Impressive

Mouminat
Believers
The name Mouminat is
mentioned in the Quran.
Variants: *Mominat,*
Mu'minat

Mouminin
Believers
The name Mouminin is
mentioned in the Quran.

Moutazah
Honored - Majestic -
Powerful

Moutiyah
Generous

Muammeerah
Long-lived
Variant of Muammirah.

Muantirah
Bold - Brave
Variants: *Mo'antira*

Muarrifah
Guide

Muawadah
Recurrence - Return

Muawidah
Returner

Muayadah
Resurgence - Return

Muayyadaa
Backed - Supported

Muayyadah
Backed - Supported

Muayyid
Eid Celebrator

Muayyidah
Eid Celebrator

Muayyidah
Advocate - Supporter

Muazzirah
Helper - Supporter

Mubaraka
Blessed
The name Mubaraka is
mentioned in the Quran
in verse 24:35.
Variants: *Mobaraka,*
Mobarakah, Mubaaraka,
Mubarakah

Mubdia
Creative - Innovative -
Inventive
Variants: *Mobdia,*
Mobdiah, Mubdi'ah,
Mubdiah

Mubin
Apparent - Clear - Self-
evident
The name Mubin is
mentioned in the Quran.

Variants: *Mobeen, Mobin, Mubeen*

Mubinaa
Apparent - Clear - Distinct - Manifest

Mubinah
Apparent - Clear - Distinct - Manifest

Mudassira
Clothed - Covered - Dressed
Variants: *Modasira, Modasirah, Modassira, Modassirah, Mudasera, Mudaserah, Mudasirah, Mudassirah, Mudathera, Mudathira, Mudathirah*

Mueena
Helper - Supporter
Variants: *Moeina, Moeinah, Mueenah, Muina, Muinah*

Mueidah
Experienced - Skilled

Mufazzalah
Gracious

Mufazzilah
Gracious

Mufidah
Beneficial

Mufizah
Gracious

Mufliha
Prosperous - Successful
Variants: *Mofliha, Moflihah, Mufleha, Muflehah, Muflihah*

Mughithah
Rescuer - Savior

Muhairah
Skilled

Muhajira
Ascetic - Avoider of Sin - Migrator
Variants: *Muajera, Muhaajera, Muhaajerah, Muhaajira, Muhaajirah, Muhajerah, Muhajirah*

Muhandamah
Beautiful

Muhannaa
Congratulated - Well Greeted

Muhannadah
Indian-made Sword
(Also used in Persian)

Muhannah
Congratulated - Well Greeted

Muhassanah
Beautified - Improved

Muhassinah
Beautifier - Improver

Muhdah
Flat Land - Plain

Muhibbat
Lovers

Muhizzat
Gracious - Honorable
(Also used in Turkish)

Muhjaa
Blood - Heart - Soul

Muhjah
Blood - Heart - Soul

Muhlah
Forbearance - Leniency

Muhsinah
Doer of Good Deeds

Muhtaramah
Honored - Respected

Muhtarimah
Respectful

Muiddah
Preparer

Mujahidah
Striver

Mujeedah
Doer of Good Deeds

Mujibah
Answerer - Responder
Mujibah means "a person who answers other's calls for help".

Mujiddah
Conscientious - Striving

Mujillah
Great - Strong

Mujirah
Rescuer - Savior

Mujtahidah
Striver

Mukafat
Recompense - Reward

Mukarramah
Honored - Respected

Mukawwinah
Builder - Creator

Mukhallisah
Chosen - Excellent - Fine
- Superior

Mukhlasah
Chosen - Purified -
Selected

Mukhlisah
Faithful - Loyal - Sincere

Mukhtarah
Chosen - Excellent - Fine
- Superior

Mulan
Gentle - Soft

Mulhah
Quip - Witticism

Mulhat
Quip - Witticism

Mulukah
Queen

Muminah
Believer in God
The name Muminah is
mentioned in the Quran.
Variants: *Momena,*
Momina, Moomina,
Moumena, Moumenah,
Moumina, Mu'minah,
Mumena, Mumenah,
Mumina, Muminah

Mumtazah
Excellent - Exceptional

Munadiyah
Caller

Munadiyat
Callers

Munajidah
Helper - Supporter

Munamirah
Leopard-like

Munaqqaa
Pure

Munar
Bright - Well-lit

Mundiyah
Generous - Giving

Muneeba
One Who Turns to God -
Virtuous
Muneebah is an Arabic
name for girls that means

"one who turns t God",
"one who does not insist
on sinning".
Variants: *Moneeba,*
Moniba, Monibah,
Muneiba, Muniba,
Munibah

Munia
Hope - Wish

Muniah
Hope - Wish

Munifah
Great - High in Status

Munira
Brilliant - Enlightening -
Illuminating - Radiant
Variants: *Moneearh,*
Moneera, Monira,
Monirah, Muneera,
Muneerah, Munirah

Munisa
Affable - Friendly
Variants: *Monisa,*
Moonesah, Mounesa,
Mounisa, Mu'nisah,
Munesa, Munesah,
Munisah

Munjidah
Rescuer - Savior

Munshidah
Reciter of Poetry

Muntasiriyyah
Victorious - Winning

Muradat
Beloved - Desired

Muraihah
Joyfulness - Liveliness

Muraziyah
Gainer of Approval -
Satisfier

Muridah
Desirous - Seeker

Murihah
Gentle - Lenient

Mursalah
Message-bearer -
Messenger

Mursalin
Messengers
The name Mursalin is
mentioned in the Quran.
Variants: *Morsalin,*
Mursaleen

Murshidaa
Guide

Murshidah
Guide

Mursilah
Disptacher

Murzaqah
Blessed - Fortunate

Murziqah
Giver of Provision

Murziyah
Pleaser - Satisfier

Musabbihah
Glorifier of God

Musadah
Glad - Happy

Musafah
Helped - Rescued

Musamma
Definite - Determined -
Specified
The name Musamma is
mentioned in the Quran.
Variants: *Mosamma,*
Musamaa

Musawiyah
Equal - Equivalent

Musawwarah
Formed - Imagined -
Pictured - Shaped

Musdiyah
Bestower - Giver -
Granter

Musefah
Helper - Rescuer

Musfira
Beautiful - Happy -
Joyous
The name Musfira is
mentioned in the Quran.
Variants: *Mosfera,*
Mosferah, Mosfira,
Mosfirah, Musfera,
Musferah, Musfirah

Mushaa
Gentle Walker

Musharrafah
Honorable

Musharrafi
Honorable

Mushiah
Radiant

Mushilah
Kindler - Lighter
Variants: *Mush'ila*

Mushirah
Gesturer - Guide

Mushrifah
Overlooking - Overseer -
Towering

Mushtaq
Desirous - Eager -
Yearning

Mushtari
Planet Jupiter

Musidah
Helper

Muskah
Intelligence - Sense

Muslihah
Doer of Good Deeds -
Improver - Reformer

Muslimaa
Muslim
Variant of Muslimah.

71

Muslimah
Muslim

Mutairah
Rain

Muteeah
Obedient

Muthailah
Exemplary - Ideal - Model

Muthalaa
Ideal - Model

Muthlaa
Exemplary - Ideal - Model

Mutmaanah
At Peace - Tranquil

Mutmainnah
At Peace - Tranquil
The name Mutmainnah is
mentioned in the Quran.

Muyassarah
Facilitated - Successful

Muyassirah
Facilitator

Muzainah
Rain-Bearing Cloud

Muzammil
Wrapped in Garments
The name Muzammil is
mentioned in the Quran.
Variants: *Mozammil,*
Muzamel, Muzamil

Muzayyanah
Adorned - Beautified

Muzdalifa
Variants: *Muzdalefa,*
Muzdalefah, Muzdalifah

Muzeeah
Radiant

Muzhirah
Blooming

Muzn
Rain-Bearing Cloud -
White Cloud
The name Muzn is
mentioned in the Quran.

Muzna
Rain-Bearing Cloud -
White Cloud

N

Naaima
Blessed - Gentle - Living in Luxury - Soft
Variants: *Naaema, Naaimah, Naema, Naemah, Naima, Naimah*

Naba
Announcement - News - Tidings

Nabahat
Vigilance - Wakefulness

Nabeela
Dignified - Gracious - Noble
Variants: *Nabeelah, Nabila, Nabilah*

Nabhanah
Aware - Vigilant - Wakeful

Nabighah
Brilliant - Outstanding

Nabihah
Aware - Honorable - Vigilant - Wakeful

Nada
Blessedness - Dew - Goodness - Rain
Variants: *Nadaa*

Naddaa
Caller - Charitable - Generous - Pleader
Variants: *Nada, Nadaa, Nadda*

Naddaa
Generous

Nadeerah
Eloquent - Fluent

Nadiaa
Caller

Nadirah
Rare - Unique

Nadiyah
Caller

Nadraa
Rare - Unique

Nadrah
Piece of Gold - Piece of Iron - Rare - Unique

Naeema
Blessed - Blissful
Variants: *Na'eemah, Na'ima, Na'imah, Naeemah, Naeemeh, Naima, Naimah, Nayima*

Naeemaat
Blessings - Bliss

Nafahat
Fragrant - Gifts - Presents

Nafeesa
Desired - Precious
Variants: *Nafeesah, Nafisa, Nafisah*

Nafizah
Influential - Powerful

Naghmat
Melody - Tune

Nahad
Honorable - Mighty - Strong

Nahar
Daytime
The name Nahar is mentioned in the Quran.
Variants: *Nahaar, Nehar*

Nahizah
Diligent - Elevated - Energetic - High - Lofty

Nahjah
Apparent - Clear

Nahran
Rivers

Nahwah
Intelligence - Wisdom

Naifah
Elevated - High - Towering

Nailawfir
Lily
(Also used in Persian)

Nailufar
Lily
(Also used in Persian)

Naira
Brilliant - Radiant

Naizak
Meteor - Shooting Star -
Short Spear

Najat
Rescue - Salvation
The name Najat is used in
the Quran.
Variants: *Najaat*

Najdah
Bravery - Rescue

Najeedah
Lion

Najeemah
Radiant

Najhah
Success

Najibah
Excellent - High-born
Variants: *Najeeba*

Najidaa
Rescuer - Supporter

Najihah
Prosperous - Successful

Najiyah
Rescued - Survivor

Najiyyah
Rescuer - Savior
Variants: *Najia*

Najlaa
Beautiful-eyed - Long
Night

Najlah
Offspring - Progeny -
Scion

Najlan
Beautiful-eyed

Najlat
Offspring - Progeny -
Scion
(Also used in Turkish)

Najm
Star
The name Najm is
mentioned in the Quran.
Variants: *Nejm*

Najma
Star
Variants: *Najmah*

Najmaa
Star

Najmiyyah
Star-like

Najud
Intelligent - Sensible -
Wise

Najumah
Radiant

Najwa
Intimate Conversation -
Whispered Speech
The name Najwa is
mentioned in the Quran.

Nakheel
Date Palms

Nakhlah
Date Palm
The name Nakhlah is
mentioned in the Quran.

Namaa
Affluence

Namiyah
Developing - Growing -
Increasing

Naoum
Blessed

Naqaawa
Cleanliness - Purity

Naqeeba
Leader - Representative
Variants: *Nakibah,*
Naqeebah, Naqiba,
Naqibah

Naqil
Copyist - Transporter

Naqilah
Copyist - Transporter

Naratain
Flowers - White Flowers

Nareen
Fresh - Passionate - Rosy
Variants: *Narin*

Naroon
Pomegranate Tree
Variants: *Narun*

Narvan
Elm Tree
Variants: *Narwan*

Nasayir
Helper - Supporter

Naseeba
Fitting - Lady-like -
Proper
Variants: *Naseebah,
Nasiba, Nasibah, Nesibe*

Naseefa
Secretly Spoken Words
Variants: *Naseefah, Nasifa,
Nesife*

Naseeraa
Helper - Supporter

Nashia
Young Generation -
Young Woman
The name Nashia is
mentioned in the Quran.

Nashidah
Praiser - Reciter of Poetry

Nashwan
Delirious - Ecstatic
Variants: *Nashuan,
Nashwaan*

Nasihah
Giver of Advice - Guide

Nasikah
Worshiper

Nasikhah
Clerk - Copyist - Editor

Nasirah
Helper - Supporter

Nasrat
Help - Support

Nasreen
White Narcissus
(Also used in Kurdish,
Persian)
Variants: *Nasrin*

Nauratan
Flowers - White Flowers

Nawal
Bestowal - Blessing - Gift
Variants: *Nawaal, Newaal,
Newal*

Nawat
Core - Kernel - Pip - Seed

Nawfaa
Great - High

Nawfah
Great - High

Nawfalah
Beautiful - Generous

Nawlaa
Gift - Present

Nawr
Radiance - White Flower

Nawraa
Beautiful - Radiant

Nawrah
Flower

Nawras
Blossoming - Budding -
Young
(Also used in Persian)

Nawwal
Generous - Noble

Nawwar
Glowing - Radiant

Nawwarah
Brilliant - Dazzling

Nawzaa
Glowing - Shimmering

Nayamee
Affluent - Blissful

Nayir
Brilliant - Radiant

Nayla
Charitable - Gracious -
Winner
Variants: *Na'ilah, Naa'ila,
Naayela, Naayla, Naela,
Naila, Nayela, Nayelah,
Nayila, Naylah*

Naylaa
Achiever - Acquirer

Naylaa
Gift

Nayyirah
Brilliant - Radiant

Nazaara
Beauty - Happiness -
Radiance

Variants: *Nadaarah,*
Nadara, Nadhaara,
Nadhara, Nazaarah,
Nazara, Nazarh

Nazeef
Clean - Virtuous

Nazeemah
Orderly - Organized

Nazeerah
Beautiful - Delicate

Nazeerah
Cautioner - Warner

Nazimah
Adjuster - Arranger -
Organizer

Nazira
Beautiful - Radiant
The name *Nazira* is
mentioned in the Quran.
Variants: *Naazerah,*
Naazira, Naazirah,
Nadherah, Nadhira,
Nadhirah, Nazerah,
Nazirah

Nazmiyyah
Orderly - Organized -
Systematic

Nazra
Beauty - Radiance
Nazra is used in the
Quran in verse 76:11.
Variants: *Nadhra, Nadra,*
Nadrah, Nazrah, Nazreh,
Nezra, Nezrah, Nezre,
Nezreh

Neem
Affluence

Nehrin
River
(Also used in Turkish)
Variants: *Nehreen*

Neima
Blessing - Favor - Gift
from God
The name Neima is
mentioned in the Quran.
Variants: *Nemah, Ni'mah,*
Nimah

Neimaat
Blessings

Neimat
Blessing

Niam
Blessings - God's Favors
The name Niam is
mentioned in the Quran.

Niamullah
God's Blessings - God's
Favors

Nida
Call - Plea - Prayer
The name Nida is
mentioned in the Quran
in verse 2:172 and others.
Variants: *Neda, Nidaa,*
Nidaa', Niyda, Nyda

Niddat
Equivalent - Opponent

Nihlah
Belief - Creed - Gift
The name Nihlah is
mentioned in the Quran.

Nijarah
Carpentry

Nijarat
Carpentry
(Also used in Turkish)

Nijdah
Rescuer - Supporter

Nilaa
Water Hyacinth
A group of flowering
plants.

Nilah
Water Hyacinth
A group of flowering
plants.

Niliyyah
Beautiful

Nimatullah
God's Blessings - God's
Favors

Nisa
Women

Nisbah
Connection - Harmony -
Relationship

Nisbat
Connection - Harmony -
Relationship

Nisbi
Comparative -
Proportional

Nismah
Soft Breeze

Nismat
Soft Breeze
(Also used in Turkish)

Niswah
Women

Niyazi
Beloved - Desired

Niyyat
Aims - Goals - Intentions

Nizalah
Strife - Struggle

Noon
Sword Blade
The name Noon is
mentioned in the Quran.

Nooni
Sharp

Noum
Affluence

Nouranghiz
Radiant

Nuaim
Delicate - Soft

Nuaimaat
Delicate - Soft

Nuaimah
Delicate - Soft

Nubla
Chivalry - Graciousness -
Nobleness

Nudairah
Rareness - Uniqueness

Nudriyyah
Rare - Unique

Nuha
Intellect - Intelligence -
Reason
The name Nuha is
mentioned in the Quran.
Variants: Noha, Nohaa,
Nouha, Nuhaa

Nuhiah
Intelligence - Wisdom

Nujaidah
Rescue

Nujaimah
Little Star

Nujud
Clarity - Elevation -
Highness

Numou
Growth - Increase

Nuqawah
Best - Finest

Nuqrah
Piece of Gold - Precious -
Valuable

Nur
Light - Radiance
The name Nur is
mentioned in the Quran.
Variants: Noor, Nour

Nura
Light - Radiance
Variants: Noorah, Noore,
Nooreh, Norah, Noura,
Nourah, Noureh, Nura,
Nurah, Nure, Nureh

Nuraa
Light

Nurahan
Good Tidings - Radiant
King
(Also used in Persian,
Turkish)

Nuralain
Bringer of Happiness -
Consoler - Remover of
Sadness
Literally means "light of
the eyes".
Variants: Nooralain,
Noorulain, Nurul Ain,
Nurulain

Nurat
Light
(Also used in Turkish)

Nureen
Brilliant - Radiant
(Also used in Persian)

Nuriyah
Brilliant - Radiant
Variants: Nooria, Noriah,

Nooriya, Nooriyah, Nuria,
Nuriah, Nuriya

Nurshah
Light of the King

Nurtaj
Crown of Light

Nusaiba
Fitting - Lady-like -
Proper
Variants: Nosaiba,
Nosaibah, Nosayba,
Nusaibah, Nusayba,
Nusaybah

Nusaimah
Soft Breeze

Nusairah
Triumph - Victory

Nushur
Resurrection
The name Nushur is
mentioned in the Quran.

Nusrah
Defense - Fortification -
Support
Variants: Nosra, Nosrah,
Nusra

Nusrat
Defense - Fortification -
Support
Nusrat is the Turkish
pronunciation of the
Arabic name Nusrah.
Variants: Nosrat

Nutou
Elevation - Greatness -
Loftiness

Nuwairah
Light - Radiance

Nuwwar
Blossoms - Flowers

Nuwwarah
Blossoms - Flowers

Nuzairah
Cautioner - Warner

Nuzairah
Flourishing - Radiant

Nuzhaa
Purity - Virtue

Nuzhah
Chastity - Stroll - Virtue

Nuzhat
Chastity - Virtue
(Also used in Turkish)

O

Ohda
Care - Custody -
Guardianship -
Responsibility -
Trusteeship
Variants: *Ohdah, Uhdah*

Omaimiya
Affectionate - Kind -
Loving
Literally "mother-like".
Variants: *Umaymiyyah*

Omniati
My Hope - My Wish
Variants: *Umniati,
Umniyyati*

Onaifa
Dignified
Variants: *Unaifah,
Unayfah*

Onaitarah
Brave

Onaysa
Consoler - Good Friend
Variants: *Unaysah*

Onshuda
Chant - Hymn
Variants: *Unshuda*

Onsiyah
Bringer of Calm and
Gladness
Variants: *Unsia*

Oraib
Intelligent - Keen -
Perceptive
Variants: *Uraib*

Oraiba
Intelligent - Keen -
Perceptive
Variants: *Uraibah*

Oraibia
Intelligent - Keen -
Perceptive
Variants: *Uraibiyyah*

Orzah
Competent - Proactive

Ouhood
Promises
Variants: *Ohood*

Oula
First - Foremost
The name Oula is
mentioned in the Quran.
Variants: *Oola, Oulaa,
Ulaa*

Owaiba
Repentant
Variants: *Uwaibah*

Owaidat
Consoler - Visitor of the
Sick

Owaiqiba
Recompense - Reward

Owaiza
Replacement

Owaria
Water Well

Oyaina
Beautiful-eyed

P

Pareesima
Fairy-like
Paree is a Persian word
meaning "fairy", while
sima is an Arabic word
meaning "complexion",
"appearance".
Variants: *Parisimaa,
Parysima*

The sound P does not
exist in Standard Arabic,
therefore there are no
Standard Arabic names
that contain this sound.

Q

Qabilaa
Accepter - Approver - Endorser

Qabilah
Accepter - Approver - Endorser

Qaddarah
Arranger - Organizer

Qadduraa
Able - Capable - Powerful

Qaddurah
Able - Capable - Powerful

Qadeerah
Able - Capable - Powerful

Qadri
Able - Powerful

Qadriyyah
Able - Capable - Powerful

Qadumah
Bold - Brave

Qaisah
Firmness - Strength

Qaleeb
Water Well

Qamar
Moon
The name Qamar is mentioned in the Quran.
Variants: *Qemer*

Qamaraat
Moons

Qamari
Moon-like

Qamariyyah
Moon-like

Qamirah
Moonlit

Qamrun
Moon

Qanita
Devoted to God - Worshiper
Variants: *Kanita, Kanitah, Qaanita, Qaneta, Qanetah, Qanitah*

Qareen
Companion - Friend
The name Qareen is mentioned in the Quran.

Qarirah
Calm - Glad - Happy - Tranquil

Qarurah
Tranquil

Qaseemah
Beautiful - Dawn

Qasmaa
Beautiful

Qassamah
Distributor - Divider

Qasumah
Beautiful

Qayyimah
Good - Proper - Upright

Qiblah
Direction - Direction of the Kaaba
The name Qiblah is mentioned in the Quran.

Qiladah
Necklace

Qindil
Oil Lamp

Qindilah
Oil Lamp

Qiraat
Recitation - Recitation of the Quran
Variants: *Qeiraat, Qeraat, Qira'ah, Qira'at*

Qismah
Fortune - Luck

Qismat
Fortune - Luck

Qiyadah
Leadership

Qiyam
Night-long Worship
The name Qiyam is mentioned in the Quran.

Qudairah
Ability - Capacity - Power

Qudrah
Ability - Capacity - Power

Qudwah
Exemplar - Ideal - Model

Qumr
Fair-skinned

Qumrah
Moonlight

Qumri
Dove
Specifically the European
turtle dove.

Qunnah
Tall Mountain

Qurb
Closeness - Nearness

Qurrah
Comfort - Consolation
Qurrah is mentioned in
the Quran in verse 28:9.
The name is used with the
meaning of "a child who
brings comfort and
consolation to her
parents".
Variants: Qorah, Qorra,
Qura, Qurah, Qurra

Qurrat
Consolation
Qurrat is the Turkish
pronunciation of the
Arabic word Qurrahm
which means
"consolation", "comfort", a
child who brings comfort
and consolation to her
parents.
Variants: Qorat, Qorrat,
Qurat

Qurratul Ain
Consolation
Qurratul Ain means "a
child who brings comfort
and consolation to her
parents".
Variants: Qurat Alain,
Qurat al-Ain, Quratulain,
Qurrat Alain, Qurrat al-
Ain, Qurratolain, Qurratul
`ain, Qurratulain

Qusaimah
Fortune - Luck

Quwa
Strength
The name Quwa is
mentioned in the Quran.
Variants: Qowa, Quah,
Quwwa, Quwwah

R

Raahima
Compassionate - Kind - Merciful
Variants: *Raahema, Raahemah, Raahimah, Rahema, Rahemah, Rahima, Rahimah*

Rabaa
Grace - Kindness

Rabab
White Cloud
Variants: *Rabaab*

Rabeeba
Queen
Variants: *Rabeebah, Rabibah*

Rabeehah
Earner - Winner

Rabiah
Constant - Fertile Firmly Set in Place - Fourth - Rainy - Stable

Rabihaat
Earners - Winners

Rabihah
Earner - Winner

Rabwah
Highland - Small Hill

Radih
Strong - Tough

Raeda
Guide - Leader - Pioneer
Variants: *Ra'eda, Ra'ida, Raaeda, Rayeda, Rayida*

Raeefah
Compassionate - Merciful

Raeesa
Chief - Leader
Variants: *Raeesah, Raesa, Raisa, Raisah*

Rafa
Compassion - Kindness - Sympathy
Rafa is mentioned in the Quran in verse 57:27.
Variants: *Ra'fah, Raafa, Raafah, Rafaa*

Rafahiyyah
Affluence - Ease - Luxury

Rafeea
High - Lofty - Sublime
Variants: *Rafeeah, Rafi'ah, Rafiah*

Rafeedah
Generous - Gracious

Rafeeqa
Companion - Gentle - Kind
Variants: *Rafeeka, Rafeeqah, Rafika, Rafiqa, Rafiqah*

Rafida
Helper - Supporter
Variants: *Raafida, Raafidah, Rafeda, Rafedah*

Rafifah
Brilliance - Gloss - Luster

Rafou
Exalted - Great - Mighty

Raghaad
Abundance - Ease - Luxury - Wealth

Raghdah
Delicate - One Who Lives in Affluence and Luxury - Soft - Sweet

Raghdiyyah
Delicate - One Who Lives in Affluence and Luxury - Soft - Sweet

Ragheebah
Desired - Wished For

Raghibah
Aspiring - Desirous - Seeking

Raghidah
Delicate - One Who Lives in Affluence and Luxury - Soft - Sweet

Raghubah
Aspiring - Desirous

Raha
Comfort - Peace of Mind - Rest
Variants: *Rahah*

Rahaa
Serene - Tranquil - Vast
Variants: *Raha*

Rahayef
Delicate - Gentle
Variants: *Rahaif*

Rahbat
Vast Expanse of Land

Rahd
Delicate - Soft

Raheebah
Generous

Raheef
Gentle - Tender
Variants: *Rahif*

Raheel
Departure - Journey
Variants: *Rahil*

Raheela
Departure - Journeying -
Traveling
Variants: *Raheelah, Rahila,*
Rahilah

Raheema
Compassionate - Kind -
Merciful
Variants: *Raheemah,*
Raheemeh, Raheima,
Raheyma, Rahiema,
Rahima, Rahimah,
Rahiyma, Rahyma

Rahifaa
Gentle - Tender
Variants: *Rahaefa*

Rahila
Journeyer
Variants: *Rahilah*

Rahimaa
Compassionate - Merciful

Rahma
Compassion - Grace -
Kindness - Mercy
The name Rahma is
mentioned in the Quran.
Variants: *Rahmah, Rehma*

Rahmanah
Compassionate - Merciful

Rahmi
Compassionate - Merciful

Rahmiyyah
Compassionate - Merciful

Rahqah
Nectar

Rahumah
Compassionate - Merciful

Raifa
Compassion - Kind -
Softhearted
Variants: *Ra'ifa, Ra'ifah,*
Raa'ifah, Raaifah, Raefa,
Rayefa, Rayfa, Rayifa

Raima
Woman Who Loves Her
Baby
Variants: *Ra'imah,*
Raaemah, Raaima,
Raaymah, Raema, Raimah,
Rayma

Rajayah
Hope - Wish

Rajihah
Predominant - Superior

Rajwaa
Hope - Wish

Rakeenah
Composed - Dignified

Rakhaa
Ease of Living - Luxury

Rakhamah
Compassion - Kindness

Rakhimah
Loving - Soft-spoken

Rakhs
Delicate - Soft

Rakhumah
Gentle - Soft-spoken

Rakidah
Calm - Tranquil

Raknah
Residence - Stay

Ramlaa
Benefit - Good Things of
Life

Ramlah
Grain of Sand

Ramlat
Grain of Sand
(Also used in Turkish)

Ramzah
Gesture - Mark - Symbol

Ramzia
Gesture - Sign - Symbl
Variants: *Ramziya,*
Ramziyah, Ramziyya,
Ramziyyah

Rana
Beautiful
Variants: *Ra'naa, Raana,*
Raanaa, Ranaa

Ranada
Fragrant Tree
Variants: *Rannada*

Randah
Fragrant Tree
Variants: *Randa*

Ranin
Buzz - Resonance
Variants: *Raneen*

Ranya
One Who Has a Loving
Gaze
Variants: *Raneya, Rania,*
Raniah, Raniya, Raniyah,
Ranyah

Raoofah
Compassionate - Merciful

Raqeema
Intelligent -
Knowledgeable -
Perceptive - Wise
Variants: *Rakeemah,*
Rakeimah, Rakima,
Rakimah, Raqeemah,
Raqima, Raqimah

Raqiah
Ascension - Elevation

Raqqah
Flat Land With Soft Dust

Rasaan
Intermittently Falling
Raindrops

Raseena
Deep-rooted - Stable -
Upstanding
Variants: *Raseenah,*
Rasina, Rasinah

Rashaa
Baby Gazelle

Rashadah
Right Guidance - Right
Path

Rashdaa
Mature - Rightly-guided

Rashidaa
Rightly-guided

Rashidah
Rightly-guided

Rashiqah
Graceful - Nimble -
Slender - Slim

Rasifah
Composed - Dignified

Rasiyah
Stable - Tall - Towering

Ratiyah
Scholar - Wise

Rawaa
Refreshing Water
Variants: *Rawa*

Rawashed
Rightly-guided
Variants: *Rawashid*

Rawashedah
Rightly-guided
Variants: *Rawashida*

Rawayeh
Fragrance
Variants: *Rawayih*

Raweeha
Good Scent - Happiness -
Relaxation
Variants: *Raweehah,*
Rawiha, Rawihah

Rawfiyyah
Mercy - Tranquility
Variants: *Rawfiya*

Rawh
Cool Breeze - Mercy -
Relaxation
Variants: *Rauh*

Rawhah
Fragrance - Fresh Breeze
Variants: *Rauha*

Rawhiya
Consolation - Fragrance -
Rest
Variants: *Rauhia, Rauhiah,*
Rauhiyyah, Rawhiyyah

Rawsan
Light Rain
Variants: *Rausan*

Raydaa
Soft Breeze
Variants: *Raida*

Raydah
Soft Breeze
Variants: *Raida*

Rayhan
Fragrance
The name Rayhan is
mentioned in the Quran.
Variants: *Raihaan, Raihan,
Rayhaan, Reehan, Reihan,
Reyhan, Rihan*

Rayyaa
Fragrance - Quenched
(not thirsty)
Variants: *Rayaa*

Rayyan
Quenched - Watered
Name of one of the gates
of Paradise.
Variants: *Raiaan, Raian,
Rayaan, Rayan, Reyan,
Reyyan, Ryan*

Razanah
Composure

Razeen
Calm - Composed -
Dignified

Razinah
Composed - Dignified

Raznah
Composure - Dignity

Razwaa
[Name of a Mountain in
al-Madinah]
Variants: *Radhwa,
Radhwaa, Radwa, Radwaa,
Razwa, Rezwa, Rezwaa*

Rebab
Covenant - Oath -
Promise
Variants: *Rebaab, Reibab,
Ribaab, Ribab*

Reem
White Gazelle
Variants: *Rim*

Reema
White Gazelle
Variants: *Reemah, Rima,
Rimah*

Rehab
Generous - Open-hearted
- Open-minded -
Spacious - Vast
Variants: *Rehaab, Reihaab,
Reihab, Reyhaab, Reyhab,
Rihaab, Rihab, Ryhab*

Reyah
Power - Scents - Victory -
Winds
Variants: *Reyaah, Riah,
Riyaah, Riyah, Ryah*

Rifa
Concord - Harmony -
Tranquility

Rifaah
Greatness - Highness of
Status

Rifaat
Greatness - Highness of
Status

Rifaq
Companions - Friends

Rifqah
Gentleness - Kindness -
Leniency

Rifqat
Gentleness - Leniency
Turkish pronunciation of
Rifqah. (Also used in
Turkish)

Riham
Light Rain
Variants: *Reham*

Rihanna
Fragrance
Variants: *Raehanah,
Raehaneh, Raihaanah,
Raihaaneh, Raihanah,
Raihaneh, Rayhaana,
Rayhana, Rayhanah,
Reihana, Reihannah,
Rihana, Rihannah*

Riqqah
Gentleness - Kindness -
Leniency

Risliyyah
Gentle - Lenient

Riza
Contentment - Having
God's Approval
Variants: *Reda, Redaa,
Redha, Redhaa, Reza, Rida,
Ridaa, Ridha, Ridhaa,
Rizaa*

Rizqaa
Blessing - Gift

Rizqah
Blessing - Gift

Rizwan
Contentment - Having
God's Approval
The name Rizwan is
mentioned in the Quran
in verse 57:20.
Variants: *Redhwan,
Rezwaan, Rezwan,
Ridhwaan, Ridhwan,
Ridwaan, Ridwan,
Rizwaan*

Rouyaa
Dream
The name Rouyaa is
mentioned in the Quran.

Ruaydaa
Gentle
Variants: *Rouaida, Ruadaa,
Ruaida, Rueyda, Rwaida*

Ruaydah
Gentle
Variants: *Roaidah, Ruaida,
Ruwaida, Ruwaidah,
Rwaida, Rwayda*

Rubaa
Blessings - Highlands -
Hills - Virtue

Rubab
Blessings - Bond - Good
Deeds
Variants: *Robaab, Robab,
Rubaab*

Rubaihah
Earner - Winner

Rufaa
Affectionate - Kind
Variants: *Rofa*

Rufah
Affectionate -
Sympathetic
Variants: *Roofa*

Rufaidah
Helper - Supporter
Variants: *Rofaida, Rufaida,
Rufaydah*

Rufaidiyyah
Helper - Supporter

Rughaidah
Delicate - One Who Lives
in Affluence and Luxury -
Soft - Sweet

Ruhab
Forbearing - Generous -
Open-minded
Variants: *Rohaab, Rohab,
Ruhaab*

Ruhaibah
Vast Expanse of Land

Ruhaila
Departer - Journeyer
Variants: *Rohailah,
Ruhailah, Ruhayla*

Ruhaimah
Light Rain
Variants: *Rohayma,
Ruhaima*

Ruhaimah
Compassionate - Merciful

Ruhan
Kind - Spiritual
Variants: *Rohaan, Rohan,
Rouhaan, Rouhan, Ruhaan*

Ruhana
Soul - Spirit
Variants: *Rohana*

Rukhaa
Soft Breeze
The name Rukhaa is
mentioned in the Quran.

Rumaisaa
Sirius
Sirius is the name of a
star.
Variants: *Romaisaa,
Rumaisa*

Rumaisah
Dispersing Wind

Ruqayya
Ascending - Elevated -
Exalted - Great
Variants: *Roqayah,
Roqayya, Roqayyah,*

Ruqaia, Ruqaya, Ruqayah,
Ruqayyah

Ruqayyat
Elevated Ones

Rushadaa
Mature Ones - Rightly
Guided Ones

Rusul
Little Girl - Messengers

Ruwaa
Beautiful Appearance -
Beautiful View

Ruwaid
Leniency - Soft Breeze
Variants: *Rowaid*

Ruwaiha
Fragrance - Relaxation -
Rest
Variants: *Rowaiha, Ruaiha,*
Ruayha, Ruayhah, Rueiha,
Ruwaihah

Ruwaizah
Beautiful Garden
Variants: *Rowaiza*

Ruwayyifah
Kind - Sympathetic
Variants: *Rowayfiah*

Ruzainah
Composed - Dignified

S

Saadaa
Happy - Successful
Variants: Sa'adaa

Saadah
Happy - Successful
Variants: Sa'ada

Saadanah
Dove - Pigeon
Variants: Sa'dana

Saadat
Happy - Successful
Variants: Sa'adat

Saadat
Leaders - Lords

Saadunah
Happy - Successful
Variants: Sa'duna

Saaebah
Intelligent - Rational -
Sensible

Saaedah
Great - Majestic
Variants: Saedah

Saaf
Pure

Saafah
Frond
Variants: Sa'fah

Saafia
Blameless - Pure -
Virtuous
Variants: Saafeya,
Saafeyah, Saafiyah, Safiya,
Safiyah

Saaiha
Flowing Water - Traveler
Variants: Saaehah,
Saaihah, Saeha, Saihah

Saairah
Avenger - Excited -
Revolutionary
Variants: Thaira

Saakinah
Tranquil
Variants: Saakena

Saalima
Intact - Pure - Virtuous
Variants: Saalema,
Saalemah, Saalimah

Saamiah
Hearer - Obedient -
Understanding
Variants: Saamia

Saatarah
Thyme - Thymus
Variants: Sa'tara

Saayah
Effort - Labor
Variants: Sa'yah

Saayerah
Returner

Saayidah
Happy - Successful
Variants: Sa'ayida

Saayidah
Chief - Dominant

Saba
Soft Breeze
Variants: Sabaa

Sabah
Complete - Whole
Variants: Thaba

Sabahah
Brilliance - Radiance

Sabbaghah
Dyer

Sabbarah
Enduring - Patient

Sabeel
Path - Road - Way
The name Sabeel is
mentioned in the Quran
in verse 27:24 and others.
Variants: Sabil, Sabyll,
Sebil, Sebill, Sybil

Sabeela
Path - Road - Way
Variants: Sabeelah,
Sabilah, Sebeelah, Sebila,
Sebylla

Sabhaa
Beautiful - Bright

Sabibah
Poured Water

Sabihah
Beautiful - Bright

Sabiqa
Advanced - Ahead
Variants: *Saabeqah,*
Saabiqa, Saabiqah, Sabeqa

Sabirah
Enduring - Patient

Sabitah
Deep-rooted -
Established
Variants: *Thabita*

Sabri
Enduring - Patient

Sabriyyah
Enduring - Patient

Sabuah
Lioness
Variants: *Saboah, Sabua*

Saburah
Enduring - Patient

Sadaaqah
Affection - Friendship

Sadadah
Rationality - Sense
Variants: *Sadada*

Sadaf
Seashell
Variants: *Sedef*

Sadafah
Conch - Shell

Sadaqaat
Acts of Charity

The name Sadaqaat is
mentioned in the Quran.

Sadaqah
Charity - Something
Given As Charity
The name Sadaqah is
mentioned in the Quran.

Sadeeqah
Friend

Sadia
Blessed - Successful
Variants: *Sadiah, Sadiya,*
Sadiyah, Sadya

Sadinah
Maintainer of the Kaaba
Variants: *Sadeena*

Sadiqah
Sincere - Truthful

Saeedaa
Happy - Successful
Variants: *Sa'ida*

Saeedah
Happy - Successful
Variants: *Sa'idah*

Saeedanah
Happy - Successful
Variants: *Sa'idana*

Safaa
Innocence - Purity
The name *Safaa* is
mentioned in the Quran.
Variants: *Safa, Sapha,*
Saphaa, Sefa, Sefaa, Sepha,
Sephaa

Safawaat
Best - Finest - Prime

Safee
Pure
Variants: *Safi, Safy*

Safeenah
Ship
Variants: *Safeena, Safina*

Safeerah
Ambassador

Safeeya
Blameless - Chosen - Pure
- Virtuous
Variants: *Safeeiah,*
Safeeyah, Safiyya, Safiyyah

Saffanah
Pearl - Shipwright
Variants: *Safaana, Saffana*

Safwah
Best - Finest - Prime

Safwana
Bright Day - Pure - Rock
Variants: *Safwaana,*
Safwaanah, Safwanah

Safwat
Best - Finest - Prime

Sahari
Deserts

Sahbah
Companionship -
Friendship

Sahela
Beach - Coast
(Also used in Persian)
Variants: *Saheleh*

Sahibah
Companion - Friend
The name Sahibah is
mentioned in the Quran.

Sahira
Moon - Unsleeping -
Wakeful
The name Sahira is
mentioned in the Quran
in verse 79:14.
Variants: *Saahera,
Saahira, Saahirah, Sahera,
Saherah*

Sahiyah
Awake - Sober - Vigilant

Sahlah
Gentle - Lenient

Sahlat
Gentle - Lenient

Saihah
Flow - Streaming - Travel

Sajdaa
Prostrator - Worshiper of
God
Variants: *Sajda*

Sajeedah
Prostrator - Worshiper
Variants: *Sajeeda*

Sajida
Prostrator - Worshiper of

God
Variants: *Saajeda,
Saajedah, Saajida,
Saajidah, Sajeda, Sajedah,
Sajidah*

Sakeenah
Composure - Dignity -
Tranquility
Variants: *Sakeena, Sakina,
Sakinah, Sekina*

Sakhiyyah
Generous - Noble
Variants: *Sakhia*

Salaat
Litany - Prayer
The name Salaat is
mentioned in the Quran.

Salama
Safety - Security
Variants: *Salaama,
Salaamah, Salamah*

Salawaat
Formal Prayer
The name Salawaat is
mentioned in the Quran.

Saleehah
Good - Pious

Saleema
Intact - Pure - Safe -
Virtuous
Variants: *Saleemah,
Salima, Salimah*

Saleemaa
Safe - Unharmed

Saleemaat
Safe - Unharmed

Sali
Amused - Cheerful
Variants: *Saly*

Saliha
Virtuous
Variants: *Saaleha, Saaliha,
Saleha, Salehah, Saliha,
Salihah, Salihe, Salyheh*

Salihat
Good Deeds - Pious Ones
The name Salihat is
mentioned in the Quran.
Variants: *Salehaat,
Salehat, Salihaat, Saulihat*

Salikah
Follower of a Path
Variants: *Saleka, Salika*

Salitaa
Eloquent - Tall

Salitah
Eloquent - Tall

Salma
Purity - Safety - Security
- Virtue
Variants: *Salmaa, Selma,
Selmaa*

Saloofah
Advancer

Saloomah
Safe - Unharmed

Salsabil
Refreshing and Tasy Drink
Variants: *Salsabeel*

Salsabilah
Refreshing and Tasy Drink
Variants: *Salsabeela*

Saltanah
Power – Rule – Sultanate
Variants: *Saltana*

Saluhah
Good – Pious

Salwa
Comfort – Consolation
The name Salwa is
mentioned in the Quran.
Variants: *Salua, Salwaa*

Salwah
Consolation

Sama
Elevated – Lofty
Variants: *Samaa*

Samaa
Heaven – Sky
The name Samaa is
mentioned in the Quran.

Samaanah
Hearer

Samaaraa
Nighttime Conversation
Alternate form
of Samaarah.
Variants: *Samara*

Samaarah
Nighttime Conversation
Companion
Variants: *Samaara,
Samara, Samarah*

Samaee
Heavenyl

Samah
Leniency – Pardon

Samahaa
Generosity – Leniency

Samahah
Generosity – Leniency

Samar
Darkness of the Night –
Night – Nighttime
Conversation
Variants: *Summer*

Samara
Nighttime Conversation
Companion

Samarah
Fruit – Product
Variants: *Samara*

Samawah
Elevation – Greatness

Samawat
Heavens – Skies
The name Samawat is
mentioned in the Quran.
Variants: *Samaawat*

Samawi
Heavenly

Sameeka
Elevated – High in Status –
Majestic
Variants: *Sameekah,
Samika, Samikah*

Sameera
Friend – Night
Conversation Partner
Variants: *Sameerah,
Sameira, Samira, Samirah,
Semira, Semire*

Samhaa
Forgiving – Lenient

Samhah
Forgiveness – Leniency

Samhiyyah
Forgiving – Lenient

Sami
Great – Lofty – Sublime
Variants: *Saami, Saamy,
Samee, Samy*

Samiha
Forgiving – Gracious
Variants: *Samihah*

Samika
Elevated – High in Status –
Majestic
Variants: *Samikah*

Samiyyan
Great – High in Status

Sammadah
Determined – Persevering
– Steadfast

Sammarah
One Who Continues
Conversation Long Into
the Night

Samraa
Mature - Ripe
Variants: *Thamraa*

Samreen
Beneficial - Fruitful -
Productive
Variants: *Samrin*

Samtah
Beauty

Samyaa
Great - Honored

Sana
Flare - Flash - Glow -
Shine - Spark
The name Sana is
mentioned in the Quran
in verse 24:43.
Variants: *Sanaa, Sena*

Sanaa
Craft - Work
Name of the capital of
Yemen.
Variants: *Sanaa', Sena, Senaa*

Sanaa
Glory - Greatness -
Honor

Sanabel
Ears of Corn - Ears of
Wheat - Plant Spikes
The name Sanabel is
mentioned in the Quran.

Variants: *Sanaabel, Sanaabil, Sanabil*

Sanai
Praise
Variants: *Thanay*

Sanan
Tradition - Way of Life

Sanaya
Honorable - Honored -
Noble
Variants: *Sanayaa, Senaia*

Sanayah
Flash of Light - Radiance
Variants: *Sanaaya, Sanaiya, Sanaya*

Sandah
Climb - Dependence -
Reliance

Saniyya
Honored - Noble -
Sublime - Superb
Variants: *Saneyah, Sania, Saniya, Saniyyah, Sanyah*

Saniyyaat
Exalted - High in Status

Sannah
Bear - Leopard

Sanubar
Cypress

Saqibah
Piercing - Sharp
Variants: *Thaqiba*

Saqrah
Falcon

Saqriyyah
Falcon-like

Sara
Delighted - Happy -
Joyous
Non-standard derivation
from the Arabic name
Sarah.
Variants: *Saara, Saaraa, Saraa*

Saraab
Mirage
The name Saraab is
mentioned in the Quran.
Variants: *Sarab*

Sarah
Delighted - Happy -
Joyous
Sarah is also the Arabic
name for the wife of
Prophet Ibrahim peace be
upon him.
Variants: *Saara, Saarah*

Sarayaa
Army Company - Brigade
Variants: *Saraya*

Sarayah
Army Company - Brigade
Variants: *Saarayah, Saraya*

Sareema
Firm Decision -
Resolution
Variants: *Sareemah, Sarima, Sarimah*

Sarihah
Shepherdess
Variants: *Saariha*

Sarima
Decisive - Resolute -
Strong-willed
Variants: *Sarimah*

Sariya
Night Cloud - Night Rain -
Night Traveler
Variants: *Saariya,*
Saariyah, Sareya, Sareyah,
Saria, Sariah, Sariyah

Sarraa
Ease and Abundance -
Happy Times
The name Sarraai is
mentioned in the Quran.
Variants: *Saraa, Sarra*

Sarraat
Ease and Abundance -
Happy Times
Variants: *Saraat, Sarat*

Sarwah
Affluence - Fortune -
Wealth
Variants: *Sarwa, Tharwa,*
Tharwah

Sarwah
Cypress - Generosity -
Selflessness

Sarwat
Affluence - Fortune -
Wealth
Turkish pronunciation of
Sarwah. (Also used in
Kurdish, Persian, Turkish,

Urdu)
Variants: *Tharwat*

Sateerah
Modest
Variants: *Satira*

Sattarah
Hider
Variants: *Satarah*

Sauba
Reward
Variants: *Saubah, Sawba,*
Sawbah, Soba, Sobah,
Souba

Sauda
Blessed - Fortunate -
Happy
Variants: *Saudah*

Sawa
Equal - Similar

Sawab
Repentant - Reward
Variants: *Thawab*

Sawaba
Repentant
Variants: *Thawabah*

Sawalih
Pious - Virtuous

Sawalihah
Pious - Virtuous

Sawbat
Repentance
Turkish pronunciation of
Sawbah. (Also used in

Turkish)
Variants: *Thawbat*

Sawda
Land With Many Palm
Trees
Name of one of the wives
of Prophet Muhammad
PBUH.
Variants: *Sauda, Saudah,*
Sawdah, Sowda, Sowdah

Sawlah
Ascendancy - Domination
- Power

Sawrah
Revolution - Uprising
Variants: *Thawrah*

Sawrat
Revolution - Uprising
Turkish pronunciation of
Sawrah.
Variants: *Thawrat*

Sawsanah
Lily

Sayibah
Rational - Sensible - Wise

Sayyadah
Hunter

Semaara
Nighttime Conversation
Variants: *Semaarah,*
Semara, Simaara, Simara,
Simarah

Senbal
Spike of Corn

Siaad
Helper
Variants: *Sead*

Siba
Childhood - Emotion -
Enthusiasm -
Youthfulness
Variants: *Seba, Sebaa,
Sibaa, Syba*

Sibgha
Color - Dye - Hue
The name Sibgha is
mentioned in the Quran.
Variants: *Sebgha, Sebghah,
Sibga, Sibghah*

Siddiqah
Saintly - Truthful -
Virtuous
The name Siddiqah is
mentioned in the Quran.
Variants: *Sediqa, Sediqah,
Siddeeqah, Siddika,
Siddiqa, Sideekah,
Sideeqah, Sidika, Sidiqah*

Sidra
Lote Tree
The name Sidra is
mentioned in the Quran
in verses 53:14 and 53:16.
It is the name of a the
name of a tree in heaven.
Variants: *Sedra, Sedrah,
Sidrah*

Sidratul Muntaha
Lote Tree of the Utmost
Boundary
The name Sidratul
Muntaha is mentioned in
the Quran. It is the name

of a tree in or near
Paradise.
Variants: *Sidrat Ul
Muntaha,
Sidratulmuntaha*

Sifah
State - Trait

Sihab
Deep Water Well

Silaam
Peace-making
Variants: *Selam*

Sima
Appearance - Complexion
- Countenance
Variants: *Seema, Simaa*

Simmaa
Brave - Lion

Simmah
Mark - Sign - Token -
Trait

Sineen
Mountain Sinai
The name Sineen is
mentioned in the Quran.
Variants: *Senin, Sinin*

Sinnah
Coulter - Double-headed
Axe

Siraa
Tradition - Way of Life

Siraayah
Night Journey
Variants: *Seraya, Siraaya*

Sirah
Tradition - Way of Life

Siraj
Cresset - Lamp - Light
Variants: *Seraa, Seraj,
Siraaj*

Sirat
Path
The name Sirat is
mentioned in the Quran.
Variants: *Serat, Siraat*

Sitr
Cover Up - Hiding
Variants: *Setr*

Siwa
Flat Land With Soft Sand

Siyadah
Glory - Greatness -
Honor - Leadership

Siyam
The name Siyam is
mentioned in the Quran.
Variants: *Fasting*

Siyaq
Articulation - Context

Sodad
Great - Honorable
Variants: *Saudad, Sawdad,
So'dad, Soudad, Sudad*

Sonbol
Ear of Corn - Ear of
Wheat - Plant Spike
The name Sonbol is
mentioned in the Quran.
Variants: *Sonbol, Sonbul,*
Sunbol, Sunbul

Sonbula
Ear of Corn - Ear of
Wheat - Plant Spike
The name Sonbula is
mentioned in the Quran.
Variants: *Sonbulah,*
Sunbula, Sunbulah

Sonya
Exalted - High in Status

Suadaa
Happy - Successful
Variants: *Suaydaa*

Suaidah
Happy - Joyful

Subahah
Beautiful - Bright

Subahah
Beautiful - Flame of a
Lamp

Subaibah
Lover

Subaihah
Morning Arriver

Subail
Pouring Rain - Spike of
Corn
Variants: *Sobail*

Subhah
Beautiful - Bright

Sudainah
Maintainer of te Kaaba
Variants: *Sodaina*

Sudaiqah
Sincere - Truthful

Sudur
Hearts
The name Sudur is
mentioned in the Quran.
Variants: *Sodur, Sudoor*

Suffah
Plaza - Square

Suha
Little Star

Suhad
Insomnia

Suhaibah
Red-brown-haired

Suhailaa
Gentle - Lenient - Soft

Suhailah
Gentle - Lenient - Soft

Suhaima
Arrow
Variants: *Sohaima,*
Sohaimah, Suhaimah

Suhaira
Unsleeping - Wakeful
Variants: *Sohaira,*
Sohayra, Sohayrah,

Suhairah, Suhayra,
Suhayrah

Suhbah
Companionship -
Friendship

Sujaydah
Prostrator - Worshiper
Variants: *Sojaida*

Sukainah
Adorable - Cute -
Energetic - Sprightly
Variants: *Sokaina*

Sukkar
Sugar
Variants: *Sokar, Sukar*

Suknah
Tranquility
Variants: *Sokna*

Sukniyyah
Tranquil
Variants: *Soknia*

Sulaimaa
Safe - Unharmed

Sulaimaat
Safe - Unharmed

Sulaimah
Safe - Unharmed

Sulaiwah
Consolation

Sulamaa
Safe Ones - Whole Ones
Variants: *Solama*

Sultanah
Queen - Ruler
Variants: *Soltana*

Sulufah
Advancement

Sulwan
Consolation - Solace
Variants: *Soluan*

Sumaihah
Forgiving - Gracious -
Lenient

Sumaira
Companion - Nighttime
Conversation Partner
Variants: *Somaira,*
Somairah, Sumairah,
Sumayra

Sumairaa
Tan-skinned

Sumama
Rescue - Salvation
Variants: *Sumamah,*
Thumama, Thumamah

Sumayya
Birthmark - Special -
Unique
Variants: *Somaya,*
Somayyah, Sumaia,
Sumaya, Sumayah,
Sumayyah

Sumou
Elevation - Greatness

Sunan
Traditions - Ways of Life

The name Sunan is
mentioned in the Quran.

Sundus
Fine Silk - Silk Brocade
The name Sundus is
mentioned in the Quran.

Sunnah
Tradition - Way of Life
The name Sunnah is
mentioned in the Quran.

Sunud
Climb - Dependence -
Reliance

Surah
Chapter of the Quran -
Greatness - Highness of
Rank
The name Surah is
mentioned in the Quran.

Sutait
Little Lady
Variants: *Sotayt*

Suwaib
Reward
Variants: *Thuwaib*

Suwaiba
Reward
Variants: *Soaiba,*
Souaibah, Suaiba,
Suwaibah, Swaiba,
Thuwaibah

Suwaida
Land With Many Palm
Trees
Variants: *Sowaida,*

Sowaidah, Suwaidah,
Suwaydah

Suwaidis
Sixth

Suwaimah
Bamboo - Gold - Mark -
Symbol

Suwairaa
Pure Gold

Sh

Shaan
Greatness - Rank - Status
The name Shaan is
mentioned in the Quran.
Variants: *Sha'n, Shan*

Shababah
Young Age - Youth

Shabibah
Young Woman

Shabinah
Beautiful Young Woman

Shabirah
Beautiful - Gracious

Shabiyyah
Great - High in Status

Shablaa
Lion Cub

Shadiyyah
Seeker of Knowledge

Shadleen
Delicate - Happy
(Also used in Persian)
Variants: *Shadlin*

Shafaq
Affection - Dawn - Pity -
Sympathy - Twilight

Shafaqat
Affection - Pity -
Sympathy

Shafeefah
Translucent -
Transparent

Shafiqa
Compassioante -
Sympathetic
Variants: *Shafeeqa,
Shafeeqah, Shafiqah*

Shafiyat
Healer

Shafiyyah
Healer

Shafyaa
Healer

Shaghf
Strong Love

Shahada
Martyrdom - Testimony
The name Shahada is
mentioned in the Quran.
Variants: *Shahadah*

Shahbaa
Gray

Shaheera
Distinguished - Well-
known
Variants: *Shaheerah,
Shahera, Shaherah,
Shahira, Shahirah*

Shahidah
Witness

Shahin
Peregrine Falcon

A type of bird. (Also used
in Persian)
Variants: *Shaheen*

Shahirah
Populizer

Shahla
Dark Blue-eyed
Variants: *Sahlaa*

Shahmah
Intelligent - Rational -
Sensible

Shaima
One Who Has Many
Beauty Marks

Shaiqah
Beautiful

Shajaa
Brave - Strong

Shajarah
Tree
The name Shajarah is
mentioned in the Quran.

Shajeeah
Brave - Strong

Shakila
Beautiful - Well-formed
(Also used in Persian)
Variants: *Shakeela,
Shakeelaa, Shakilaa*

Shakirat
Thankful

Shakiriyyah
Thankful

Shakkarah
Thankful

Shakura
Appreciative - Thankful
Variants: *Shakoora,*
Shakoorah, Shakurah

Shalal
Waterfall

Shamikha
Great - High - Lofty -
Towering
Variants: *Shamekhah,*
Shamikhah

Shamisah
Bright - Sunlit

Shamkhah
Greatness - Highness of
Status

Shammam
Muskmelon

Shammamah
Muskmelon

Shamra
Fennel
Variants: *Shamrah*

Shams
Light and Radiance
The name *Shams* is
mentioned in the Quran.

Shams Jahan
Radiant
Literally "sun of the
world".

Shamsa
Radiant - Sun
Variants: *Shamsah,*
Shemsa, Shemsah, Shemse

Shaqaaiq
Heavy Rain

Shaqeerah
Fair-skinned

Shaqhaa
Fair-skinned

Shaqhah
Fair-skinned

Shaqrah
Fair-skinned

Shaqriyyah
Fair-skinned

Sharaa
Beautiful

Sharah
Beautiful

Shararah
Flare - Spark

Shari
Beautiful

Sharifah
Glorious - High in Status -
Honored

Shariqah
Variants: *Glowing, Radiant*

Sharraqah
Bright - Briliant

Sharufah
Glorious - Honorable -
Noble

Shawab
Young Woman

Shawq
Desire - Longing

Shawqat
Desire - Longing
(Also used in Turkish)

Shawqiyyah
Desirous - Longing

Shawraa
Beautiful

Shayiqah
Beautiful

Shaykhaa
Great - High in Status

Shazah
Special - Unique

Shazrah
Little Pearl - Lump of
Gold

Sheefa
Cure - Healing

Sheemah
Character - Natural
Disposition - Nature

Shiblah
Lion Cub

Shifa
Cure - Healing - Remedy
The name Shifa is
mentioned in the Quran.
Variants: *Shefa, Shefaa,
Shifaa*

Shira
Beautiful

Shoulah
Flame
(Also used in Persian)
Variants: *Sholeh, Shouleh,
Shu'lah, Shuleh*

Shufafah
Clear - Translucent -
Transparent

Shufaiqah
Mercy - Pity

Shuhada
Martyrs - Witnesses
The name Shuhada is
mentioned in the Quran.
Variants: *Shohada,
Shohadaa, Shuhadaa*

Shuhaibah
Little Shooting Star

Shuhaidah
Witness

Shuhairah
Famous - Month

Shuhbah
Grayness

Shuhdah
Hony-containing
Honeycomb

Shujayaah
Brave - Strong

Shulaikhah
Origin - Root

Shuqairaa
Fair-skinned

Shuqrah
Fairness of Skin

Shuqriyyah
Fair-skinned

Shuqur
Blondness - Fairness of
Skin
Variants: *Shoqur*

Shuraa
Consultation - Council -
Honeycomb Cell - View

Shurafaa
High in Status -
Honorable

Shurah
Beauty

Shuruq
Sunrise

Shuwaihah
Artemisia
A group of plants that
include tarragon.

T

Taal
Ascending - Come
The name can be a
command ("come!") or a
description of the state of
something that ascends.

Taaliah
Reciter
Variants: *Talalia, Taliya,
Taliyah*

Taazaz
Honor - Might - Power

Tabarak
Blessed

Tabarruk
Blessedness

Tabiah
Follower - Successor

Tabseer
Education -
 Enlightenment

Tadbir
Contrivance -
Organization -
Procurement

Tadris
Research - Study

Tafheem
Elaboration - Illustration
Variants: *Tafhim, Tefhim*

Taflah
Delicate - Gentle - Soft

Tafli
Delicate - Gentle - Soft

Taghrid
Singing

Tahani
Congratulations

Taheerah
Pure - Virtuous

Tahillah
Gladness - Happiness

Tahira
Pure
Variants: *Taahera,
Taahira, Tahera*

Tahmeed
Praising of God
Variants: *Tahmid, Tehmid*

Tahrir
Liberation

Tahsin
Beautification -
Improvement
Variants: *Tahseen, Tehsin*

Tahzeeb
Edification - Purification -
Rectification - Refinement

Taiba
Repentant - Virtuous
Variants: *Ta'ibah, Taaebah,*

*Taaiba, Taaibah, Taeba,
Taebah, Taibah*

Taibah
Good - Wholesome
Also another name for the
city of Medina.
Variants: *Teibah*

Taidah
Compassion - Kindness

Taihaa
Vast
Variants: *Taiha, Tayha,
Tayhaa, Teiha, Teihaa*

Tajallah
Crown of God
Variants: *Taj Ullah,
Tajullah*

Takreem
Graciousness - Honor -
Respect
Variants: *Takrim, Tekrim*

Talaah
Aspect - Countenance -
Face

Talaat
Aspect - Countenance -
Face
Turkish pronunciation of
Talaah. (Also used in
Turkish)

Talibah
Pursuer - Seeker - Seeker
of Knowledge
Variants: *Taaliba, Taleba,
Talebah, Taliba*

Tamanna
Hope - Wish
Variants: *Tamana,*
Tamanaa, Tamannaa

Tamassuk
Adherence

Tamasul
Similarity

Tamheed
Facilitation - Preparation

Tamirah
Date Merchant

Tammamah
Date Merchant

Taneem
Blessedness
Variants: *Tan'im, Taneim,*
Tanim

Taqadum
Advancement - Progress

Tarashud
Guidance

Tareefah
Exquisite - Quaint - Rare

Tarheeb
Graciousness -
Spaciousness - Vastness

Tariqa
Star
Variants: *Taareqa,*
Taareqah, Taariqa,

Taariqah, Tareqa,
Tareqah, Tariqah

Tarkheem
Mellowing - Softening

Tarkhunah
Tarragon

Tarqiyah
Ascension

Tasaad
Happy - Successful

Tasahir
Vigils

Tasamuh
Forbearance -
Forgiveness - Pardon

Taskeen
Tranquility

Tasmia
Naming
The name Tasmia is
mentioned in the Quran.
Variants: *Tasmiah,*
Tasmiya, Tasmiyah

Tasmira
Fruit - Investment -
Product - Profit
Variants: *Tasmirah,*
Tathmira

Tasneem
Falling Water - Fountain
in Paradise
Variants: *Tasnim*

Tasteer
To Author - To Write

Tasweer
To Describe - To Paint -
To Picture

Tatheer
Purification
The name Tatheer is
mentioned in the Quran.
Variants: *Tateheer, Tathir*

Tawadud
Affection - Love

Tawaf
Circumambulation
Variants: *Tawaaf, Tewaf*

Tawaqur
Calmness - Composure -
Solemnity

Tawbaat
Repntance

Tawfiqah
Success

Tawhidah
Monotheism

Tawilah
Long - Tall

Tawlah
Elevation - Highland

Tawus
Beautiful - Peafowl

Tawwabah
Repenting

Tawwad
Affection - Love

Tayibat
Acts of Virtue - Good
Things - Pure Things
The name Tayibat is
mentioned in the Quran.
Variants: *Taibaat, Tayebat,*
Tayyebat, Tayyibaat,
Tayyibat

Tayilah
Generous - Great

Taymurah
Iron
(Also used in Turkish)

Taysirah
Ease - Facilitation

Tayyibah
Good - Virtuous -
Wholesome
The name Tayyibah is
mentioned in the Quran.

Taza
Active - Fresh - Happy
(Also used in Persian)

Tazayyun
Adornment -
Beautification

Tazeen
Adornment -
Beautification

Variants: *Tazieen,*
Tazyeen, Tazyin

Tazkiah
Growth - Improvement -
Purification

Teeha
Vast
Variants: *Teehah, Tiha,*
Tihah

Tibhaj
Beauty - Radiance

Tibrah
Gold Ore

Tina
Fig
Variants: *Teena, Tinaa*

Tinat
Figs

Tinjal
Beauty of the Eyes

Tirhab
Graciousness -
Spaciousness - Vastness

Tiymah
Beautiful

Tooba
The name Tooba is
mentioned in the Quran.
Variants: *Blessedness,*
Bliss, Goodness

Tufan
Cataclysm - Deluge -

Flood
The name Tufan is
mentioned in the Quran.

Turaifah
Blessing - Luxury

Turas
Inheritance
The name Turas is
mentioned in the Quran.

Turfah
Blessings – Luxuries

107

Th

Thameenah
Precious - Valable
Variants: *Sameenah*

Thamirah
Fruit-bearing -
Productive
Variants: *Samirah*

Thanaa
Praise
Variants: *Sanaa*

Tharaa
Affluence - Prosperity -
Wealthiness
Variants: *Saraa'*

Thayeba
Repentant
Variants: *Thayebah,*
Thayiba

Thurayya
Chandelier - Pleiades
Pleiades is a group of
stars.
Variants: *Soraia, Surayya*

Thurayyat
Chandeliers
Variants: *Surayyat*

TRADITIONAL AND MODERN ARABIC BABY NAMES

U

Ubaidah
Servant of God -
Worshiper of God

Ubayaa
Beautiful

Ubayaat
Beautiful

Udaina
Eden - Place of
Everlasting Bliss
Variants: Odaina,
Odainah, Odayna, Odeina,
Udainah

Ufairah
Gazelle
Variants: Ofaira, Ofairah,
Ofayra, Ofayrah, Ufaira,
Ufayrah

Uhaidah
Covenant - Promise

Ulya
Highest - Sublime -
Supreme
Ulya is mentioned in the
Quran in verse 9:40.
Variants: Oliaa, Olya,
Olyaa, Ulia, Uliaa, Ulyaa

Umaima
Mother
Diminutive form of
umm ("mother").
Variants: Omaima,

Oumaima, Umaimah,
Umayma

Umaira
Performer of Umrah -
Pilgrim
Variants: Omaira,
Omairah, Umairah,
Umayra, Umayrah

Umamah
Three Hundred Camels
Variants: Oumama,
Umaama, Umama

Umm Aiman
Blessed

Umm Hamdi
Grateful - Thankful

Ummah
Community - Nation
The name Ummah is
mentioned in the Quran.
Variants: Omma, Ommah,
Uma, Umah, Umma

Ummul Hanaa
Happy - Peaceful
Variants: Ummulhana

Umniya
Hope
The name Umniya is
mentioned in the Quran
in verse 22:52.
Variants: Omniya Umnia,
Umnea, Umneya

Umrah
Minor Pilgrimage -
Overhaul - Restoration -
Revival

The name Umrah is
mentioned in the Quran.

Unayzee
Agile - Beautiful - Gazelle
Variants: Onaizee, Onayzi,
Unayzi

Uraifah
Fragrant - Good Scent

Urwah
Ever-green Tree -
Handhold - Lion
The name Urwah is
mentioned in the Quran
in verse 31:22.
Variants: Orwa, Orwah,
Urwa

Usmanah
Baby Houbara - Baby
Snake

Usraat
Refuge - Shelter

Utaiqah
Generosity - Virtue

Utairah
Fragrant

Uzaibah
Fresh Water

Uzaizah
Honor - Might - Power

Uzrat
Virginity

TRADITIONAL AND MODERN ARABIC BABY NAMES

W

Waad
Promise
The name Waad is
mentioned in the Quran.
Variants: Wa'd, Wad

Waafiyah
Faithful - Loyal - Perfect -
Whole

Waaliyah
Governor - Ruler

Waddaa
Affection - Love

Waddah
Affection - Love

Wadida
Affectionate - Loving
Variants: Wadeeda,
Wadeedah, Wadidah

Wadiyah
Valley

Waelah
Clan - Tribe

Wafa
Completion - Faithfulness
- Fulfillment - Loyalty

Wafeeqah
Appropriate - Companion
- Friend - Harmonious

Wafiyyah
Faithful - Loyal

Variants: Wafeeya, Wafiya,
Wafiyah

Wafqah
Accord - Harmony

Wahbah
Bestowal - Gift

Wahbiyyah
Bestowal - Gift

Wahdah
Alliance - Unity
Variants: Wahda

Wahdat
Wahdat is the Turkish
pronunciation of Wahdah.

Waheebah
Bestowal - Gift

Waheeda
Peerless - Singular -
Unique
Variants: Waheedah,
Wahida, Wahidah

Wahibah
Bestower - Giver

Wahida
Singular - Unique
The name Wahida is
mentioned in the Quran.
Variants: Wahidah

Wajahah
Distinction - Glory -
Honor - Prestige

Wajahat
Distinction - Prominence

Wajeedaa
Affectionate - Loving

Wajeedah
Affectionate - Loving

Wajeehah
Honorable - Noble -
Prestigious

Wajibah
Essential - Imperative -
Obligatory

Waleedah
Girl - Infant - New -
Newborn

Waleeya
Caretaker - Companion -
Custodian - Patron
Variants: Waleeyah, Walia,
Waliah, Waliya, Waliyah,
Waliyya, Waliyyah

Waniya
Breeze - Gentle Breeze
Variants: Waaniya,
Wanea, Waneya, Wania,
Waniyah

Waqida
Brilliant - Kindled
Variants: Waqidah

Waqqaa
Guardian - Protector -
Shield

Ward
Flower - Rose
Variants: Werd

Wardaa
Flower - Rose
Variants: Warda

Wardah
Flower - Rose
The name Wardah is
mentioned in the Quran.
Variants: Warda

Wardiyyah
Rose-like - Rosy

Wareefah
Blooming - Flourishing

Warida
Aware - Experienced -
Learned
Variants: Waareda,
Wareda, Waredah,
Waridah

Waritha
Inheritor - Long-lived
Variants: Waarisah,
Waretha, Warisa,
Warithah

Warqaa
Female Pigeon
Variants: Warqa

Wasamah
Beauty

Wasaya
Behests - Teachings
Precepts - Tenets

Waseela
Instrument - Path - Route
- Track
The name Waseela is
mentioned in the Quran.
Variants: Waseelah,
Wasila, Wasilah

Waseema
Beautiful
Variants: Waseemah,
Wasima, Wasimah

Wasfah
Description - Praise

Wasfia
Praiseworthy
Variants: Wasfia, Wasfiah,
Wasfiyya, Wasfiyyah

Washan
Elevated Land - Highland

Washana
Elevated Land - Highland

Wasifa
Describer - Praiser
Variants: Waasefa,
Waasifa, Waasifah,
Wasefa, Wasefah, Wasifah

Wasiya
Gracious - Patient
Variants: Wasi'ah, Wasia,
Wasiah, Wasya

Wasiyyah
Behest - Tenet - Will

Wasmaa
Beautiful

Wathiqa
Confident - Sure
Variants: Waseqa, Wasiqa,
Wathiqah

Wazeenah
Creative - Original

Wazhaa
Beautiful

Wazhah
Clarity - Prominence

Wazia
Distributor - Protector
Variants: Wazi'ah,
Waziyah

Wazihaa
Apparent - Clear - Visible

Wazihah
Apparent - Clear - Visible

Wazin
Collator - Comparer -
Weigher

Wazira
Assistant - Helper -
Minister
Variants: Wazeera,
Wazeerah, Wazirah

Waznah
Intelligent - Petite

Wazzaa
Beautiful - Clean -
Radiant

Wiam
Concord - Harmony -
Peace - Rapport
Variants: Wi'am, Wiaam

Wid
Affection - Harmony -
Love
Variants: Widd

Widad
Affection - Harmony -
Love
Variants: Wedaad, Wedad,
Widaad

Wifaq
Harmony - Sympathy -
Unity
Variants: Wefaaq, Wefaq,
Wfaaq

Wijdan
Affection - Conscience -
Fondness - Soul -
Tenderness
Variants: Wejdaan,
Wejdan, Wijdaan

Wiqaa
Protection - Shield

Wirad
Flowers - Roses
Variants: Werad, Wiraad

Wisal
Communion - Reunion
Variants: Wesal, Wisaal

Wisama
Attractiveness - Beauty
Variants: Wesama,

Wesamah, Wisaama,
Wisaamah, Wisamah

Wuhaibah
Bestowal - Gift

Wuraidah
Little Flower

Wurud
Flowers - Roses
Variants: Worud, Wurood

Y

Yalina
Gentleness - Leniency -
Softness
Variants: *Yaleena,*
Yaleenah, Yaleina,
Yalinah, Yelina, Yelinah

Yamam
Dove
Variants: *Yamaam*

Yamama
Dove
Variants: *Yamaama,*
Yamaamah, Yamama

Yamar
Alive - Life - Long-lived
Variants: *Ya'mar, Yaamar,*
Yaamer, Yamer

Yameena
Blessed - Prospering -
Righteous
Variants: *Yameenah,*
Yamina, Yaminah

Yameenaa
Blessed - Favored

Yaminah
Blessed

Yaqeen
Certainty
The name Yaqeen is
mentioned in the Quran.
Variants: *Yaqin*

Yaqeena
Certain
Variants: *Yaqeenah,*
Yaqina, Yaqinah

Yaqoot
Ruby
The name Yaqoot is
mentioned in the Quran.
Variants: *Yaqut*

Yaquta
Ruby
Variants: *Yaooqtah,*
Yaqoota, Yaqutah

Yaseera
Blessed - Easy
Variants: *Yaseerah, Yasira,*
Yasirah

Yashal
Brilliant - Radiant
Variants: *Yash'al*

Yasira
Lenient
Variants: *Yaasira,*
Yaasirah, Yaserah, Yasirah

Yasm
Jasmine
(Also used in Persian)
Variants: *Yaasm*

Yasma
Jasmine
(Also used in Persian)
Variants: *Yaasmah,*
Yasmah, Yasmeh

Yasmin
Jasmine

(Also used in Persian)
Variants: *Yasmeen*

Yasmina
Jasmine
(Also used in Persian)
Variants: *Yaasmina,*
Yasminah, Yasmineh

Yazeedah
Growth - Increase

Yumna
Blessed
Variants: *Yumna, Yumnaa,*
Yuwmna, Yuwmnaa

Yumnaat
Blessedness - Blessings

Yumnah
Blessed - In the Grace of
God
Variants: *Yomna, Yomnah,*
Yumna

Yusra
Blessedness - Comfort -
Ease
The name Yusra is
mentioned in the Quran.
Variants: *Yosra, Yosraa,*
Yousra, Yusraa

Yusraat
Affluence

Yusrah
Affluence

Yusriya
Living in Luxury -
Needless - Rich

Variants: *Yosriyah,*
Yosriyya, Yosriyyah,
Yusria, Yusriah, Yusriyah,
Yusriyya, Yusriyyah

Yusrullah
God's Blessing

Z

Zaada
Increasing - Prosperous
Variants: *Zaadah, Zadah*

Zaakiyah
Blessed - Virtuous
Variants: *Zakiah*

Zabi
Gazelle

Zabira
Knowledgeable - Wise
Variants: *Dhabira, Zaabirah, Zabirah*

Zabiyyah
Gazelle

Zafaa
Growth - Increase - Proximity - Side

Zafar
Triumph - Victory - Win
Variants: *Dafar, Dhafar, Zafer*

Zafeera
Successful
Variants: *Dhafeera, Dhafeerah, Dhafirah, Zafeerah, Zafira, Zafirh*

Zafira
Successful
Variants: *Dhafirah, Zaafira, Zaafirah, Zafirah*

Zaghalil
Adorable
Variants: *Zaghaleel*

Zaghlula
Baby Pigeon
Variants: *Zaghloola, Zaghloolah, Zaghlulah, Zagloolah*

Zahaa
Morning

Zahab
Gold
The name *Zahab* is mentioned in the Quran.
Variants: *Dahab, Dehab, Dhahab, Zehab*

Zahabia
Golden
Variants: *Dahabia, Dahabiyyah, Dhahabia, Zahabeya, Zahabiah, Zahabiyah, Zahabiyyah*

Zaheena
Intellectual - Intelligent - Sagacious
Variants: *Daheena, Dahina, Zahina, Zahinah*

Zaheera
Brilliant - Radiant
Variants: *Zaheerah, Zahira, Zahirah*

Zaheeraa
Radiant
Variants: *Zahira*

Zahia
Beautiful - Breeze - Radiant
Variants: *Zaheya, Zaheyah, Zahiah, Zahiya, Zahiyah*

Zahian
Bright Day - Brilliant
Variants: *Dhahian, Zahiaan, Zahyaan, Zahyan*

Zahidah
Ascetic
Variants: *Zaheda*

Zahira
Bright Star - Glowing - Radiant
Variants: *Zahirah*

Zahou
Beautiful View - Blooming Plant
Variants: *Zahu, Zahu*

Zahou
Beautiful View - Blooming Plant

Zahraa
Brilliant - Radiant
Variants: *Zahra, Zahraa', Zehra, Zehraa*

Zahrah
Flower
The name *Zahrah* is mentioned in the Quran.
Variants: *Zahra, Zahreh, Zehra, Zehrah, Zehre, Zehreh*

119

Zahriyyah
Flower-like
Variants: *Zahria*

Zahwah
Beauty - Freshness - Vista
Variants: *Zahua, Zahuah,*
Zahwa

Zahyaa
Bright - Moonlit Night -
Pure

Zaida
Generous
Variants: *Zaaeda, Zaaedah,*
Zaaida, Zaaidah, Zaayda,
Zaaydah, Zaayeda,
Zaayedah, Zaeda, Zayda,
Zaydah, Zayeda, Zayedah

Zaigham
Lion
Variants: *Zaygham*

Zaighama
Lioness
Variants: *Zaighamah*

Zaina
Adornment - Beauty -
Excellence
Variants: *Zainah, Zayna,*
Zaynah, Zeinah, Zeineh

Zainabah
The name of a tree with
fragrant flowers. It is
unclear what tree it is
exactly.
Variants: *Zainaba*

Zaira
Guest - Visitor
Variants: *Zaaera, Zaaerah,*
Zaaira, Zaairah, Zaera,
Zaerah, Zayra

Zaitun
Olive - Olive Tree
The name Zaitun is
mentioned in the Quran.
Variants: *Zaitoon,*
Zaytoon, Zaytun, Zeitoon,
Zeitun, Zeytun

Zaituna
Olive - Olive Tree
The name Zaituna is
mentioned in the Quran.
Variants: *Zaitoona,*
Zaitoonah, Zaitunah,
Zaytoona, Zaytoonah,
Zaytuna, Zaytunah

Zakaa
Intelligence - Keenness
Arabic for "intelligence",
"cleverness".
Variants: *Zaka*

Zakat
Alms - Purification
The name Zakat is
mentioned in the Quran.
Variants: *Zakaat, Zekat*

Zakawat
Intelligence - Keenness
Turkish pronunciation of
Zakawah. (Also used in
Turkish)
Variants: *Zakaawat*

Zakhira
Rich - Wealthy - Wise

Variants: *Zaakhira,*
Zaakhirah, Zakhera,
Zakherah, Zakhirah

Zakiya
Fragrant - Innocent -
Pure
Variants: *Zakeyah,*
Zakeyyah, Zakia, Zakiah,
Zakiyah, Zakiyya,
Zakiyyah

Zaluj
Nimble - Sprightly
Variants: *Zalooj*

Zamaair
Consciences - Hearts -
Minds
Variants: *Zamaaer,*
Zamaer, Zamair

Zameela
Colleague - Companion
Variants: *Zameelah,*
Zamila, Zamilah

Zameer
Conscience - Heart -
Mind
Variants: *Dameer, Dhamir,*
Zamir, Zemir

Zaminah
Guarantor - Surety

Zamira
Fit - Lean
Variants: *Damira,*
Zaamera, Zaamerah,
Zaamira, Zaamirah,
Zamera, Zamerah,
Zamirah

Zanbaqi
Lily-like
Variants: *Zanbaqy*

Zanera
Intelligent - Sensible
(Also used in Persian)
Variants: *Zaneereh,*
Zanireh

Zanurah
Intelligent - Keen
Variants: *Zanoora*

Zara
Excellent - Pinnacle - Top
Plural of Zirwah.
Variants: *Daraa, Dharaa,*
Zaraa

Zareefa
Charming - Intelligent -
Witty
Variants: *Dharifah,*
Zareefah, Zarifa, Zarifah

Zareera
Fragrant Plant
Known as Reseda in
English. (Also used in
Persian)
Variants: *Zareerah, Zarira,*
Zarirah

Zarfaat
Courteous - Elegant -
Refined - Witty

Zarghama
Brave - Lionness -
Warrior
Variants: *Zarghamah*

Zariya
Scattering Wind
Variants: *Dhariya, Zarea,*
Zareia, Zaria, Zarya

Zarnab
Fragrant Plant
Scientific name: Taxus
baccata. (Also used in
Persian)
Variants: *Zarnaab*

Zarqa Bano
Blue-eyed Lady
Variants: *Zarqaa Banu*

Zarqa Habiba
Blue-eyed Beloved

Zarqa Sultana
Blue-eyed Queen

Zarqaa
Blue-eyed
Arabic for "blue eyed".
Variants: *Zarqa*

Zarra
Pilgrim - Visitor
Arabic for "visitor",
"pilgrim".
Variants: *Zaraa, Zarraa*

Zaufishan
Radiant - Spreader of
Light
(Also used in Persian)
Variants: *Zaufeshan,*
Zaufishaan, Zofishan,
Zowfishan

Zawal
Sundown
Variants: *Zawaal*

Zawala
Sundown
Variants: *Zawaala,*
Zawaalah, Zawalah

Zaweela
Motion - Movement
Variants: *Zaweelah,*
Zawila, Zawilah

Zayana
Adorner - Beautifier -
Decorator
Variants: *Zayaana,*
Zayaanah, Zayyana,
Zayyanah, Zeyaana,
Zeyana, Zeyyana,
Zeyyanah

Zayanaa
Adorner - Beautifier
Variants: *Zayaana*

Zayda
Fortune - Increase -
Progress
Variants: *Zaayedah,*
Zaayida, Zaayidah, Zaydah
Zayida, Zayeda, Zayidah

Zayirah
Roaring Lion
Variants: *Zayera*

Zayn
Adornment - Beauty -
Excellence - Grace -
Virtue
Variants: *Zain, Zaine,*
Zane, Zayne, Zein, Zeine,
Zeyn, Zeyne

Zayyan
Adorner - Beautifier -

Decorator
Variants: *Zaiaan, Zaian, Zaiane, Zayaan, Zayan, Zayyaan, Zayyaane, Zayyane, Zeyan, Zeyyan*

Zeeana
Adornment - Beautification
Variants: *Zeana, Zeanah, Ziana, Zianah, Ziyaana, Ziyaanah, Ziyana, Ziyanah, Zyaanah, Zyana, Zyanah*

Zeenah
Adornment - Beauty
The name Zeenah is mentioned in the Quran in verse 57:20.
Variants: *Zeena, Zeinah, Zeinah, Zeineh, Zienah, Zinah, Zynah*

Zehak
Laughter
Variants: *Dhihak, Zeihak, Zihak*

Zehn
Intellect - Psyche - Reason
Variants: *Zihn*

Zeifa
Guest
Variants: *Zaifa, Zaifah, Zayfa, Zayfah*

Zia ul Qamar
Moonlight
Variants: *Ziaul Qamar, Ziyaul Qamar*

Ziara
Visit - Visitation
Variants: *Ziaara, Ziaarah, Ziarah, Ziyara, Ziyarah, Zyaara, Zyaarah, Zyara, Zyarah*

Zibaa
Gazelles

Zibriqan
Crescent - Moon

Zifaf
River Bank - Shore - Side

Zihaka
Happy - Laughing
Arabic for "one who laughs often", "happy".
Variants: *Zehaakah, Zehaka, Zihaaka*

Zihni
Intellectual - Reasonable - Understanding
Arabic for "intellectual", "understanding", "reasonable", "deep thinker".
Variants: *Dhehni, Zehni, Zihnee, Zihny*

Zihniyyah
Intelligent - Wise

Zikr
Mention - Remembrance
The name Zikr is mentioned in the Quran.
Variants: *Dhekr, Dhikr, Dikr, Zekr*

Zikra
Memory - Recollection - Remembrance
The name Zikra is mentioned in the Quran.
Variants: *Dekra, Dekraa, Dhikra, Dhikraa, Dikra, Dikraa, Zekra, Zekraa, Zikraa, Zykra*

Zikrayat
Memories - Recollections - Reminiscences

Zil Allah
God's Mercy - God's Protection
Literally meaning "shade of God".
Variants: *Zell Allah, Zilallah*

Zil Elahi
God's Mercy - God's Protection
Literally meaning "shade of God". (Also used in Urdu)
Variants: *Zill Elahi*

Zil Yazdan
God's Mercy - God's Protection
Literally meaning "shade of God". (Also used in Persian, Urdu)
Variants: *Zil Yazdaan*

Zil-e-Qamar
Dark Side of the Moon
Urdu for "the dark side of the moon". Arabic version is Zil al-Qamar or Zilil Qamar. In Urdu it can also

be written as Zili Qamar and Zil e Qamar.
Variants: *Zil E Qamar, Zilleqamar*

Zilal
Shade
The name Zilal is mentioned in the Quran.
Variants: *Zelaal, Zelal, Zilaa, Zylal*

Zill
Shade - Shadow
Variants: *Zel, Zell, Zil*

Zilla
Shade - Shadow
Variants: *Zella, Zellah, Zila, Zilah, Zillah*

Zimal
Garment - Robe
Variants: *Zemaal, Zemal, Zimaal, Zymaal, Zymal*

Zirwa
Pinnacle - Superb - Top
Variants: *Dherwa, Dhirwa, Thirwa, Zerwa, Zirua, Zyrua, Zyrwa*

Ziya
Light - Radiance
The name Ziya is mentioned in the Quran.
Variants: *Dea, Deea, Deia, Deya, Deyya, Dhea, Dheea, Dheia, Dheya, Dhia, Dhiaa, Dhiya, Dhiyaa', Dhiyya, Dhiyyaa, Dhya, Dhyya, Dia, Diaa, Diea, Diya, Dya, Dyaa, Zea, Zeea, Zeia, Zeiya, Zeya, Zeyaa, Zia,*
Ziaa, Ziea, Zieya, Ziya, Ziyaa, Zya

Ziyada
Increase - Progress
The name Ziyada is mentioned in the Quran.
Variants: *Ziaada, Ziada, Ziadah, Ziyaada, Ziyaadah*

Zoeya
Brilliant - Radiant
Variants: *Zaw'iyyah, Zawiyah, Zawiyyah, Zoeyyah, Zouiyyah*

Zohra
Bright White Color - Radiant - Venus
Variants: *Zohrah, Zohreh, Zuhra, Zuhrah*

Zonera
Variant of Zunairah.
Variants: *Zonerah, Zuneera, Zunera, Zunerah*

Zoona
Adornment - Beautification
Variants: *Dhuna, Doona, Zona, Zonah, Zoonah, Zouna, Zounah, Zuna, Zunah*

Zoona
Gazelle

Zoraiz
Enlightener - Spreader of Light
(Also used in Persian)
Variants: *Dhuraiz, Zoreez, Zoriz, Zouraiz, Zuriz*

Zoreza
Radiant
Literally "spreader of light".
Variants: *Zooriza, Zoureza, Zourizah, Zureeza, Zuriza, Zurizah*

Zubaida
Excellent - Soft-bodied - Superb
Variants: *Zobaida, Zobaidah, Zobayda, Zobaydah, Zubaidah, Zubayda, Zubaydah*

Zubi
Gazelle

Zuha
Forenoon
The name Zuha is mentioned in the Quran.
Variants: *Doha, Duha, Zohaa, Zuhaa*

Zuhaa
Radiance
Variants: *Zoha*

Zuhaibah
Lump of Gold

Zuhaira
Flower - Radiant
Variants: *Zohaira, Zohairah, Zuhairah, Zuhayra, Zuhayrah*

Zuhairaa
Little Flower - Radiant
Variants: *Zohaira*

Zuhayyah
Radiant
Variants: *Zohaya*

Zuhdiyyah
Ascetic
Variants: *Zohdia*

Zuhniyyah
Intelligent - Wise

Zuhr
Radiant
Variants: *Zohr*

Zuhriyyah
Florid - Pink - Rosy
Variants: *Zohria*

Zuhur
Flowers
Variants: *Zohur, Zuhoor*

Zulfaa
Closeness - Nearness -
Rank - Station
The name Zulfaa is
mentioned in the Quran.
Variants: *Zolfa, Zolfaa,
Zulfa*

Zulhijjah
12th Month of the Hijri
Calendar

Zulla
Shade
The name Zulla is
mentioned in the Quran.
Variants: *Zolla, Zollah,
Zula, Zulah, Zullah*

Zultan
King - Leader
Urdu variant of
Arabic Sultan. (Also used
in Urdu)
Variants: *Zultaan*

Zultana
Leader - Queen
Urdu variant of Arabic
Sultana. (Also used in
Urdu)
Variants: *Zultanana*

Zumar
Groups - Throngs
The name Zumar is
mentioned in the Quran.
Variants: *Zomar, Zomer,
Zumer*

Zumard
Emerald
Urdu variant of the Arabic
word Zumurrud. (Also
used in Urdu)
Variants: *Zomard*

Zumurrud
Emerald
Variants: *Zomorrud,
Zumurud*

Zumurruda
Emerald
Variants: *Zomorrudah,
Zumrudah, Zumurrdah,
Zumurudah*

Zurafaa
Beautiful - Elegant -
Graceful
Variants: *Dhurafa, Zorafa,
Zorafaa, Zurafa*

Zurfah
Charm - Elegance - Wit

Zurmah
Lavender

Zuwaila
Motion - Movement
Variants: *Zuwailah,
Zuwaylah*

Zuwailah
Adorable

Zuwainah
Blessing

Zuwaiten
Little Olive
Variants: *Zowayten*

Zyan
Adornment -
Beautification -
Decoration
Variants: *Zeyan, Ziyaan,
Ziyan, Zyaan*

Arabic Names for Boys

A

Aabid
Devoted to God -
Worshiper
The name Aabid is
mentioned in the Quran.
Variants: Aabed, Abed, Abid

Aabidullah
Servant of God -
Worshiper of God
Variants: Abidulla,
Abidullah

Aabir
Crossing - Passing By -
Traveling
Variants: Aaber, Aber, Abir

Aabis
Fierce - Grim
Variants: Aabes, Abes, Abis

Aadil
Excellent - Fair - Just -
Moderate - Virtuous
Variants: Aadel, Adel, Adil

Aaf
Forgiver - Pardoner
Variants: Aaff, Af

Aafaaq
Horizons
The name Aafaaq is
mentioned in the Quran.
Variants: Aafaq, Afaaq,
Afaq

Aafiq
Generous - Great -
Superb - Wise
Variants: Afiq

Aaidun
Returning Ones
The name Aaidun is
mentioned in the Quran.

Aaiz
Replacement - Successor
Variants: Aa'idh, Aaez,
Aedh, Aez

Aakif
Devoted Worshiper of
God
The name Aakif is
mentioned in the Quran.
Variants: Aakef, Aakif,
Akef, Akif

Aala
Exalted - High in Status -
Supreme
The name Aala is
mentioned in the Quran.
Variants: A'la, Alaa

Aalam
World
Variants: Alam

Aali
Great - Lofty - Sublime
The name Aali is
mentioned in the Quran.
Variants: Aalee, Aaly, Alee,
Aly

Aalif
Amiable - Friendly
Variants: Aalef, Alef, Alif

Aamad
Ages - Eras - Periods of
Time
Variants: Aamad, Amaad,
Amad

Aameen
Arabic for "Oh Allah,
accept our prayer".
Variants: Aamin, Ameen

Aamin
Safe - Secure - Unharmed
Variants: Amen, Amin

Aamir
Full of Life - Prosperous
Variants: Aamer, Amer,
Amir

Aaqil
Discerning - Reasonable -
Sensible - Wise
Variants: Aaqel, Aqel, Aqil

Aaraf
Heights
Variants: Aaref, Aref, Arif

Aarib
Successful
Variants: Aareb, Areb, Arib

Aariz
Rain-Bearing Cloud
The name Aariz is
mentioned in the Quran.
Variants: Aaredh, Aarez,
Aaridh, Arez, Aridh, Ariz

Aasal
Evenings
The name Aasal is
mentioned in the Quran.

Variants: Aasaal, Asaal, Asal

Aasir
Captivator - Warrior
Variants: Aaser, Aser, Asir

Aati
Bestower - Giver
Variants: Aatee, Aaty, Atee

Aatik
Generous - Pure
Variants: Aatek, Atek, Atik

Aatiq
Baby Pigeon - Free
Variants: Aateq, Ateq, Atiq

Aayiz
Replacement - Restitution

Aazam
Great - Mighty
Variants: A'zam, Aadham

Aazz
Great - Mighty
Variants: A'az, Aaz

Ababil
Bundles - Crowds - Flocks
- Groups
Variants: Abaabil, Ababeel

Aban
Clear - Eloquent - Lucid
Variants: Abaan

Abbad
Servant of God -
Worshiper of God

Variants: Abaad, Abad, Abbaad

Abbas
Lion
Variants: Abaas, Abas

Abbood
Servant of God -
Worshiper of God
Variants: Abbud, Abood, Abud

Abda
Power - Strength
Variants: Abdah, Abduh

Abdaal
Replacements -
Successors
Variants: Abdal

Abdar
Early - Full Moon - Moon
- Quick
Variants: Abder, Ebder

Abdul Aakhir
Servant of God

Abdul Aala
Servant of God

Abdul Afuw
Servant of God

Abdul Ahad
Servant of God
Variants: Abdulahad

Abdul Akram
Servant of God

Abdul Aleem
Servant of God

Abdul Awwal
Servant of God

Abdul Azim
Servant of God

Abdul Aziz
Servant of God

Abdul Baatin
Servant of God

Abdul Baseer
Servant of God

Abdul Basit
Servant of God

Abdul Birr
Servant of God

Abdul Elah
Servant of God

Abdul Fattah
Servant of God

Abdul Ghaffar
Servant of God

Abdul Ghafoor
Servant of God

Abdul Ghani
Servant of God

Abdul Haafiz
Servant of God

Abdul Hadi
Servant of God
Variants: *Abdolhadi, Abdul Hady, Abdulhadi*

Abdul Hafee
Servant of God

Abdul Hafeez
Servant of God

Abdul Hai
Servant of God

Abdul Hakam
Servant of God

Abdul Hakeem
Servant of God

Abdul Halim
Servant of God

Abdul Hameed
Servant of God

Abdul Haq
Servant of God

Abdul Haseeb
Servant of God

Abdul Jabar
Servant of God

Abdul Jaleel
Servant of God

Abdul Jameel
Servant of God

Abdul Kabir
Servant of God

Abdul Karim
Servant of God

Abdul Khabir
Servant of God

Abdul Khaliq
Servant of God

Abdul Khallaq
Servant of God

Abdul Latif
Servant of God

Abdul Maalik
Servant of God

Abdul Majeed
Servant of God

Abdul Maleek
Servant of God

Abdul Manaan
Servant of God

Abdul Mateen
Servant of God

Abdul Mawla
Servant of God

Abdul Mubeen
Servant of God

Abdul Muhaimin
Servant of God

Abdul Muheet
Servant of God

Abdul Mujeeb
Servant of God

Abdul Muqaddim
Servant of God

Abdul Muqit
Servant of God

Abdul Muqtadir
Servant of God

Abdul Musawwir
Servant of God

Abdul Mutaal
Servant of God

Abdul Mutaali
Servant of God

Abdul Naseer
Servant of God

Abdul Qadeer
Servant of God

Abdul Qadir
Servant of Allah
Variants: *Abdulqaadir, Abdulqader*

Abdul Qahir
Servant of God

Abdul Qareeb
Servant of God

Abdul Qawee
Servant of God

Abdul Qawi
Servant of Allah

Variants: *Abdolqawee,*
Abdulqawi

Abdul Qayyum
Servant of God

Abdul Quddus
Servant of Allah
Variants: *Abd Ul Quddus,*
Abd e Quddus, Abdol
Quddus, Abdulquddus

Abdul Shaheed
Servant of God

Abdul Shakoor
Servant of God

Abdul Tawwab
Servant of God

Abdul Wadud
Servant of God

Abdul Wahaab
Servant of God

Abdul Wahid
Servant of God

Abdul Wakeel
Servant of God

Abdul Waleei
Servant of God

Abdul Waris
Servant of God

Abdulbary
Servant of God

Abdullah
Servant of Allah
The name Abdullah is
mentioned in the Quran.
Variants: *Abdollah*

Abdur Rab
Servant of God

Abdur Raheem
Servant of God

Abdur Rahman
Servant of God

Abdur Raoof
Servant of God

Abdur Raqeeb
Servant of God

Abdur Razzaq
Servant of God

Abdus Salam
Servant of Allah
Variants: *Abd Ul Salam,*
Abd al-Salam, Abdosalam,
Abdossalam, Abdul Salam,
Abdusalam, Abdussalam

Abdus Samad
Servant of God

Abdus Samee
Servant of God

Abduz Zaahir
Servant of God

Abeed
Servant of God -
Worshiper of God

Abhaj
Better - Brilliant -
Successful

Abhar
Brilliant - Lucid -
Renowned
Variants: *Abher*

Abi
Dignified - Reserved
Variants: *Abee, Abeei,*
Abeey, Abei

Abidain
Worshipers

Abideen
Servant of God -
Worshiper of God
Variants: *Aabidin, Abedin*

Abkar
Early - On Time
Variants: *Abker*

Ablagh
Eloquent - Mature

Ablaj
Brilliant - Clear - Lucid

Abou
Beauty - Radiance

Abqar
Extraordinary -
Supernatural

Abraj
Beautiful-eyed

Abraq
Brilliant - Radiant
Variants: *Abrak, Abreq*

Absaar
Insight - Intellect -
Perception - Vision
The name Absaar is used
in the Quran.
Variants: *Absar, Absar*

Absaar
Eye-sights - Insights -
Perceptions - Visions
The name Absaar is
mentioned in the Quran

Abu Bakr
Young - Young Man -
Youthful
The name Abu Bakr is
from Abu ("father of",
"like") and Bakr (ancient
name of Arabian tribes,
"young man").
Variants: *Abubaker,
Abubakir, Abubakr*

Abu Firas
Lion
Variants: *Abu Feras, Abu
Firaas, Abufiras*

Abuda
Servant of God -
Worshiper of God
Variants: *Abooda, Aboodah,
Abudah*

Abudain
Worshiper

Abudi
Worshiper

Abul Fazl
Gracious
Variants: *Abulfazl*

Abwan
Handsome - Radiant

Abyan
Clear - Distinct -
Eloquent
Variants: *Abyen*

Abyaz
Bright - Pure - White
Variants: *Abyad, Abyez*

Adalat
Fairness - Justice
Turkish pronunciation of
Adalah.
Variants: *Adaalat*

Adam
Dust
The name Adam is
mentioned in the Quran.
According to some
scholars it is related to
Adeem, which means
"dust", since God created
prophet Adam from dust.

Addal
Fair - Just

Adeel
Excellent - Fair - Just -
Moderate - Virtuous
Variants: *Adil*

Adeen
Obedient - Righteou
Variants: *Adin, Azeen, Azin*

Adham
Black - Dark
Variants: *Adhem, Adhum,
Edhem*

Adl
Fairness - Justice
The name Adl is
mentioned in the Quran.
Variants: *Edl*

Adlan
Fair - Just

Adli
Fair - Just
Variants: *Adlee, Adly*

Adnan
Inhabitant - Resident
Variants: *Adnaan*

Adr
Heavy Rain

Adwam
Eternal - Everlasting -
Lasting - Stable
Variants: *Aduam*

Adyan
Creeds - Religions
Variants: *Adiaan, Adian,
Adyaan*

Afeen
Forgiver - Pardoner
Variants: *Afin*

Affan
Chaste - Modest -
Virtuous

Variants: *Afaan, Afan, Affaan*

Afif
Chaste - Modest -
Righteous
Variants: *Afeef, Afef*

Afnan
Spreading Branches of
Trees
The name Afnan is
mentioned in the Quran.
Variants: *Afnaan*

Afrad
Matchless - Unique

Afsah
Eloquent - Expressive -
Fluent
The name Afsah is
mentioned in the Quran.
Variants: *Efseh*

Afseruddin
Supporter of Islam
Literally "crown of the
faith".

Aftabuddin
Supporter of Islam
Literally "sun of the faith".
(Also used in Persian)

Afzaal
Good Deeds - Kind Deeds
Variants: *Afdhaal, Afdhal, Afzal*

Aghla
Precious - Valuable
Variants: *Aghlaa*

Aghlab
Conqueror - Superior -
Victor

Ahad
One - Peerless - Unique
The name Ahad is
mentioned in the Quran.

Ahbab
Beloved Ones
Variants: *Ahbaab*

Ahdaf
Goals - Objectives -
Targets

Ahdawi
Faithful - Loyal

Ahdee
Faithful - Loyal
Variants: *Ahdy*

Ahibun
Prepared - Ready

Ahid
Caretaker - Promiser
Variants: *Aahed, Aahid, Ahed*

Ahin
Ascetic
Variants: *Aahen, Aahin, Ahen*

Ahkam
Decisive - Wise
The name Ahkam is
mentioned in the Quran.
Variants: *Ahkem, Ehkem*

Ahmad
Noble - Praiseworthy
One of the names of
Prophet Muhammad
(pbuh). The
name Ahmad is
mentioned in the Quran.
Variants: *Ahmat, Ahmed, Ahmet, Ehmet*

Ahmar
Red - Red-colored
Variants: *Ahmer*

Ahnaf
Upright - Worshiper of
God
Variants: *Ehnef*

Ahram
Pyramids
Variants: *Ahraam*

Ahsan
Beautiful - Best -
Handsome
The name Ahsan is
mentioned in the Quran.
Variants: *Ehsen*

Ahwas
Brave
Variants: *Ahuas*

Ahyam
Starless Night
Variants: *Ahiam*

Ahyan
Moments - Times
Variants: *Ahiaan, Ahian, Ahyaan*

Ahyas
Brave
Variants: Ahias

Aidan
Tall Palm Tree
Variants: Aidaan, Aydan,
Eidan, Eydan

Ain
Fountain - Spring
The name Ain is
mentioned in the Quran,
such as in verse 88:12.
Variants: Aene, Aine, Ayn,
Ayne, Eiyn

Aish
Life - Livelihood
Variants: Aysh

Ajaar
Rewards
Variants: Ajar

Ajab
Amazement - Wonder
The name Ajab is
mentioned in the Quran.

Ajam
Date Seed - Foreign -
Persian

Ajaweed
Acts of Kindness -
Generosity

Ajeeb
Amazing - Wondorous
The name Ajeeb is
mentioned in the Quran.

Ajeel
Quick
Variants: Ajil

Ajiad
Generous - Gracious -
Noble
Variants: Ajyad

Ajmal
Beautiful - Delightful
Variants: Ajmel

Ajmi
Intelligent - Wise

Akbar
Great - Magnificent
The name Akbar is
mentioned in the Quran.
Variants: Akber, Ekber

Akfah
Black
Akfah refers to the color
"black".

Akhas
Excellent - Special
Akhas is an indirect
Quranic name for boys
that means "special",
"excellent". It is derived
from the KH-SAAD-SAAD
root which is used in the
Quran.
Variants: Excellent, Special

Akhlaq
Decency - Integrity -
Morality
Akhlaq is an indirect
Quranic name for boys
that means "morality",

"integrity", "decency". It is
derived from the KH-L-Q
root which is used in
many places in the
Quran.
Variants: Akhlaaq

Akhmad
Calm - Silent - Tranquil

Akhtab
Falcon

Akhtaf
Slender - Slim
Akhtaf is an indirect
Quranic name for boys
that means "slender",
"slim". It is derived from
the KH-T16-F root which
is used in the Quran.

Akhyar
Good - Virtuous
The name Akhyar is
mentioned in the Quran.
Variants: Akhiar, Akhyaar

Akhzam
Serpent - Snake
Ancient Arabic name.

Akhzar
Green - Green-colored

Aki
Textile Merchant
Variants: Akee, Aky

Akmal
Complete - Perfect -
Whole
Variants: Akmel

Aknan
Covers - Shelters
The name Aknan is
mentioned in the Quran.
Variants: *Aknaan*

Akram
Gracious - Honorable -
Honored
The name Akram is used
in the Quran.
Variants: *Ekrem*

Akrama
Female Pigeon
Akrama is the Urdu
variant of the Arabic name
Ikrimah. (Also used in
Urdu)
Variants: *Akramah*

Akwan
Cosmos - Universes
Variants: *Akuaan, Akuan,
Akwaan*

Akyas
Intelligent - Wise
Variants: *Akias*

Alaa
Greatness - Highness
Variants: *Ala*

Aladdin
Supporter of Islam
Literally "supremacy of
the faith".

Alamat
Emblem - Gesture - Sign
- Symbol
Turkish pronunciation of

Alamah.
Variants: *Alaamat*

Alamgir
World Conqueror
Variants: *Alamgeer,
Alamghir*

Alamguir
World Conqueror
(Also used in Persian)
Variants: *Alam Ghir,
Alamgeer, Alamghir*

Aleef
Compassionate - Friendly
- Good Friend - Kind
Variants: *Alif*

Aleem
Intellectual -
Knowledgeable - Learned
The name Aleem is
mentioned in the Quran.
Variants: *Alim*

Alhasan
Gentle - Good -
Handsome - Virtuous

Alhusain
Good-looking -
Handsome - Virtuous
Variants: *Alhosain*

Ali
Exalted - Great - High -
Sublime - Superb
The name Ali is
mentioned in the Quran.
Variants: *Alee, Aleei, Aliy,
Aliyy*

Alim
Knowledgeable - Scholar
Variants: *Aalem, Aalim,
Alem*

Allaam
Extremely Wise -
Knowledgeable
The name Allaam is
mentioned in the Quran.

Allamah
Extremely Wise -
Knowledgeable

Altaaf
Gentleness - Kindness
Variants: *Altaf*

Altaf
Gentle - Kind

Alyan
Great - High - Sublime
Variants: *Aliaan, Alian,
Alyaan*

Amad
Age - Era - Period of Time

Aman
Peace of Mind - Safety -
Security

Amanat
Devotion - Guardianship -
Trust
Turkish pronunciation of
Amanah. (Also used in
Persian, Turkish, Urdu)
Variants: *Amanaat*

Amara
Fleet - Tribe
Variants: *Amaara,*
Amaarah, Amarah

Amdad
Expansion - Gain -
Growth - Increase

Ameed
Chief - Leader - Prefect
Variants: *Amid*

Ameen
Loyal - Trustworthy -
Virtuous
The name *Ameen* is
mentioned in the Quran.
Variants: *Amein, Amin,*
Amyne, Emeen, Emin,
Umeen

Amial
Lighthouses
Variants: *Amyaal, Amyal*

Amil
Hoper - Striver - Worker
Variants: *Aamel, Aamil,*
Amel

Amir
Chief - Commander -
Leader - Ruler
Variants: *Ameer, Emeer,*
Emir

Amiri
Leader
Variants: *Ameeri, Ameree,*
Ameri, Amiree, Amiry

Amiri
Enlivener - Reviver

Amiruddin
Supporter of Islam
Literally "leader of the
faith".
Variants: *Amir Uddin*

Amjaad
Distinction - Glory -
Honor
Variants: *Amjad*

Amjad
Distinguished - Glorious -
Honorable
Variants: *Amjed*

Amlas
Delicate - Smooth - Soft

Ammam
Leader

Amman
Citizen - Resident
Also name of the capital of
Jordan.
Variants: *Amaan, Aman*

Ammar
Long-lived - Pious -
Reviver
Variants: *Amaar, Amar,*
Ammaar

Ammuni
Away From Harm - Safe
Variants: *Amuni*

Amnan
Safe - Secure
Variants: *Amnaan*

Amr
Life - Revival

Amrullah
God's Command
Variants: *Amr Ullah*

Amsal
Best - Exemplary -
Optimal
The name Amsal is
mentioned in the Quran.
Variants: *Amthal*

Amyali
Ambitious - Desirous
Variants: *Amialy*

Anar
Glowing - Radiant
Variants: *Anaar*

Anas
Comforter - Consoler -
Friend

Anasat
Comfort - Tranquility
Turkish pronunciation of
Anasa.
Variants: *Anaasat*

Anasi
Consoler - Goo Friend
Variants: *Anasee*

Anbas
Lion

Andaleeb
Nightingale
(Also used in Urdu)
Variants: *Andalib*

Andalus
Andalusia

Andalusi
From Andalusia
Variants: *Andaloosi*

Anees
Close Friend - Comforter
Variants: *Aneis, Anis*

Anfa
Dignity - Self-respect
Variants: *Anfah*

Anfani
Dignified

Anfas
Breaths - Souls - Spirits
Variants: *Anfaas*

Anhar
Rivers
Variants: *Anhaar*

Aniq
Attractive - Elegant -
Graceful - Stylish
Variants: *Aneek, Aneeq,
Aneiq, Anik*

Anjam
Star
Variants: *Anjaam*

Anjud
Heights - Plateaus
Variants: *Anjod*

Anjum
Stars
Variants: *Anjom, Anjoum*

Anmar
Tigers
Variants: *Anmaar*

Ansab
Better - Worthier

Ansam
Breezes
Variants: *Ansaam*

Ansar
Advocates - Defenders -
Supporters - Upholders
The name Ansar is
mentioned in the Quran.
Variants: *Ansaar*

Ansari
Supporter of Islam
Variants: *Ansaari, Ansary*

Antar
Brave

Anum
God's Blessings - God's
Favors
The name Anum is
mentioned in the Quran.
Variants: *Anom, Anoum*

Anumullah
God's Blessings - God's
Favors

Anush
Beautiful - Handsome

Anwaar
Lights - Radiant
Variants: *Anwar*

Anwaaraddin
Supporter of Islam
Literally "radiance of the
faith".
Variants: *Anuaruddin*

Anwar
Clear - Eloquent -
Enlightened
Variants: *Anwer*

Anwari
Radiant
Variants: *Anuari*

Aqeeb
Follower
Variants: *Aqib*

Aqeed
Aqid
Variants: *Under Oath*

Aqeel
Discerning - Reasonable -
Sensible - Wise
Variants: *Aqil, Aquil,
Aquille*

Aqiq
Agate
(Also used in Persian)
Variants: *Aqeeq*

Aql
Intelligence - Mind -

Sense - Thought - Wisdom
Variants: *Akl*

Aqlan
Intelligent - Keen

Aqrab
Scorpion
Variants: *Akrab*

Aqsaa
Farthest
Name of the third holiest site in Islam: Masjid al-Aqsa (al-Aqsa Mosque) in Palestine.
Variants: *Aksa, Aqsa*

Aqsad
Achiever - Moderate - Modest - Righteous
Variants: *Aksad, Eqsed*

Aqwa
Strong - Strongest
Variants: *Aqua, Aqwaa*

Araabi
Eloquent - Fluent

Arandas
Fierce Lion

Arar
Lent Lily - Wild Daffodil
A type of flower.

Arbab
Chiefs - Masters
The name Arbab is used in the Quran.
Variants: *Arbaab*

Arbad
Lion - Snake

Arban
Eloqent - Fluent

Ardas
Lion

Areeb
Intelligent - Wise
Variants: *Areib, Arib*

Areef
Knowledgeable - Learned - Wise
Variants: *Arif*

Areej
Fragrance
Variants: *Arij*

Areeq
Deep-rooted - High-born - Noble
Variants: *Ariq*

Arf
Fragrance - Scent

Arfa
Elevated - Exalted - Great
Variants: *Arfa', Arfaa*

Arfaan
Spiritual Knowledge - Wisdom
Non-standard variant of the name Irfan.
Variants: *Arfan*

Arhab
Gracious - Open-minded

Variants: *Arheb, Arhub, Erheb*

Arham
Compassionate - Kind - Merciful
The name Arham is mentioned in the Quran in verse 12:64.

Arish
Builder - Maker
Variants: *Aarish, Aresh*

Arkan
Leaders - Pillars
Variants: *Arkaan*

Aroof
Learned - Skilled - Wise
Variants: *Arouf, Aruf*

Arqam
Snake

Arsh
Power - Throne
The name Arsh is mentioned in the Quran.

Arshad
Mature - Well-guided - Wise
Variants: *Arshed*

Arshan
Thrones
Variants: *Arshaan*

Arshi
Royal
Literally meaning "worthy

of a throne".
Variants: *Arshee, Arshy*

Arz
Breadth - Mountain -
Width

Asaad
Fortunate - Happy
Variants: *As'ad*

Asad
Lion
Variants: *Esed*

Asah
Correct - Healthy -
Proper
Variants: *Aseh*

Asar
Mark - Print - Sign -
Work
Variants: *Aser, Athat,
Ather*

Asbah
Beautiful
Variants: *Esbeh*

Asbat
Deep-rooted - Firmly
Established - Reliable -
Steady
Variants: *Athbat*

Aseel
Creative - Deep-rooted -
Evening Time - High-born
- Nighttime - Original
The name Aseel is
mentioned in the Quran.
Variants: *Asil, Assil*

Asfiya
Pure Ones
Variants: *Asfiaa, Asfiyaa*

Asfour
Bird
Variant of Arabic Osfur.
(Also used in Urdu)
Variants: *Asfoor, Asfur*

Asghar
Junior - Smaller -
Younger

Ashaab
Companions - Friends
The name Ashaab is
mentioned in the Quran.
Variants: *Ashab*

Ashaar
Fierce
Variants: *Ash'ar, Ashar*

Ashal
Brilliant - Kindled -
Radiant
Variants: *Ash'al, Ashaal*

Ashbal
Lion Cubs

Asheeq
Beloved - In Love
Variants: *Ashiq*

Ashhab
Lion

Ashham
Composed - Dignified

Ashhar
Famous - Renowned
Variants: *Ashher*

Ashhub
Shooting Stars
Variants: *Ashhob*

Ashiq
In Love - Obsessed

Ashja
Brave
Variants: *Ashja'*

Ashmal
Inclusive

Ashqar
Blond - Fair-skinned
Variants: *Ashqer*

Ashraf
Honorable - Noble

Ashtar
Name of a companion of
Ali bin Abi Talib. The
meaning is "one whose
eyelashes are curved
backwards", "one whose
eye is torn".

Ashwaq
Longing - Yearning
Variants: *Ashuaq, Ashwaaq*

Asif
Fierce - Powerful - Strong
The name Asif is
mentioned in the Quran.
Variants: *Aasef, Aasif, Acef,
Aceph, Aseph*

Asim
Protector - Rescuer -
Shield
The name Asim is
mentioned in the Quran.
Variants: *Aasem, Aasim,*
Asem

Asjad
Prostrator - Worshiper of
God

Askar
Soldier

Aslam
Intact - Safe

Asmar
Brown - Tan
Describes a person whose
skin color is not too dark
and not too light.

Asrar
Mysteries - Secrets
Variants: *Asraar*

Assab
Gazelle

Aswab
Correct - Rational -
Sensible
Variants: *Asuab*

Asyaf
Swords
Variants: *Asiaf, Asyaaf*

Ata
Gift from God
The name Ata is

mentioned in the Quran.
Variants: *Ataa*

Ataullah
Gift from God
Variants: *Ata Ullah,*
Ataaullah

Ataur Rahman
Gift from God
Variants: *Ataurrahman*

Ateeb
Gentle - Tender

Ateeq
Ancient - Freed -
Liberated - Noble
The name Ateeq is
mentioned in the Quran.
Variants: *Atiq*

Ateer
Fragrant
Variants: *Atir*

Atf
Affection - Compassion

Atfat
Affection - Compassion

Atheel
Deep-rooted - High-born
- Noble
Variants: *Aseel, Asil*

Atheer
Glint - Luster - Radiance
- Shimmer
Literal meaning is
"shimmer of a sword
blade".

Variants: *Aseer, Asir,*
Atheir, Athir, Esir

Atif
Affectionate -
Sympathetic
Variants: *Aatef, Aatif, Atef*

Atik
Generous - Pure

Atoof
Affectionate -
Compassionate -
Sympathetic
Variants: *Atouf, Atuf*

Attaf
Affectionate -
Compassionate

Attar
Perfume-maker
Variants: *Ataar, Atar,*
Attaar

Auraq
Dust-colored - Sand-
colored
Variants: *Awraaq*

Ausan
Relaxed - Resting
Variants: *Awsan*

Awad
Compassion - Goodness -
Kindness
Variants: *Awaad*

Awadil
Fair Ones - Just Ones

139

Awadili
Fair - Just

Awadini
Eternal - Everlasting

Awamil
Active - Industrious

Awamir
Full of Life - Inhabited

Awamiri
Long-lived

Awan
Moment - Time
Variants: Awaan

Awani
Helper - Supporter

Awasim
Fighters of Corruption
Variants: Awathim

Awatif
Emotions - Instincts -
Passions
Variants: Awaatef,
Awaatif, Awatef

Awayed
Habit - Tradition

Awb
Repentance
Variants: Aub

Awbi
Repentant
Variants: Awby

Awd
Return

Awdaq
Friendly - Genial -
Intimate
Variants: Audaq

Awfa
Faithful - True
The name Awfa is
mentioned in the Quran.
Variants: Aufa, Awfaa

Awfar
Plenty
Variants: Aufar

Awhad
Unique
Variants: Auhad

Awj
Height - Pinnacle - Top
(Also used in Persian)
Variants: Auj

Awla
Worthier
Variants: Aulaa

Awlan
Returner
Variants: Aulan

Awlya
Close Friends -
Supporters
Variants: Auliya

Awmani
Skilled Swimmer

Awmar
Long-lived

Awmari
Long-lived

Awn
Aid - Friend - Help -
Helper
Variants: Aun

Awni
Helper - Supporter

Awrad
Rose-colored - Rosy
Variants: Aurad

Awsal
Becoming Closer to God
Variants: Ausaal

Awsam
Badges of Honor
Variants: Awsaam

Awsat
Middle - Moderate
The name Awsat is
mentioned in the Quran.

Awshan
Guest
Variants: Aushan

Awthal
Dutiful
Variants: Ausal

Awwab
Repentant - Virtuous
The name Awwaab is
mentioned in the Quran.

Variants: *Auab, Awaab, Awab*

Awwad
Compassionate - Kind

Awwadi
Compassionate - Kind

Awwak
Compassionate - Sympathetic
Variants: *Awak*

Awwal
First
The name Awwal is mentioned in the Quran.
Variants: *Aual, Awal*

Awwalan
Advanced Ones - First Ones
Variants: *Awalaan*

Awwam
Skilled Swimmer
Variants: *Awam*

Awwaz
Restitutioner
Variants: *Awaz, Awwadh*

Ayad
Able - Capable - Powerful
Ayad should not be confused with Ayyad, though both are derived from the same Arabic root.
Variants: *Aiad, Ayaad*

Ayamin
Blessed Ones - Fortunate Ones
Variants: *Ayaamin, Ayamen*

Ayan
Era - Time
The name Ayan is mentioned in the Quran in verse 51:12.
Variants: *Ayaan, Ayyan*

Ayd
Power - Strength
Variants: *Aid, Eyd*

Aydarus
Lion
Variants: *Aidaroos, Aidarus*

Aydarusi
Brave
Variants: *Aydaroosy*

Aydi
Hands - Power - Strength
The name Aydi is mentioned in the Quran.
Variants: *Aidi, Aidy, Aydee*

Aydin
Hands - Power - Strength
The name Aydin is mentioned in the Quran in verse 51:47.
Variants: *Aiden, Aidin, Ayden, Eyden, Eydin*

Ayed
Returner - Visitor
Variants: *Aayed, Aayid, Ayid*

Ayiq
Larkspur
A flowering plant.

Ayish
Alive - Prosperous

Aykon
Nest
Variants: *Aikon, Aikun*

Ayman
Blessed - Fortunate
The name Ayman is mentioned in the Quran.
Variants: *Aiman, Aimen, Aymen*

Aynan
Two Fountains
The name Aynan is mentioned in the Quran.
Variants: *Ainan*

Aysar
Easy - Left-handed - Lenient
Masculine form of Yusra.
Variants: *Aisar, Ayser*

Ayyad
Fortifier - Strengthener - Supporter
Ayyad is an indirect Quranic name for boys that means "able strengthener", a person who is powerful and adds strength to others. It is derived from the Y-D-Y root which is mentioned in many places in the Quran, such as 38:17: Bear with their words

patiently. Remember Our servant David, a man of strength who always turned to Us. Ayyad should not be confused with Ayad. Both names are derived from the same root, but they have different, though close, meanings.
Variants: *Ayyaad*

Ayyam
Days
Variants: *Aiam, Ayaam*

Ayyan
Beautiful-eyed - Observant - Perceptive
Variants: *Ayaan, Ayan*

Ayyash
Alive - Prospering
Variants: *Ayash*

Ayyashi
Alive - Prospering
Variants: *Ayashi*

Ayyub
Repentance
Ayyub is the name of one of the prophets mentioned in the Quran.
Variants: *Aiub, Ayoob, Ayub, Ayyoob*

Azaan
Announcement - Call
The name Azaan is mentioned in the Quran.
Variants: *Azan*

Azal
Eternity - Perpetuity
(Also used in Persian)

Azali
Eternal
(Also used in Persian)
Variants: *Azalee, Azaly*

Azb
Fresh - Sweet
The name Azbi is mentioned in the Quran.

Azban
Fresh Water

Azeeb
Fresh Water

Azeem
Great - Magnificent
The name Azeem is mentioned in the Quran.
Variants: *Adheem, Adhim, Azim*

Azfaar
Triumphs - Victories
Variants: *Adfaar, Adhfar, Azfar*

Azfar
Overcomer - Victor - Victorious
Variants: *Azfer, Ezfer*

Azhar
Brilliant - Radiant

Azil
Guardian - Protector
Variants: *Aazel, Aazil, Azel*

Azim
Determined - Resolute - Resolved

Aziz
Beloved - Dear - Exalted - Great - Noble
The name Aziz is mentioned in the Quran.
Variants: *Azeez*

Azka
Better - Purer
The name Azka is mentioned in the Quran.
Variants: *Azkaa*

Azm
Aim - Determination - Resolve
The name Azm is mentioned in the Quran.
Variants: *Ezm*

Azmat
Greatness - Importance - Might

Azmi
Brave - Determined - Resolute
Variants: *Azmee, Azmey, Azmy*

Azoom
Determined - Resolved

Azraf
Charming - Intelligent - Witty
Variants: *Adhraf*

Azyan
Adornments -

Decorations - Virtues
Variants: *Azian*

Azzam
Lion
Variants: *Azaam, Azam,*
Azzaam

Azzami
Fierce - Lion-like

Azzan
Beloved - Cherished -
Dear - Excellent - Lofty
Variants: *Azaan, Azzaan*

Azzat
Gazelle
Turkish pronunciation of
Azzah. (Also used in
Turkish)

TRADITIONAL AND MODERN ARABIC BABY NAMES

B

Baadi
Bedouin
Variants: *Bady*

Baashir
Bringer of Good Tidings
Variants: *Basher*

Bab
Door
The name Bab is
mentioned in the Quran
in verse 12:67.
Variants: *Baab*

Badaah
Plains
Variants: *Baddah*

Badawi
Bedouin

Baddar
Early - On Time -
Punctual

Badeed
Example - Sample -
Specimen

Badeel
Replacement - Successor
Variants: *Badil*

Badhaa
Initiation - Start

Badih
Creative - Intuitive -

Witty
Variants: *Badeeh*

Badilayn
Replacements -
Substitutes

Badir
Full Moon - Moon
Variants: *Baader, Baadir,
Bader*

Badr
Full Moon
This name is mentioned in
the Quran.
Variants: *Bedir*

Badr al Din
Supporter of Islam
Literally "full moon of the
faith".
Variants: *Badruddin*

Badran
Beautiful - Radiant
Literally "like the full
moon".

Badrawi
Handsome - Radiant
Literally "like the full
moon".

Badri
Autumn Rain - Fullness of
the Moon
In Islamic history this
word means "one who
took part in the Battle of
Badr".
Variants: *Badry*

Baghish
Light Rain

Baha
Beauty - Brilliance
Variants: *Bahaa*

Baha al Din
Supporter of Islam
Literally "brilliance of the
faith".
Variants: *Bahauddin*

Bahat
Beauty
Variants: *Bahaat*

Bahat
Pure - Spotless

Baheej
Beautiful - Radiant
Variants: *Bahij*

Baheen
Cheerful

Baheer
Handsome - Radiant -
Talented

Bahhas
Researcher - Scholar
Variants: *Bahaas, Bahas*

Bahi
Brilliant - Radiant
Variants: *Bahee, Bahy*

Bahir
Brilliant - Lucid -
Renowned

Variants: *Baaher, Baahir, Baher*

Bahiri
Brilliant - Renowned

Bahiriya
Brilliant - Renowned

Bahirun
Brilliant - Lucid - Renowned
Variants: *Baherun*

Bahis
Explorer - Learner - Researcher - Seeker
Variants: *Baahes, Baahis, Bahes, Bahith*

Bahjat
Beautiful - Radiant
Variants: *Behjet*

Bahlul
Cheerful - Smiling
Variants: *Bahlool*

Bahoos
Researcher - Seeker
Variants: *Bahus*

Bahoosh
Cheerful - Relaxed

Bahr
Ocean - Sea
The name Bahr is mentioned in the Quran.

Bahradin
Knowledgeable - Scholar - Wise

Literally "ocean of the faith".

Bahri
Ocean-like - Vast
Variants: *Bahree, Bahry*

Bahuj
Energetic - Handsome - Lively
Variants: *Bahooj*

Bahur
Brilliant - Lucid
Variants: *Bahoor*

Bahzar
Respected - Wise

Baihas
Brave - Lion
Variants: *Bayhas*

Bailul
Freshness - Wetness
Variants: *Baylul*

Baitaar
Expert - Veterinarian

Bajdan
Inhabitant - Resident
Variants: *Bajdaan*

Bajes
Warrior
Variants: *Baajes, Bajis*

Bajli
Cheerful - Happy

Bakeel
Elegant - Good-looking

Bakheet
Fortunate
Variants: *Bakhit*

Bakhit
Fortunate - Lucky

Bakhti
Fortunate - Lucky

Bakkar
Early Riser

Bakkur
Early - New - On Time

Bakr
New - Untouched - Virgin
Variants: *Bekir*

Bakrun
Fresh - New

Balagh
Announcement - Maturity - Proclamation
Variants: *Balaagh*

Baleegh
Eloquent - Far-reaching
The name Baleegh is mentioned in the Quran.
Variants: *Baligh*

Balooj
Radiant

Bandar
Port - Port City
(Also used in Persian)
Variants: *Bander*

Bani
Builder - Founder Creator
Variants: *Banee, Bany*

Banna
Builder - Founder
Variants: *Bana, Banaa, Bannaa*

Baqaa
Eternity - Perpetuity
Variants: *Baqa*

Baqee
Enduring - Everlasting
The name Baqee is mentioned in the Quran.
Variants: *Baqi, Baqy*

Baqian
Everlasting - Perpetual

Baqir
Discoverer -
Knowledgeable - Lion
Variants: *Baaqir, Baqer*

Baraa
Blameless - Healed -
Innocent
The name
Baraa mentioned in the
Quran.
Variants: *Bara*

Baraaem
Fresh - Innocent -
Unopened Flower Bud -
Young
Variants: *Bara'im*

Barahim
Variant of Ibrahim.

Baraj
Handsome

Barakat
Abundance - Blessings
Variants: *Barakaat*

Barayek
Blessed

Bareek
Blessed
Variants: *Barik*

Bareeq
Glow - Sheen
Variants: *Bariq*

Bariq
Brilliant - Flashing

Bariz
Prominent - Visible
Variants: *Baarez, Baariz, Barez*

Barizi
Prominent - Visible

Barjees
Planet Jupiter
Urdu variant of Birjis.
(Also used in Urdu)
Variants: *Barjis*

Barkhan
Great Chief
(Also used in Turkish)
Variants: *Baarkhan*

Barraq
Brilliant - Radiant -
Shining

Barraz
Clear - Prominent

Barzan
Powerful - Prominent -
Visible
Variants: *Barzaan*

Basam
Happy - Smiling
Variants: *Basaam, Bassam*

Basar
Eyesight - Insight -
Perception - Vision -
Wisdom
The name Basar is
mentioned in the Quran.

Baseel
Brave - Lion
Variants: *Basil*

Baseer
Discerning - Insightful -
Perceptive
The name Baseer is
mentioned in the Quran.
Variants: *Basir*

Baseerat
Insight - Perception -
Wisdom
Turkish pronunciation of
Baseera.
Variants: *Basirat*

Basel
Brave - Lion
Variants: *Baasel, Baasil, Basil*

Basem
Cheerful - Smiling

Variants: *Baasem, Baasim, Basim*

Bashar
Bringer of Good News - Bringer of Good Tidings
Variants: *Bashaar*

Bashash
Charming - Cheerful
Variants: *Bashaash*

Basheer
Bringer of Good News - Bringer of Good Tidings
Variants: *Bashir, Beshir*

Basheesh
Cheerful - Optimistic

Bashiri
Bringer of Good Tidings

Bashirun
Bringers of Good Tidings

Bashu
Cheerful - Optimistic
Variants: *Bashoo*

Bashur
Bringer of Good News
Variants: *Bashoor*

Bashwan
Classy - Good-mannered

Bashwi
Classy - Good-mannered

Basili
Brave

Basimi
Happy - Smiling

Basiq
High - Lofty - Soaring - Towering
Variants: *Baaseq, Baasiq, Baseq*

Basit
Friendly - Generous - Kind
The name Basit is mentioned in the Quran.
Variants: *Baaset, Baasit, Baset*

Basmat
Smile
Turkish pronunciation of Basmah.
Variants: *Besmet*

Basmin
Cheerful Ones - Happy Ones - Smiling Ones
Variants: *Basmeen*

Basoom
Cheerful - Smiling

Bassaar
Insightful - Perceptive

Batal
Brave - Hero

Batek
Sharp Sword
Variants: *Baatek, Baatik, Batik*

Bathr
Plain
A type of land.
Variants: *Basr*

Batil
Ascetic - Devoted to God - Virtuous
Variants: *Baatel, Baatil, Batel*

Battaal
Ascetic - Chaste - Modest
Variants: *Bataal*

Bayan
Declaration - Elucidation - Exposition - Illustration
Variants: *Baian, Bayaan*

Bayhas
Courageous - Lion
Variants: *Beihas, Beyhas*

Baz
Northern Goshawk
A type of bird of prey.
Variants: *Baaz*

Bazigh
Radiant - Shining
The name Bazigh is mentioned in the Quran.
Variants: *Baazigh*

Bazij
Adorner - Beautifier
Variants: *Baazij*

Bazir
Sower
One who plants seeds
Variants: *Baazir, Bazer*

Bazullah
God's Hawk

Bidar
Earliness - Punctuality

Bidayat
Beginning - Genesis -
Inception
Turkish pronunciation of
Bidayah.

Bikr
New - Untouched - Virgin
Variants: *Bekir, Bekr*

Bilal
Water
Variants: *Belaal, Belal*

Birjees
Planet Jupiter
Variants: *Berjees, Berjis*

Bisharah
Good Tidings

Bishr
Cheerfulness - Optimism
Variants: *Beshr*

Bishry
Cheerful - Glad -
Optimistic

Bodaad
Fortune - Share

Bokhur
Incense

Boshry
Gladness - Happiness

Budaid
Example - Sample -
Specimen

Budaili
Replacement

Budair
Full Moon
Variants: *Bodair*

Budaiwi
Bedouin

Budool
Ascetic - Honored -
Respected

Budur
Full Moons
Variants: *Bodoor*

Buhair
Lake

Buhur
Oceans - Seas
Variants: *Bohoor, Buhoor*

Bujaij
Beautiful-eyed - Large-
eyed

Bujud
Residence - Stay
Variants: *Bojud*

Bukair
New - Untouched

Bukhari
One Who Comes From
Bukhara

Bukhara is a city and
region in modern-day
Uzbekistan. Some
important Islamic
scholars come from this
area. (Also used in
Persian)

Bukran
Dawn

Bulbul
Nightingale
Variants: *Bolbol*

Bunyan
Buildings - Institutions -
Structures
The name Bunyan is
mentioned in the Quran.

Buraik
Blessed

Burhan
Demonstration - Evidence
- Proof - Proof of God's
Greatness
Burhan is used in the
Quran in verse 2:111 and
others.
Variants: *Borhaan,
Borhan, Burhaan*

Busraq
Yellow Sapphire
Variants: *Busraaq*

Buzur
Seeds

D

Daaem
Constant - Continual - Perpetual

Dabir
Ancestry - Origins - Root
The name Dabir is mentioned in the Quran.
Variants: *Daaber, Daabir, Daber*

Daeb
Conscientious - Diligent

Daeej
Beautiful-eyed

Dahaa
Intelligence - Sense - Wisdom

Dahban
Gold-plated

Dahee
Clever - Intelligent
Variants: *Dahi*

Dahus
Lion

Daleel
Guide - Mentor
The name Daleel is mentioned in the Quran.
Variants: *Dalil*

Dalu
Well Bucket

The name Dalu is mentioned in the Quran.

Daneer
Radiant

Daqeeq
Delicate - Fine
Variants: *Daqiq*

Daqr
Thriving Garden

Dareeb
Experienced - Trained

Dareeq
Fixer - Mender

Daris
Researcher - Seeker of Knowledge - Student
Variants: *Daares, Daaris*

Darkan
Perceptive - Understanding

Darrak
Intelligent - Perceptive
Variants: *Daraak, Darak*

Daruj
Fast - Swift

Daulah
Power - State
Variants: *Daula, Dawla, Dawlah*

Daulat
Power - State
Turkish pronunciation of

Daulah.
Variants: *Dawlat*

Davut
Beloved Friend
Davut is the Turkish form of Dawood, Arabic form of David.

Dawood
Beloved Friend
Originally from Hebrew.
The name Dawood is mentioned in the Quran.
Variants: *Dawoud, Dawud*

Dawub
Conscientious - Diligent
Variants: *Da'ub, Daoob, Daub, Dawood*

Dawwas
Brave - Strong

Dayyar
Inhabitant - Resident

Dayyin
Devout - Religious

Deeb
Wolf

Deen
Creed - Religion
The name Deen is mentioned in the Quran.
Variants: *Dean, Dein, Din*

Dibaaj
Silk Cloth
A type of silk cloth.

Dilf
Bold

Dinar
Gold Coin
The name Dinar is
mentioned in the Quran.
Variants: *Deenar*

Diras
Scholar - Student

Dirbas
Lion

Dirgham
Lion

Diryas
Lion

Duhat
Intelligent - Sensible

Duhr
Noon
Variants: *Dohr*

Duryab
Finder of Pearls
Variants: *Doryab, Duryaab*

E

Eeda
Commitment - Consignment
Variants: *Idaa'*

Eezah
Clarification - Elucidation
Variants: *Izaah*

Eid
Celebration - Festival
The name Eid is mentioned in the Quran.
Variants: *Eed, Eyd*

Eidi
Eid Gift
Variants: *Eedy*

Eifa
Faithfulness - Loyalty
Variants: *Eefaa, Ifaa*

Eihab
To Bestow - To Confer a Gift - To Endow With
Variants: *Eyhab, Ihaab, Ihab*

Eiham
Fantasy - Illusion
Variants: *Eyham, Iham*

Eimam
Chief - Leader
Variants: *Eemam*

Einas
Comfort - Consolation - Peace of Mind
Variants: *Eenas*

Eira
Kindling - Starting a Fire
Variants: *Eera, Eiraa, Eyra, Ira*

Eisun
Capable - Competent
Variants: *Esoun, Isoon*

Eisuni
Capable - Competent
Variants: *Isoony, Isuni*

Eithar
Love - Preferring Another Person to Yourself
Variants: *Isaar, Isar*

Eiwa
Guardianship - Protection
Variants: *Eewaa, Eiwaa, Eywa, Eywaa, Iwa, Iwaa, Iywa*

Elaf
Safety - Security Promise
The name Elaf is used in the Quran.
Variants: *Elaaf, Ilaaf, Ilaf*

Elias
Yahweh is my God
The name Elias is mentioned in the Quran. It is the name of a prophet mentioned in the Quran, in English known as Elias and Elijah. The meaning of "Yahweh is my God" is acceptable since "Yahweh" is a synonym of "Allah".
Variants: *Eliaas, Elyaas, Elyas, Iliaas, Ilias, Ilyaas, Ilyas*

Eshaal
Excitation - Kindling
Variants: *Eshal, Ish'al, Ishaal, Ishal*

Etemad
Reliance - Trust
Variants: *I'timad, Itimad*

Etizaaz
Glory - Greatness - Honor
Variants: *Itizaaz, Ittizaz*

Ewazi
Replacement

Eyazi
Replacement
Variants: *Iyazi*

F

Faahim
Intelligent -
Understanding
Variants: *Faahem, Fahem,
Fahim*

Faaiz
Successful
Variants: *Faaez, Faez, Faiz,
Faize, Faizz, Fayez, Fayiz*

Faalan
Productive

Faariq
Differentiator - Judge

Fabil
Heavy Rain

Fadi
Heroic - Self-sacrificing
Variants: *Faady, Fadee,
Fady*

Faeq
Excellent - Extraordinary
- Superb
Variants: *Faaek, Faaiq,
Faiq, Fayeq, Fayik, Fayiq*

Faham
Intelligent -
Understanding
Variants: *Fahham*

Fahd
Leopard

Fahdi
Brave - Leopard-like

Fahduddin
Leopard of the Faith

Fahdullah
Leopard of God

Faheem
Intelligent - Keen -
Perceptive -
Understanding
Variants: *Fahim, Fehim*

Fahis
Investigator - Tester
Variants: *Faahes, Faahis,
Fahes*

Fahm
Comprehension -
Understanding

Fahmat
Comprehension -
Understanding

Fahmawi
Comprehending -
Intelligent

Fahmee
Intelligent -
Understanding
Variants: *Fahmi, Fahmy*

Fahmun
Comprehending -
Intelligent

Faih
Fragrant - Scent
Variants: *Fayh, Feih*

Faihami
Comprehending -
Intelligent

Faihan
Fragrant

Fairuz
Successful - Victor
(Also used in Kurdish,
Persian, Urdu)
Variants: *Fairooz, Fayrooz,
Fayruz*

Faisal
Decisive
Variants: *Faysal, Feisal,
Feysal*

Faitah
Right Guidance

Faiz
Plenty

Faizan
Beneficence - Grace -
Philanthropy
Variants: *Faidhaan,
Faidhan, Faizaan, Fayzan*

Faizee
Abundance - Gracious -
Virtuous
Variants: *Faidhi, Faizy*

Faizullah
Bounty from God

Faizurrahman
Bounty from God

Fajr
Dawn - Daybreak
The name Fajr is
mentioned in the Quran.

Fajruddin
Dawn of the Faith

Fajrul Islam
Dawn of Islam

Fakhir
High Quality - Luxurious
Variants: *Faakher, Faakhir,
Fakher*

Fakhr
Glory - Honor - Pride
Variants: *Fekhr*

Fakhri
Cause for Pride - Glorious
Variants: *Fakhry*

Fakhrjahan
Pride of the World

Fakhruddin
Supporter of Islam
Literally "pride of the
faith".
Variants: *Fakhr al-Din*

Falah
Prosperity - Success
Variants: *Falaah*

Falak
Cosmos - Orbit - Ship -
Space

The name Falak is used in
the Quran.
Variants: *Felek*

Falaq
Dawn - Daybreak
The name Falaq is used in
the Quran.

Faleeh
Successful

Falih
Prosperous - Successful
Variants: *Faaleh, Faalih,
Faleh*

Falihi
Successful - Winner

Fallah
Farmer

Falooh
Successful

Fannan
Artist
Variants: *Fanaan, Fanan,
Fannaan*

Faqeeh
Expert - Knowledgeable -
Learned - Scholar
Variants: *Faqih*

Farahaat
Happiness - Joy
Variants: *Farahat*

Faraj
Comfort - Ease - Relief

Farajuddin
Relief of the Faith

Farajullah
God's Relief - God's
Rescue

Farasat
Acumen - Foresight -
Keenness - Vision
Variants: *Faraasat*

Farazdaq
Loaf of Bread

Fardain
Peerless - Unique

Fardan
Unique
Variants: *Fardaan*

Fardun
Peerless - Unique

Fareed
Matchless - Unique
Variants: *Farid*

Fareeq
Band - Crew - Group
The name Fareeq is
mentioned in the Quran.
Variants: *Fariq*

Farhaat
Happiness - Joy
Variants: *Farhat*

Farhan
Happy - Joyous -
Rejoicing
Variants: *Farhaan, Ferhan*

Farhand
Full-bodied - Muscular

Farhatullah
Happiness Coming From
God

Farheen
Happy - Joyous
(Also used in Urdu)
Variants: *Farhin*

Farhi
Happy

Farhiyyan
Happy

Farih
Happy

Faris
Horseman - Rider

Farman
Command -
Commandment
(Also used in Persian)

Farmanullah
God's Command

Farood
Peerless - Unique

Farrad
Independent-minded -
Original

Farraj
Happy - Joyous

Farrooh
Happy

Faruq
Differentiator -
Distinguisher
Variants: *Farooq*

Farwa
Crown - Wealth
Variants: *Farua, Faruah,*
Farwah

Farwan
Living in Luxury -
Wealthy
Variants: *Faruaan, Faruan,*
Farwaan

Faseeh
Eloquent - Fluent

Fateem
Weaned Off Breast Milk

Fateen
Brilliant - Intelligent

Fath
Beginning - Conquest -
Guidance
The name Fath is
mentioned in the Quran.

Fathan
Conqueror - Guide

Fathi
Conqueror - Guide

Fathuddin
Guidance of the Faith

Fathullah
God's Guidance - God's
Help

Fatih
Conqueror - Initiator

Fatihi
Conqueror - Initiator

Fatin
Intelligent - Perceptive
Variants: *Faatin, Faten*

Fatnan
Clever - Keen - Skilled

Fatooh
Conqueror - Guide

Fattah
Conqueror - Victor
The name Fattah is
mentioned in the Quran.

Fauz
Victory - Win
The name Fauz is
mentioned in the Quran.
Variants: *Fawz, Fouz, Fowz*

Fawaid
Beneficial Things -
Benefits

Fawaz
Successful - Winner
Variants: *Fawaaz,*
Fawwaaz, Fawwaz

Fawiz
Successful - Winner

Fawzan
Successful
Variants: *Fauzaan, Fauzan,*
Fawzaan, Fouzan, Fowzan,
Fozan

Fayid
Benefiter - Winner

Fayyaz
Charitable - Doer of Good
Deeds
Variants: *Fayaad, Fayaadh,*
Fayaaz, Fayad, Fayaz,
Fayyaaz, Fayyad

Fazeel
Excellent - Praiseworthy

Fazil
Admirable and
Praiseworthy - Exalted -
High Status - Noble -
Sublime and Superb

Fazl
Courtesy - Noble Deed
The name Fazl is
mentioned in the Quran.
Variants: *Fadhl, Fadl*

Fazli
Gracious - Praiseworthy

Fazluddin
Excellence of the Faith

Fazlullah
God's Bounty

Fazlurrahman
God's Bounty

Fikr
Concept - Intellect -
Thought

Fikrat
Concept - Idea -
Thoughts
Turkish pronunciation of
Fikrah.

Fikri
Conceptual - Perceptive -
Thoughtful

Firas
Skilled Horseman

Firhad
Full-bodied - Muscular

Firtan
Cool Fresh Water

Firwad
Independent-minded

Fizzi
Silvery

Fuad
Conscience - Heart
The name Fuad is
mentioned in the Quran
in verse 28:10.
Variants: *Fo'ad, Foaad,*
Fowad, Fu'aad, Fu'ad,
Fuaad, Fuwaad, Fuwad,
Fwaad, Fwad

Fuhaid
Little Leopard

Fuhaim
Comprehending -
Intelligent

Fulaih
Successful

Fulaihan
Successful

Furaij
Relief

Furat
Cool Fresh Water
The name Furat is
mentioned in the Quran.

Furhud
Full-bodied - Lion Cub

Fursat
Opportunity - Right Time
(Also used in Turkish)

Furud
Uniqueness

Futaih
Beginning - Conquest -
Guidance

Futaim
Weaned Off Breast Milk

Futain
Brilliant - Intelligent

Futooh
Conquests

Fuzail
Excellent - Praiseworthy

Fuzailan
Excellent - Praiseworthy

Fuzzal
Excellent - Praiseworthy

TRADITIONAL AND MODERN ARABIC BABY NAMES

Gh

Ghaanim
Winner

Ghadeer
Little Stream

Ghadfan
Generous

Ghadi
Early Riser

Ghadif
Generous

Ghaffari
Forgiver - Forgiving

Ghafir
Forgiving
The name Ghafir is
mentioned in the Quran.
Variants: *Ghafer*

Ghafiri
Forgiving

Ghafr
Forgiveness - Pardon

Ghafur
Ghafoor - Ghafour -
Ghefur
The name Ghafur is
mentioned in the Quran.

Ghafuri
Forgiving

Ghaidan
Delicate - Gentle

Ghailam
Handsome

Ghailum
Handsome

Ghaisullah
God's Bounty

Ghali
Dear - Respected -
Valuable

Ghalib
Victor and Winner
The name Ghalib is
mentioned in the Quran.

Ghalibi
Victor

Ghallab
Victor

Ghamidi
Sword Sheath

Ghamiq
Black - Dark

Ghaneem
Winner

Ghani
Needless - Rich - Self-
sufficient
The name Ghani is
mentioned in the Quran.
Variants: *Ghanee, Ghaniy,
Ghany*

Ghanimi
Winner

Ghanum
Winner

Ghanyan
Needless - Wealthy

Gharab
Gold - Silver

Gharam
Devotion - Infatuation -
Love
The name Gharam is
mentioned in the Quran.

Ghareeb
Rare - Strange - Stranger
Variants: *Gharib*

Ghareer
Affluence - Good Manners
- Inexperienced - Young

Gharibi
Stranger

Gharisullah
Young Tree Planted by
God

Gharras
Tree Planter

Gharsan
Planter of Trees

Ghasasini
Handsome

Ghasharab
Lion

Ghasin
Beautiful - Handsome
Variants: *Ghaasin, Ghasen*

Ghasini
Beautiful

Ghaslan
Forest

Ghassan
Beautiful - Handsome
Variants: *Ghasan*

Ghassani
Handsome

Ghawalib
Victor

Ghawsaddin
Rescuer of the Faith

Ghayat
Aim - End Goal

Ghayid
Gentle - Soft

Ghayoor
Fervent - Protective

Ghays
Rain
The name Ghays is
mentioned in the Quran.

Ghayyas
Doer of Good Deeds

Ghazanfar
Lion

Ghazanfari
Lion

Ghazeer
Plenty
Variants: *Ghazir*

Ghazi
Warrior

Ghaziyyat
Enduring - Patient

Ghazni
From Ghazni

Ghazwan
Attacker - Raider

Ghimd
Sword Sheath

Ghufran
Forgiveness - Pardon
The name Ghufran is
mentioned in the Quran.

Ghulam
Boy - Young Male Servant
The name Ghulam is
mentioned in the Quran.

Ghumair
Saffron

Ghumr
Saffron

Ghur
Fair-skinned - Honored

Chief
Variants: *Ghorr*

Ghuraib
Gold - Silver

Ghurais
Newly Planted Tree

Ghurrah
Chief - Leader - Moonrise

H

Haaiz
Acquirer - Getter

Haayi
Bashful - Modest

Habaq
Basil - Ocimum
A type of plant.

Habbab
Affectionate - Loving

Habban
Loving

Habib
Beloved - Lover
Variants: *Habeeb*

Habibur Rahman
Loved by God
Variants: *Habeebur
Rahman, Habiburrahman*

Habiri
Colorful Clouds

Habqar
Hail

Habr
Blessings - Happiness -
Scholars - Virtuous

Habrur
Blessed - Living in Luxury
Variants: *Habroor*

Hadal
Mistletoe
A type of plant.

Haddal
Cooing Pigeon

Hadeed
Iron - Penetrating - Sharp
The name Hadeed is used
in the Quran.
Variants: *Hadid*

Hadees
Hadeeth - Hadis - Hadith
- Hedis
The name Hadees is
mentioned in the Quran.

Hadi
Guide
The name *Hadi* is
mentioned in the Quran.
Variants: *Haadi, Haadie,
Hadie, Hady*

Hadir
Good-mannered

Hafeel
Plenty

Hafeesh
Candid - Loyal - True-
hearted

Haffaz
Protective - Protector

Haib
Seriousness - Solemnity

Haidar
Lion
Variants: *Hayder, Hyder*

Haidaru
Lion

Hairaz
Guardian - Protector

Haizar
Lion

Hajid
Night-long Worshiper -
Sleeper

Hajir
Emigrant - Excellent -
Migrator

Hakeem
Decisive - Wise
The name *Hakeem* is
mentioned in the Quran.
Variants: *Hakeim, Hakim,
Hekeem, Hekeime,
Hekeimm, Hekiem, Hekim,
Hukeem*

Haleef
Ally

Haleej
Rain-Bearing Cloud

Halif
Oath-taker

Halil
Clear - Prominent

Hallam
Enduring - Forbearing -
Lenient

Halooj
Cloud That Gives Off
Lightning

Halul
Pouring - Torrential

Halyan
Adorned

Hamd
Praise
The name Hamd is
mentioned in the Quran.
Variants: *Hemd*

Hamdan
Praise - Praiser
Variants: *Hamdaan*

Hamdat
Praise
Turkish pronunciation of
Hamdah. (Also used in
Turkish)

Hamdi
Praise - Praiseworthy
Variants: *Hamdee*

Hamdun
Praise - Praiseworthy

Hameed
Laudable - Praiseworthy
The name Hameed is
mentioned in the Quran.
Variants: *Hamed, Hamid*

Hameef
Virtuous

Hameez
Cute - Intelligent - Strong

Hamidat
Praiseworthy
Turkish pronunciation of
Hamidah.

Hamim
Close Friend
The name Hamim is
mentioned in the Quran.
Variants: *Hameem*

Hammad
Praiser
Variants: *Hamaad, Hamad*

Hammadah
Praiser
Variants: *Hamada*

Hammadi
Praiseworthy

Hammud
Praiseworthy

Hammuzah
Lion

Hamool
Enduring - Patient

Hanafi
Devout Believer -
Monotheist

Hanan
Love - Sympathy

The name Hanan is
mentioned in the Quran.
Variants: *Hanaan*

Hanif
Devout Believer -
Monotheist
Variants: *Haneef*

Hanin
Affectionate -
Sympathetic

Haq
Truth
The name Haq is
mentioned in the Quran.
Variants: *Hak, Haqq,
Haque*

Haqiq
Befitting - Worthy
Variants: *Haqeeq*

Haraz
Guardian - Protector
Variants: *Harraz*

Harees
Desirous - Eager - Keen
The name Harees is
mentioned in the Quran.
Variants: *Haris*

Harith
Cultivator - Farmer - Lion
Variants: *Haares, Haareth
Haris, Haaris, Haarith,
Hares, Hareth, Harith,
Harres, Harris*

Haritha
Cultivator - Farmer - Lion
Variants: *Haaretha,*

Haarethah, Haaritha, Haarithah, Haresah, Haretha, Harethah, Harithah

Haroona
Mountain
Haroona is the Arabic feminine form of Harun. Harun is not an Arabic word, some Arabic sources say it means "mountain".
Variants: *Haroonah, Haruna, Harunah*

Harun
Mountain
The name Harun is mentioned in the Quran.
Variants: *Haroon, Haroun*

Harz
Guardianship - Protection

Harzan
Guardian - Protector

Hasab
Generosity - Good Deed - Lineage - Pedigree

Hasan
Gentle - Good - Good-mannered - Handsome - Virtuous
The name Hasan is mentioned in the Quran.

Haseef
Judicious - Reasonable
Variants: *Hassif*

Haseem
Assiduous - Diligent - Persevering
Variants: *Hasim*

Haseen
Handsome
Variants: *Hasin*

Hasees
Perceptive - Sensitive
Variants: *Hasis*

Hashaam
Breaker
Variants: *Hashim*

Hashim
Breaker - Destroyer of Evil
Variants: *Haashem, Haashim, Hashem*

Hasil
Acquirer - Harvester - Producer

Hasim
Conclusive - Decisive - Determinate

Hasin
Handsome

Hasoun
Chaste - Virtuous

Hassan
Charitable - Good-mannered - Handsome
Not to be confused with Hasan (name of one of the Prophet's grandsomes

PBUH).
Variants: *Hasaan, Hassaan, Hessan*

Hassun
Handsome
Variants: *Hasoon*

Hatim
Decisive - Wise
Variants: *Haatim, Hatem*

Hattab
Woodcutter

Hattal
Heavy Rain

Hawari
Apostle - Follower - Supporter

Hawas
Brave

Hawis
Brave

Hayat
Life
The name Hayat is mentioned in the Quran.
Variants: *Hayaat*

Hayl
Heaped Sand

Hayyan
Alive - Awake - Dignified n
Variants: *Hayaan, Hayan, Hayyaan*

Hayyee
Bsahful - Modest

Hayyin
Facilitated - Lenient
The name Hayyin is
mentioned in the Quran.

Hazar
Cautious - Vigilant
Variants: *Hazzar*

Hazeem
Intelligent - Wise
Variants: *Hazim*

Hazeem
Continuous Rain -
Thunder

Haziq
Brilliant - Excellent -
Sagacious - Skillful
Variants: *Haazeq, Haaziq,
Hadeq, Hadiq*

Hazir
Prepared - Present -
Ready
The name Hazir is
mentioned in the Quran.

Hazzar
Generous - Laughing

Hibr
Ink - Scholar - Virtuous
Variants: *Hebr*

Hikma
Wisdom
The name Hikma is
mentioned in the Quran.

Variants: *Hekma, Hekmah,
Hikmah*

Hikmat
Wisdom
Variants: *Hekmat, Hikmet*

Hilal
Beginning of Rain -
Crescent Moon

Hilf
Alliance - Treaty

Hilmi
Enduring - Forbearing -
Lenient

Himaa
Harbor - Haven -
Hideaway

Himayat
Care - Defense -
Protection - Safekeeping
Turkish pronunciation of
Himayah. (Also used in
Turkish)

Hisham
Gracious - Honorable -
Noble
Variants: *Heshaam,
Hesham, Hishaam*

Hishmat
Modesty - Virtue
(Also used in Turkish)
Variants: *Heshmat*

Hobb
Affectionate - Love
The name Hobb is
mentioned in the Quran.

Hubaibi
Beloved

Hubair
Ink - Little Scholar
Variants: *Hobair*

Hubbee
Loving

Hufaiz
Protector
Variants: *Hofaidh*

Hulm
Forbearance - Patience

Humaid
Praise

Humaidan
Praiseworthy

Humaisun
Brave

Humam
Elite - Honored - Noble

Hunain
Hunain is the name of a
valley between at-Taif
and Mecca in which a
battle took place. The
literal meaning of the
word is not known.
Variants: *Honain, Honayn,
Hunayn*

Huraira
Cat - Kitten
Variants: *Horaira,*

Horairah, Hurairah,
Hurayrah

Husaim
Assiduous - Diligent -
Persevering
Variants: *Hosaim*

Husam
Sharp Sword - Sword
Blade
Variants: *Hosam*

Husni
Good - Handsome
Variants: *Hosnee, Hosni,*
Husnee, Husny

Hussein
Gentle - Handsome -
Virtuous
Variants: *Hosain, Hosein,*
Husain, Husein, Hussain

Hutaim
Judge - Pure
Variants: *Hotaim*

Huyai
Alive - Flourishing

Huzaifah
Sheep
Variants: *Hozaifa,*
Hudhaifa

Huzair
Laughter

I

Ibad
Servants of Allah
The name Ibad is
mentioned in the Quran
in verse 20:77.
Variants: *Ebaad, Ebad,
Ibaad*

Ibadah
Worship
The name Ibadah is
mentioned in the Quran.

Ibadullah
Worshipers

Ibhar
Breadth - Graciousness
Variants: *Ebhar, Ibhaar*

Ibrahim
The name Ibrahim is
mentioned in the Quran.
It is the name of a
Prophet, the same as
Biblical Abraham, who is
the ancestor of the
prophets Isaac, Jacob,
Joseph, Moses, John, Jesus
and Muhammad (peace be
upon them).
Variants: *Ebraheem,
Ebraheim, Ebrahim,
Ibraaheem, Ibraheem,
Ibrahem*

Ibreez
Gold
Variants: *Ebreez, Ebriz,
Ibriz*

Ibtihal
Humble Prayer -
Supplication
Variants: *Ebtehal*

Ibtisam
Smile
Variants: *Ebetesam,
Ebtesaam, Ibtesam,
Ibtisaam*

Idris
Idris is the name of one of
the prophets mentioned
in the Quran. The
meaning of the name is
not known for certain.
Variants: *Edrees, Edris,
Idrees*

Iffat
Chastity - Modesty
Turkish pronunciation of
Iffah.

Ifra
Enjoining of Good
Variants: *Efra, Efraa, Ifraa*

Ihdaf
Closeness - Proximity
Variants: *Ihdaaf*

Ihkam
Decisiveness - Mastery
Variants: *Ehkaam, Ehkam,
Ihkaam*

Ihlal
Clarity - Radiance
Variants: *Ehlal*

Ihram
Prohibition

The word ihram is used to
refer to a pilgrim's
entering into a state of
prohibition once he starts
his pilgrimage, in which
many things are
prohibited to him, such as
hunting or wearing
perfume.

Ihsan
Generosity - Good Deeds
- Graciousness - Kindness
The name Ihsan is
mentioned in the Quran.
Variants: *Ehsaan, Ehsan,
Ihsaan, Ihsan*

Ihtiram
Consideration - Esteem -
Regard
Variants: *Ehteram,
Ehtiram, Ihteram*

Ijlal
Greatness - Majesty
Variants: *Ejlaal, Ejlal, Ijlaal*

Ikha
Brotherhood - Friendship
Variants: *Ekha, Ekhaa,
Ikhaa, Ikhaa'*

Ikhlas
Faithfulness - Loyalty -
Sincerity
Variants: *Ekhlaas, Ekhlas,
Ikhlaas*

Ikhwan
Brothers
The name Ikhwan is
mentioned in the Quran.

Variants: Ekhuan, Ekhwan, Ikhuan, Ikhwaan

Ikleel
Crown
Variants: Iklil

Ikrimah
Female Pigeon
Variants: Ikrima

Ilan
Announcement - Proclamation
Variants: Elaan, Ilaan

Ilhan
Eloquence
Variants: Elhaan, Elhan, Ilhaan

Ilm
Knowledge - Science
The name Ilm is mentioned in the Quran.

Ilya
Great - High in Status - Noble
Variants: Elia, Eliah, Ilia, Iliah, Ilyah

Imad
Pillar - Supporter
The name Imad is mentioned in the Quran.
Variants: Emaad, Emad, Imaad

Imad ad-Din
Supporter of Islam
Literally means "pillar of the faith".

Variants: Imad Uddin, Imaduddin

Imamuddin
Supporter of Islam
Literally "leader of the faith".
Variants: Imam Uddin

Imara
Construction - Revival - Visit
The name Imara is mentioned in the Quran.
Variants: Emara, Emarah, Imaara, Imaarah, Imarah

Imdad
Help - Support
Variants: Emdad, Imdaad

Imhal
Forbearance - Leniency
Variants: Emhal, Imhaal

Imran
The name Imran is mentioned in the Quran. It is the name of the father of Mariam (Mary), mother of Prophet Isa (Jesus), peace be upon them.
Variants: Emraan, Emran, Imraan

Imtiaz
Distinction - Prominence - Superiority
Variants: Imtyaz

Imtiazuddin
Supporter of Islam
Literally "superiority of

the faith".
Variants: Imtyaz Uddin

Imtisal
Adoration - Imitation - To Follow
Variants: Emtisal

Inab
Grape
The name Inab is mentioned in the Quran.

Inam
Blessings - God's Favors
Variants: Enaam, In'am, Inaam

Inam ul Haq
Gift from God
Literally "blessing from al-Haq". al-Haq means "the Truth" and is one of the names of God.

Inamurrahman
Gift from God
Variants: Inamur Rahman

Inbihaj
Cheerfulness - Delight - Mirth
Variants: Enbihaj, Inbehaaj

Inbisat
Cheerfulness - Joyfulness - Relaxation
Variants: Enbisat, Inbesaat

Infisal
Distance - Divergence - Separation
Variants: Infesal

Inhal
Pouring of Rain
Variants: *Enhal*

Injah
Success
Variants: *Injaah*

Injeel
Messenger - The Gospels
The name Injeel is
mentioned in the Quran.
Variants: *Enjil*

Ins
Relaxation - Tranquility
Variants: *Ens*

Insaf
Fairness - Justice
Variants: *Insaaf*

Inshad
Chanting - Singing
Variants: *Enshad, Inshaad*

Inshiraf
Glory - Greatness -
Honor
Variants: *Insheraaf*

Insijam
Harmony - Symmetry
Variants: *Ensejam,
Insejam*

Intiha
Completion - Conclusion
- End
Variants: *Intehaa*

Intisar
Triumph - Victory
Variants: *Entisar, Intesaar*

Intishal
Healing - Recovery
Variants: *Entishal,
Intishaal*

Intizar
Anticipation - Expectation
- Wait
Variants: *Intezaar*

Iqbal
Boldness - Success
Variants: *Eqbaal, Eqbal,
Iqbaal*

Iqdam
Boldness
Variants: *Eqdam*

Iqleem
Country - Land - Region -
Zone
Variants: *Eqlim, Iqlim*

Iqyan
Gold

Iraq
River Bank - Shore

Irfan
Wisdom - Enlightenment
Variants: *Erfaan, Erfan,
Irfaan*

Irmas
Strong - Tough

Irtiqa
Ascension - Ascent -
Improvement - Promotion
Variants: *Ertiqa, Ertiqaa,
Irteka, Irteqa, Irtika,
Irtiqaa*

Isa
God is Salvation
Originally from Hebrew.
Arabic form of "Jesus".
The name Isa is
mentioned in the Quran.
Variants: *Eesa, Eisa, Esa,
Esaa, Eysa, Eysaa, Issa*

Isam
Bond - Connection -
Promise
Variants: *Esaam, Esam,
Isaam*

Ishraq
Daybreak - Emergence -
Illumination - Sunrise -
Vividness
The name Ishraq is
mentioned in the Quran.
Variants: *Eshraaq, Eshraq,
Ishraaq*

Iskandar
Defender of Humanity
Iskandar is the Arabic
form of Alexander.
Variants: *Eskander,
Iskander*

Islam
Submission
The name Islam is
mentioned in the Quran.

Israr
Determination -
Insistence - Resolve

Istiqlal
Independence -
Sovereignty
Variants: *Esteqlal, Estiqlal,
Istiqlaal*

Itqan
Mastery - Proficiency -
Skill
Variants: *Etqaan, Etqan,
Itqaan, Itqan*

Iwazallah
God's Restitution

Iyad
Able - Capable - Powerful
Variants: *Eiaad, Eiaade,
Eiad, Eyaad, Eyad, Iyaad*

Iyadi
Consoler - Visitor of the
Sick
Variants: *Eyaadi*

Iyan
Era - Time
The name Iyan is
mentioned in the Quran.
It is an alternate reading
of the word Ayyan used in
verse 27:65.
Variants: *Eyaan, Eyan,
Eyyan, Iyaan, Iyyan*

Iyas
Replacement - Restitution
Variants: *Eyas, Iyaas*

Izaad
Advocacy - Loyalty

Izaan
Acceptance - Obedience -
Submission
Variants: *Ezaan, Iz'an*

Izfaar
Help - Support
Literally "to help someone
attain victory".
Variants: *Ezfaar, Ezfar,
Izfar*

Izzaddin
Honor of the Faith

Izzat
Greatness - Majesty -
Might

J

Jaamil
Handsome

Jaar
Neighbor
Variants: *Jar*

Jaari
Neighborly
Variants: *Jary*

Jabbad
Attractive - Charming

Jabir
Fixer - Improver -
Mender
Variants: *Jaaber, Jaabir,
Jaber*

Jaboor
Mender - Strong

Jabr
Brave

Jabran
Brave

Jabreel
Gabriel
Variant of Jibreel.

Jadir
Spring Bloom - Spring
Sprout
Variants: *Jader*

Jadud
Fortunate - Great - Lucky

Jadur
First Sprout of Spring

Jaed
Generous - Gracious -
Torrential Rain
Variants: *Jaaed*

Jafar
River - Stream

Jafaran
Two Rivers

Jafur
River

Jahd
Strife - Struggle

Jahhad
Striver

Jahid
Striver

Jalee
Clear - Lucid

Jalib
Attractive - Captivating
Variants: *Jaaleb, Jaalib,
Jaleb*

Jalis
Sitter

Jalwan
Discoverer of the Truth

Jamal
Beauty
The name Jamal is

mentioned in the Quran.
Variants: *Jamaal*

Jameelu
Beautiful - Handsome

Jamiloun
Handsome

Janis
Ripe Fruit

Jaram
Date (fruit) - Kernel -
Seed

Jaran
Ally - Neighbor
Variants: *Jaaran*

Jarum
Big-bodied - Fruit
Collector

Jaseer
Bold - Brave

Jasim
Hulking - Muscular -
Strong
Variants: *Jasem*

Jasir
Bold - Brave
Variants: *Jaser*

Jassar
Bold - Brave

Jawabir
Mender - Orphan's
Caretaker

Jawad
Generous - Gracious -
Noble
Variants: *Javad, Jawaad, Jewaad, Jewad*

Jawd
Torrential Rain

Jawdat
Goodness - Virtue

Jawhar
Essence - Jewel -
Precious Stone
Variants: *Johar, Jouhar, Jowhar*

Jayed
Generous - Giving

Jayesh
Night Traveler

Jayyid
Good - Gracious

Jazaa
Recompense - Reward
The name Jazaa is
mentioned in the Quran.
Variants: *Jaza, Jaza', Jeza, Jezaa*

Jazal
Delight - Happiness

Jazal
Generous - Great

Jazee
Advocate
Variants: *Jazi*

Jazeel
Great - Tremendous

Jazim
Determined - Resolute
Variants: *Jazem*

Jazoon
Advocate
Variants: *Jazun*

Jazub
Attractive - Charming

Jibal
Mountains
The name Jibal is
mentioned in the Quran.
Variants: *Jebaal, Jebal, Jibaal*

Jibillah
Nation
The name Jibillah is
mentioned in the Quran.

Jibraeel
Gabriel
Variant of Jibreel.

Jibran
Consolation -
Recompense - Redress
Variants: *Jebraan, Jebran, Jibraan*

Jibreel
Gabriel
Name of the angel of
revelation. The name
Jibreel is used in the
Quran.

Jibriyal
Gabriel
Variant of Jibreel.

Jihad
Struggle
Jihad is mentioned in the
Quran.
Variants: *Jehaad, Jehad, Jihaad*

Jodd
Beach - Coast - Fortunate
- Side

Johd
Strife - Struggle

Joud
Generosity -
Graciousness

Juayfir
Stream

Jubair
Mender - Unbreaker
Variants: *Jobair, Jobayr, Jubayr*

Jubran
Consolation -
Recompense - Redress
Variants: *Jobraan, Jobran, Jubraan*

Jumail
Nightingale

Jumal
Handsome

Junada
Helper - Soldier - Warrior
Variants: *Junaada,*
Junadah

Junaid
Soldier - Warrior
Variants: *Jonaid, Jonayd,*
Junayd

Juraiw
Cub

Jusair
Bold - Brave

Jusam
Hulking - Muscular

Juwaid
Generous - Gracious

K

Kaabir
Great - Powerful

Kaarim
Excellent - Generous -
Gracious - Noble
Variants: *Kaarem, Karem,*
Karim

Kabir
Chief - Great - Powerful
The name Kabir is
mentioned in the Quran.
Variants: *Kabeer, Kebir*

Kafi
Sufficient
The name Kafi is
mentioned in the Quran.

Kahal
One Who Has Beautiful
Dark Eyelids

Kahul
One Who Has Beautiful
Black Eyes

Kalamuddin
Supporter of Islam
Literally "speech of the
faith", meaning "orator of
the faith".

Kamal
Completeness -
Perfection - Wholeness
Variants: *Kamaal, Kemaal,*
Kemal

Kamaluddeen
Virtuous
Literally means
"perfection of the faith".

Kamayel
Complete - Perfect -
Whole

Kameel
Complete - Perfect -
Whole

Kamil
Complete - Perfect -
Whole
Variants: *Kaamel, Kaamil,*
Kamel

Kamilan
Complete - Perfect -
Whole

Kamlan
Complete - Perfect -
Whole

Kamush
Bold - Brave

Kanz
Treasure
The name Kanz is used in
the Quran.
Variants: *Kenz, Kinz*

Kanzuddin
Treasure of the Faith

Karam
Generosity -
Graciousness

Karamullah
God's Graciousness

Karawan
Curlew
A type of bird.

Kareem
Excellent - Generous -
Gracious - Noble
The name Kareem is
mentioned in the Quran.
Variants: *Karim, Kerim*

Karman
Gracious

Karram
Generous - Gracious

Karrum
Gracious

Kashaaf
Discoverer - Finder
Variants: *Kashshaf, Keshaf*

Kasir
Plenty

Kasoor
Plenty

Kasran
Plenty

Kassab
Earner - Winner

Kathir
Plenty
The name Kathir is
mentioned in the Quran.

Variants: *Kaseer, Kasir, Khatheer*

Katib
Intellectual - Scholar - Writer
The name Katib is mentioned in the Quran in verse 2:283.
Variants: *Kaateb, Kaatib, Kateb*

Kattam
Keeper of Secrets

Kawnain
Beings - Existences - Universes

Kayani
Kingly - Royal
Variants: *Kaiani, Kayaani, Kayany*

Kazim
One Who Controls His Own Anger

Keyan
Being - Existence
Variants: *Keyaan, Kiaan, Kian, Kyaan, Kyan*

Kibaar
Great Ones Leaders

Kifah
Strife - Struggle
Variants: *Kefaah, Kefah, Kifaah*

Kifayatullah
God's Contentment

Contentment that is bestowed by God.

Kifl
Example - Fortune - Luck
The name Kifl is mentioned in the Quran.

Kinan
Covering - Veil - Wrap

Kindi
Mountain-dweller

Kiswa
Clothing - Garment
Refers to the black silk cloth that covers the Kaaba in Mecca, Saudi Arabia.
Variants: *Keswa, Keswah, Kiswah*

Kohl
Kohl

Kufah
Mound of Sand

Kumail
Complete - Perfect - Whole
Variants: *Komail, Komayl, Komeil, Kumayl, Kumeil*

Kundas
Magpie
A type of bird.

Kuraiman
Gracious

Kuram
Gracious Ones - Honorable Ones

Kh

Khaalud
Immortal

Khabir
Experienced - Expert
The name Khabir is
mentioned in the Quran.
Variants: *Khabeer*

Khadamullah
Servant of God

Khadeej
Born Preterm
Variants: *Khadij*

Khafid
Agile - Fast

Khafif
Nimble - Sprightly
Variants: *Khafeef*

Khailad
Immortal

Khair
Good - Wealth
The name *Khair* is
mentioned in the Quran.
Variants: *Cair, Caire,
Kaire, Kayr, Kayre, Keir,
Keire, Ker, Kere, Keyr,
Keyre, Khaire, Khayr,
Khayre, Kheir, Kheire,
Kher, Khere, Kheyr, Kheyre*

Khairullah
God's Blessings

Khaldan
Immortal

Khaldun
Immortal
Variants: *Khaldoon*

Khaleed
Immortal

Khaleef
Leader - Successor
Variants: *Kaleef, Khaleif,
Khalif*

Khaleefa
Leader - Successor
The name *Khaleefa* is
mentioned in the Quran.
Variants: *Kalifa, Kalifah,
Khaleefah, Khalifa,
Khalifah*

Khaleel
Companion - Friend
The name *Khaleel* is
mentioned in the Quran.
Variants: *Helil, Kaleel,
Kalil, Khalil, Khelil*

Khalees
Brave - Skilled - Vigilant

Khalfun
Successor - Virtuous Son

Khali
Bygone - Solitary

Khalidin
Immortal Ones
The name Khalidin is

mentioned in the Quran.
Variants: *Khalideen*

Khalidun
Everlasting - Immortal
The name Khalidun is
mentioned in the Quran.
Variants: *Khaledun,
Khalidoon*

Khalifat
Successor

Khalis
Pure
The name Khalis is
mentioned in the Quran.
Variants: *Khaalis, Khales*

Khalud
Immortal

Khaluq
Good-mannered

Khaseeb
Fertile - Fruitful -
Productive

Khassab
Blessed
Variants: *Khasaab*

Khassal
Victor

Khateeb
Orator - Speaker

Khateer
Dangerous - Honorable -
Important - Noble
Variants: *Khatir*

Khatir
Heart - Idea - Notion

Khattar
Lion - Perfume-maker

Khawatir
Ideas - Notions -
Thoughts

Khawli
Chief - Foreman

Khayal
Fantasy - Imagination -
Vision

Khayyar
Good - Virtuous

Khayyir
Good - Noble - Virtuous
Variants: *Khayir, Khayyer*

Khazeer
Greenery - Sea

Khazran
Green-colored - Soft
Grass

Kheer
Generosity - Honor -
Virtue

Khidr
Green
Name of a personality
mentioned in the Quran
(not by name though),
who met prophet Musa
(Moses) and taught him.
Variants: *Kheder, Khedr,*

Khezer, Khezr, Khidhr,
Khidir, Khizr

Khilal
Companionship -
Friendship
The name Khilal is
mentioned in the Quran
in verse 14:31.
Variants: *Kelal, Khelaal,*
Khelal, Khilaal, Khylal,
Kilal

Khisb
Blessedness - Growth
Variants: *Khesb*

Khitab
Dispatch - Letter -
Speech

Khitam
Final - Finale - Seal

Khiyar
Doers of Good Deeds -
Virtuous Ones

Khosrau
King
(Also used in Persian)
Variants: *Khosro, Khosrou*

Khoulad
Immortal

Khufaf
Clever - Intelligent
Khufaf is an Arabic name
for boys that means
"clever", "intelligent".

Khufair
Guardianship - Modesty -
Protection

Khulaid
Immortal

Khulaif
Successor

Khulaifah
Successor

Khulum
Devoted Friend

Khuml
Devoted Friend

Khusaib
Fruitfulness - Growth -
Productivity

Khusaif
Dust-colored

Khushdel
Happy - Joyful

Khuwailid
Immortal

Khuzaimah
Gabal Elba Dragon Tree
A type of tree.

L

Laaiq
Eligible - Qualified -
Suitable

Labeeb
Intelligent - Sagacious

Labis
Coverer - Wearer

Lahiq
Following - Reaching

Lahiq
White-colored

Laidan
Gentle - Good-mannered

Lail
Night
The name Lail is
mentioned in the Quran.
Variants: *Layl, Leil, Leyl*

Lailan
Two Nights

Laith
Lion

Laithi
Brave - Lion-like

Lamaan
Glimmer - Shine

Lameek
One Who Has Beautiful
Dark Eyelids

Lamees
Smooth - Soft - Sun

Lamis
Toucher

Latafat
Gentleness - Kindness

Lateef
Gentle - Kind
The name Lateef is
mentioned in the Quran.
Variants: *Latif*

Latifi
Gentle - Kind

Lawahiz
Eyes - One Who Glances

Layiq
Fitting - Proper - Suitable

Lazim
Desired - Wished For

Liaqat
Aptitude - Competence -
Worthiness

Lisanuddin
Supporter of Islam

Luay
Strong
Variants: *Loae, Loai, Loay,
Louay, Loway, Luae, Luai,
Luway*

Lubaib
Pure

Luham
Great

Lujain
Silver

Luqman
Luqman is the name of a
person mentioned in the
Quran.
Variants: *Loqmaan,
Loqman, Luqmaan*

Lutah
Intelligent - Sensible

Lutaif
Gentle - Kind

Lutf
Gentleness - Kindness -
Leniency

Lutfan
Gentleness - Kindness -
Leniency

Lutfi
Gentle - Kind

Lutfullah
God's Mercy

Lutfurrahman
God's Mercy

Luwaibid
Little Lion

Luwaih
Apparent - Manifest -
Visible

M

Maabad
Temple - Worship

Maad
Afterlife - Hereafter -
Recurrence
The name Maad is
mentioned in the Quran.

Maadil
Method - Road - Way

Maadin
Metal - Mineral

Maadini
Metallic

Maadun
Inhabited - Settled

Maalam
Milestone - Road Sign

Maali
Greatness - Highness of
Status

Maamour
Inhabited - Restored
The name Maamour is
mentioned in the Quran.

Maan
Beneficial - Helpful
Variants: Ma'n

Maany
Meanings - Virtues

Maarif
Knowledge - Wisdom

Maarij
Ascents - Routes of
Ascent - Stairs
The name Maarij is
mentioned in the Quran.

Maarufi
Doer of Good Deeds

Maash
Livelihood - Sustenance
The name Maash is
mentioned in the Quran.

Maashar
Folk - Group of People -
Kinsfolk
The name Maashar is
mentioned in the Quran.
Variants: Ma'shar

Maashir
Communities Societies

Maasib
Chiefs - Masters

Maatuq
Freed - Freed From
Slavery

Maayish
Livelihood - Sustenance
The name Maayish is
mentioned in the Quran.

Maayush
Alive - Prosperous

Maaz
Refuge - Shelter

Maazim
Dignified - Enduring -
Patient

Maazir
Excuses

Maazur
Blameless - Excused

Maazuz
Powerful - Strong

Mabkhut
Lucky - Protected
Variants: Mabkhoot

Mabruk
Blessed

Mabrur
Blessed - Proper - Valid

Madar
Circuit - Cycle - Orbit

Maddah
Praiser

Madeeh
Praise

Madih
Praiser

Madkhal
Access - Admittance -
Entrance - Entry

183

Maeesh
Life - Lifetime - Livelihood

Mafakhir
Glorious Deed - Glorious Trait

Maftooh
Free - Open
Variants: Maftuh

Maghayis
Rainfalls

Maghazi
Content - Essence - Gist - Intent

Mahaad
Comforter - Facilitator
Variants: Mahad

Mahal
Forbearing - Lenient

Mahbub
Adored - Loved

Mahbur
Affluent - Blessed

Mahd
Cradle - Place of Comfort - Starting Point
The name Mahd is mentioned in the Quran.
Variants: Mehd

Mahdi
Well-guided

Maheer
Wise

Mahfuz
Guarded - Protected
The name Mahfuz is mentioned in the Quran.

Mahid
Comforter - Facilitator
Variants: Maahed, Maahid, Mahed

Mahir
Adept - Proficient - Skilled

Mahjan
Flourishing - Pure

Mahmud
Laudable - Praiseworthy
The name Mahmud is mentioned in the Quran.
Variants: Mahmood, Mahmoud, Mehmood, Mehmud, Mehmut

Mahrus
Guarded - Protected

Mahsub
Measured - Quantified

Mahsum
Decided - Determined - Resolved

Mahsun
Beautified - Improved

Mahul
Forbearance - Leniency

Mahzuz
Fortunate - Lucky

Maidan
Arena - Plaza

Maiz
Distinguisher
Variants: Maaez, Maaiz, Maez

Majal
Chance - Elbowroom - Opportunity - Space

Majd
Distinction - Glory - Honor
Variants: Mejd

Majdan
Glorious - Praiseworthy

Majdi
Laudable - Praiseworthy

Majduddin
Supporter of Islam
Literally "glory of the faith".

Majeed
Glorious - Majestic - Praiseworthy
Variants: Majid, Mejid

Majeedan
Glorious - Laudable - Praiseworthy

Majeedi
Laudable - Praiseworthy

Majjad
Glorious - Praiseworthy

Majjadin
Praiseworthy Ones

Majzub
Attracted

Makan
Place
The name Makan is
mentioned in the Quran.
Variants: *Makaan*

Makki
Meccan

Makram
Generosity - Honor -
Respect

Makrimi
Generosity - Honor

Makrur
Recurring - Repeating

Maktub
Decreed - Recorded -
Written

Maleed
Gentle - Soft

Maleeh
Charming - Handsome -
Witty
Variants: *Malih*

Maleek
King - Master - Owner

The name Maleek is
mentioned in the Quran.

Maleekan
Kings - Masters

Malih
Charming - Handsome -
Witty
Variants: *Maaleh, Maalih,
Maleh*

Malmus
Touchable - Within Reach

Malouf
Beloved - Friend - Well-
known
Variants: *Maluf*

Mamdud
Extensive - Great
The name Mamdud is
mentioned in the Quran.

Mamduh
Praiseworthy

Mamun
Honorable - Loyal -
Trustworthy
Variants: *Ma'mun,
Maamun, Mamoon,
Mamoun*

Manaf
Great - High in Status

Manafi
Benefits
The name Manafi is
mentioned in the Quran.

Manari
Radiant

Manarul Islam
Lighthouse of Islam

Manazir
Flourishing - Radiant

Maneeh
Generous

Manhal
Fountain - Spring - Water
Well

Mansar
Advocacy - Support

Mansur
Backed - Supported -
Victor
The name Mansur is
mentioned in the Quran.

Mansuri
Victor

Manzur
Anticipated - Foreseen -
Seen - Visible

Maooni
Helper - Supporter

Maqasid
Destinations - Goals -
Intentions

Maqbul
Accepted - Approved

Maqdeed
Powerful - Strong

Maqdum
Accepted - Begun -
Initiated

Maqdur
Achievable - Doable -
Feasible

Maqsud
Desired - Sought

Maraheeb
Generosity - Hospitality -
Welcome

Marahi
Exuberant - Lively

Marashid
Right Guidance

Maratib
Ranks - Stations

Marbuh
Earned

Marduf
Followed - Succeeded

Mareekh
Lead Monoxide
A chemical used in
Medieval times in
alchemy and medicine.

Mareen
Gentle - Lenient

Mareer
Resolved - Strong

Marghab
Desire - Wish

Marin
Forgiving - Lenient

Marooh
Gleeful - Lively

Marshud
Well-guided

Marshudi
Well-guided

Maruf
Acceptable - Customary -
Good
The name Maruf is
mentioned in the Quran.
Variants: *Ma'ruf, Maroof,
Marouf*

Marukh
Perfume-wearer

Marur
Crossing - Passage

Marwan
Fragrant Tree - Quartz
Variants: *Marwaan*

Marwani
Quartz-like

Marzi
Approved - Beloved -
Chosen - Liked

Marzooq
Blessed - Gifted
Variants: *Marzuq*

Marzun
Calm - Composed -
Dignified

Marzuqi
Blessed by God - Given
Provision

Marzuqullah
Blessed by God

Masad
Hunting Ground

Masadiq
Faithful - Loyal

Masajid
Mosques - Places of
Worship

Masakin
Habitation - Residence
The name Masakin is
mentioned in the Quran.

Masari
Path - Road

Masarrat
Gladness - Happiness -
Joy

Masbat
Place of Rest - Place of
Sleep

Masd
Highland - Plateau

Masduq
Credible - Trusted
Variants: *Masdooq,*
Masdouq

Maseeri
Destiny - Fate

Mashahid
Landscapes - Panoramas
- Scenes

Mashal
Lantern - Light
Variants: *Mash'al, Mashaal*

Mashar
Honeycomb Cell

Mashariq
East - Eastern Lands -
Orient
The name Mashariq is
mentioned in the Quran.

Mashawir
Honeycomb Cells

Masheedi
Great - High in Status

Mashhad
Scene - View
The name Mashhad is
mentioned in the Quran.

Mashhur
Distinguished - Well-
known
Variants: *Mashhoor*

Mashiyat
Will - Willpower

Variants: *Masheat,*
Masheeat, Mashi'at,
Mashiat, Mashiyyat

Mashkur
Appreciated - Thanked
The name Mashkur is
mentioned in the Quran.

Mashkuri
Appreciated - Thanked

Mashqur
Fair-skinned

Mashriq
East - Orient
The name Mashriq is
mentioned in the Quran.

Mashriqi
Eastern - Oriental

Mashruh
Explained - Open -
Relaxed

Mashta
Winter Resort

Masik
Grasper - Holder

Masir
Destiny - Fate
The name Masir is
mentioned in the Quran.
Variants: *Maseer, Massir*

Masjid
Mosque - Place of
Worship

The name Masjid is
mentioned in the Quran.

Maskun
Inhabited - Occupied

Masrur
Glad - Happy
The name Masrur is
mentioned in the Quran.

Mastoor
Covered - Hidden -
Modest
The name Mastoor is
mentioned in the Quran.

Masud
Blessed - Happy -
Successful
Variants: *Masood, Masoud*

Masudi
Glad - Happy

Masus
Unripe Date

Mataf
Place of Tawaf - Place of
Visitation
Variants: *Mataaf*

Matahir
Cleansers - Purifiers

Matalib
Demands - Desires

Matar
Rain
The name Matar is
mentioned in the Quran.

Matari
Rain-like

Matee
Good - Virtuous
Variants: *Mati, Mati'*

Mateer
Rainy

Mateeri
Rain-like

Mathnawi
Binary - Couplet
Usually refers to a type of
poetry.

Mathwa
Abode - Home
The name Mathwa is
mentioned in the Quran.

Matir
Fast-running Horse -
Rainy Day

Matlab
Demand - Desire

Matlub
Desired - Sought
The name Matlub is
mentioned in the Quran.

Mattali
Smith - Sword-maker

Mauddin
Miner

Mawfoud
Agent - Delegate - Deputy

Mawhab
Gifted - Given

Mawhad
One - Singular

Mawhub
Bestowed - Gifted - Given
Freely

Mawjud
Accessible - Existing -
Obtainable

Mawoud
Appointed - Determined -
Promisee
The name Mawoud is
mentioned in the Quran.

Mawthuq
Trusted - Trustworthy

Maymun
Blessed - Prosperous
Variants: *Maimoon,
Maimun, Maymoon*

Mazahir
Scenes - Views

Mazamin
Guarantee - Guarantor

Mazeed
Abundance
The name Mazeed is
mentioned in the Quran.

Mazhur
Apparent - Clear

Mazin
Rain-Bearing Cloud
Variants: *Maazen, Maazin,
Mazen*

Mazir
Elegant - Witty

Mazkur
Mentioned - Remembered
The name Mazkur is
mentioned in the Quran.

Mazman
Bail - Duty - Guarantee -
Obligation

Mazmun
Content - Meaning -
Significance - Substance

Miad
Appointment

Mibshar
Glad - Happy

Midadi
High - Tall

Midhat
Poem of Praise
(Also used in Turkish)

Midrar
Abundant - Copious -
Flowing

Mieshar
One Tenth

Mietaf
Affectionate -

Compassionate - Sympathetic

Mietawi
Generous

Mifrah
Happy - Joyous
Variants: *Mefraah, Mefrh, Mifraah*

Miftah
Guide - Key

Miftahuddin
Guide of the Faith

Mifyaz
Gracious

Mihad
Cradle - Place of Comfort - Plain
The name Mihad is mentioned in the Quran.
Variants: *Mehaad, Mehad, Mihaad*

Mihlal
Happy

Mihraz
Fixer - Improver

Mihwar
Axis - Pivot

Mijbar
Improver - Mender

Mijdad
Great - Strong

Mijhan
Young Man

Mikhaeel
Mikhaeel is the name that Arab Christians use to refer to the angel Mikaeel/Michael.
Variants: *Mikhael*

Milad
Birth Day - Noble Lineage - Parentage

Milhaan
Pure White Color
Variants: *Melhaan, Melhan, Milhan*

Milhas
Brave

Minhaj
Clear Path - Clear Way - Curriculum - Method
The name Minhaj is mentioned in the Quran.

Minhajuddin
Curriculum of the Faith - Path of the Faith

Minhal
Generous - Honorable

Minhali
Generous - Honorable

Minsar
Victor - Winner

Miqdad
Powerful - Strong

Miqdadi
Powerful - Strong

Miqdam
Bold - Brave

Miradi
Powerful - Strong

Miraf
Intelligent - Perceptive

Miraj
Ascent - Route of Ascent - Stars
Variants: *Mi'raj*

Mirajuddin
Ascent of the Faith

Mirfiq
Beneficial - Helpful

Mirghad
Doer of Good Deeds

Mirkhas
Gentle - Lenient - Soft

Mirrikh
Planet Mars - Wolf

Mirsab
Forbearing - Lenient

Mirsad
Lookout - Observatory - Place of Ambush

Mirsal
Message-bearer - Messenger

Mirshadi
Well-guided

Mirshaq
Nimble - Sprightly

Mirwaf
Compassionate - Kind

Mirzai
Content - Satisfied

Mirzaq
Affluent

Misam
Beautiful
Variants: Meesam,
Meysam, Miesam, Mysam

Misaq
Covenant
The name Misaq is
mentioned in the Quran.
Variants: Meesaq,
Meethaq, Misaaq, Mithaaq,
Mithaq

Misbah
Lamp - Lantern - Light -
Oil Lamp
The name Misbah is
mentioned in the Quran.
Variants: Mesbaah,
Mesbah, Misbaah

Misbahi
Radiant

Misbaq
Advanced - Ahead

Misdad
Faultless - Reasonable -
Sensible

Mishal
Lantern - Light
Variants: Mesh'al, Meshaal,
Meshal, Mish'al, Mishaal

Mishdad
Strong - Tough

Mishkat
Niche
The name Mishkat is
mentioned in the Quran.
Variants: Meshkaat,
Meshkat, Mishkaat

Mishraq
Brilliant - Radiant

Misk
Musk
The name Misk is
mentioned in the Quran.

Miski
Musk-like

Misri
Egyptian

Mithal
Ideal - Model

Mizan
Balance - Measure -
Scales - Weigth
The name Mizan is used
in the Quran.
Variants: Mezaan, Mezan,
Mizaan

Mizhir
Filled With Flowers

Mizn
Rain-Bearing Cloud -
White Cloud

Mizyan
Beautiful

Moein
Helper - Supporter
Variants: Moeen, Mouin,
Mueen, Muin

Moez
One Who Honors Others
- One Who Values Others
Variants: Moeiz, Muizz

Mouhib
Generous - Giving

Moujab
Amazed - Impressed -
Pleased

Moujib
Amazing - Impressive -
Pleasing

Moujid
Creator

Moumin
Believer
The name Moumin is
mentioned in the Quran.
Variants: Momin, Mu'min,
Mumen, Mumin

Mouminin
Believers

The name Mouminin is mentioned in the Quran.

Mouminun
Believers
The name Mouminun is mentioned in the Quran.
Variants: *Mu'minun*, *Muminun*

Moumir
Long-lived

Mouqib
Rewarder

Mourib
Eloquent - Fluent

Mousir
Needless - Wealthy

Moutaaz
Honored - Mighty - Powerful

Moutabir
Introspective - Tester

Moutadil
Balancec - Straight

Moutamad
Aim - Goal - Reliable

Moutamid
Reliant

Moutaq
Freed - Freed Slave

Moutaqad
Belief - Conviction - Faith - Tenet

Moutaqid
Believer - Faithful

Moutasam
Recourse - Refuge

Moutasim
Shelter-taker - Taker of Refuge

Moutaz
Honored - Majestic - Powerful

Moutazim
Determined - Persevering - Resolved

Mouti
Generous

Moutif
Elevated - Great - High in Status

Moutiq
Slave-liberator

Muaddal
Corrected - Reformed - Tuned

Muaddil
Equalizer - Rectifier

Muain
Helper - Supporter

Mualla
Exalted - Raised

Muallam
Educated - Learned - Tauht
The name Muallam is mentioned in the Quran.

Mualli
Exalter - Glorifier - Raiser

Muallim
Teacher
Variants: *Mu'allim*

Muameer
Long-lived
Variant of Muammir.

Muammal
Desired - Hoped For

Muammar
Long-lived

Muarrif
Guide

Muarrifi
Guide

Muashir
Close Friend - Companion - Fellow

Muawini
Helper - Supporter

Muawwal
Dependable - Reliable

Muayyad
Backed - Supported

Muaz
Guarded - Protected

Muazid
Helper - Supporter

Muazzid
Fortifier - Strengthener

Muazzim
Resolute - Resolved

Muazzir
Helper - Supporter

Mubarak
Blessed
The name Mubarak is
mentioned in the Quran.

Mubariz
Warrior
Variants: *Mobaariz,*
Mobarez, Mubaariz

Mubarrik
Rain-Bearing Cloud

Mubashir
Bringer of Good News -
Bringer of Good Tidings
The name Mubashir is
mentioned in the Quran.
Variants: *Mobashir,*
Mubasher

Mubdih
Praiseworthy

Mubdir
One Who the Full Moon
Shines Upon

Mubin
Apparent - Clear - Self-
evident
The name Mubin is
mentioned in the Quran.
Variants: *Mobeen, Mobin,*
Mubeen

Mudassir
Clothed - Covered -
Dressed
The name Mudassir is
mentioned in the Quran.
Variants: *Modasir,*
Modasser, Modassir,
Modathir, Mudasir,
Mudasser, Mudather,
Mudathir

Mueid
Experienced - Skilled

Mueidi
Experienced - Skilled

Mueinuddin
Supporter of the Faith

Mufakkir
Thinker

Mufazzil
Gracious

Mufid
Beneficial

Muflah
Successful

Muflih
Prosperous - Successful
Variants: *Mofleh, Moflih,*
Mufleh

Muflihi
Successful

Mufzil
Gracious

Mughamir
Adventurous - Daring

Mugharbal
Chosen - Pure - Select

Mughir
Attacker - Raider

Mughirah
Attacker - Raider

Mughith
Rescuer - Savior

Mughithi
Rescuer - Savior

Mughithuddin
Savior of the Faith

Mughram
In Love - Obsessed

Mughtin
Needless - Rich

Muhab
Fearsome - Mighty -
Strong

Muhabbab
Beloved

Muhabbib
Endearer

Muhafaz
Guarded - Protected
Muhafaz is an Arabic
name for boys that means
"protected", "guarded".

Muhaffiz
Giver of Knowledge

Muhafiz
Conservative - Keeper -
Protector

Muhajir
Ascetic - Avoider of Sin -
Migrator
The name Muhajir is used
in the Quran in verse
29:26.
Variants: *Mohaajir,
Mohaajir, Mohajer,
Mohajir, Muhaajer,
Muhaajir, Muhajer*

Muhammad
Admirable - Noble -
Praiseworthy
The name *Muhammad* is
mentioned in the Quran.
Variants: *Mohamad,
Mohamat, Mohamed,
Mohamet, Mohammad,
Mohammat, Mohammed,
Mohammet, Mohemad,
Mohemat, Mohemed,
Mohemet, Mohemmad,
Mohemmat, Mohemmed,
Mohemmet, Muhamad,*

*Muhamat, Muhamed,
Muhamet, Muhammat,
Muhammed, Muhammet,
Muhemad, Muhemat,
Muhemed, Muhemet,
Muhemmad, Muhemmat,
Muhemmed, Muhemmet*

Muhannad
Indian-made Sword

Muhassan
Beautified - Improved

Muhassin
Beautifier - Improver

Muhawwin
Facilitator

Muhazab
Backed - Supported

Muhazib
Advocate - Supporter

Muhazzab
Courteous - Educated -
Refined

Muhazzib
Educator - Teacher

Muhazzim
Defeater

Muhib
Lover

Muhibbudin
Lover of the Faith

Muhif
Elevated - Towering

Muhiyyuddin
Reviver of the Faith

Muhiz
Gracious - Honorable

Muhizzat
Gracious - Honorable
(Also used in Turkish)

Muhsad
Sensible - Wise

Muhsin
Doer of Good Deeds
The name Muhsin is
mentioned in the Quran.

Muhsinin
Doers of Good Deeds
The name Muhsinin is
mentioned in the Quran.
Variants: *Mohsinin*

Muhtad
Well-guided

Muhtadi
Well-guided

Muhtarim
Respectful

Muhtasab
Sufficient

Muhtashim
Chaste - Modest -
Virtuous

Variants: *Mohtashem,*
Mohtashim, Muhtashem

Muhtasib
Seeker of God's Rewards

Muidd
Preparer

Muinudeen
Supporter of Islam
Variants: *Moeinuddin,*
Muin Uddin, Muinuddin

Muizzawi
Enduring - Patient

Mujahid
Striver

Mujammal
Adorned - Beautified -
Improved

Mujawir
Neighbor

Mujayed
Praiseworthy

Mujeed
Doer of Good Deeds

Mujeedan
Doer of Good Deeds

Mujeedi
Doer of Good Deeds

Mujfar
Great

Mujib
Answerer - Responder
The name Mujib is
mentioned in the Quran.

Mujiran
Protector - Rescuer -
Savior

Mujtaba
Chosen - Selected
Variants: *Mojtaba,*
Mojtabaa, Mujtabaa

Mujtahid
Striver

Mukabbir
Glorifier of God

Mukafat
Recompense - Reward

Mukaibir
Exalter - Glorifier

Mukairim
Honorable - Respectful

Mukairiman
Honorable - Respectful

Mukallaf
Entrusted - Obligated -
Responsible

Mukarram
Honored - Respected

Mukhallis
Chooser - Picker -
Purifier - Selector

Mukhlas
Chosen - Purified -
Selected
The name Mukhlas is
mentioned in the Quran.

Mukhlis
Faithful - Loyal - Sincere
The name Mukhlis is
mentioned in the Quran.

Mukhlisi
Faithful - Loyal - Sincere

Mukhtar
Chosen
Variants: *Mokhtaar,*
Mokhtar, Mukhtaar

Mukhtari
Chosen - Excellent - Fine
- Superior

Muktafi
Content - Needless

Muktamil
Complete - Whole

Muladin
Gentle

Mulahib
Beautiful

Mulaisen
Eloquent - Fluent

Mulatif
Gentle - Kind

Mulayin
Gentle - Kind

Multamas
Desired - Wished For

Multamis
Desirer - Seeker

Muluk
Kings
The name Muluk is
mentioned in the Quran.

Mumajjad
Extolled - Glorified

Mumajjid
Extoller - Glorifier

Mumtaz
Excellent - Exceptional

Munaam
Blessed - Given Blessings
Variants: Mounaam,
Mounam, Mun'am

Munabbahan
Awake - Vigilant -
Wakeful

Munadi
Caller
The name Munadi is
mentioned in the Quran.

Munajji
Rescuer - Savior

Munal
Giver

Munaqqi
Pure

Munar
Bright - Well-lit

Munawwar
Radiant - Well-lit

Munawwir
Enlightener - Radiant

Mundi
Generous - Giving

Muneeb
One Who Turns to God -
Virtuous
The name Muneeb is
mentioned in the Quran
in verse 75:11.
Variants: Moneeb, Monib,
Muneib, Munib

Munif
Great - High in Status

Munir
Brilliant - Enlightening -
Illuminating - Radiant
The name Munir is
mentioned in the Quran.
Variants: Moneer, Monir,
Mounir, Muneer, Muner

Munis
Comforting Friend -
Consoling Friend

Muniym
Blessed - Giver of Charity
- Wealthy
Variants: Mounim,
Mun'im, Muneim

Munji
Rescuer - Savior

Munjid
Rescuer - Savior

Munshid
Reciter of Poetry

Munsif
Fair - Just

Muntaha
Aspiration - Goal
The name Muntaha is
mentioned in the Quran.

Muntaqa
Chosen - Pure - Purified -
Selected

Muntasaf
Middle

Muntasir
Conqueror - Victorious -
Winner

Muntazar
Awaited - Expected

Muntazir
Awaiting - Expecting

Munzir
Cautioner - Harbinger -
Portent - Warner
The name Munzir is
mentioned in the Quran.
Variants: Monzer, Monzir,
Munzer

Muqaddam
Beginning - Brought
Forward - Offered - Start

Muqarab
Brought Close - Muqarrab

Muqassam
Balanced - Symmetric

Muqassim
Distributor - Divider

Muqazi
Arbitrator - Judge -
Peace-maker

Muqid
Kindler - Lighter

Muqrin
Brave - Strong - Uniter

Muqsit
Fair - Just

Muqtadir
Capable - Powerful
The name Muqtadir is
mentioned in the Quran.

Murabbi
Trainer

Murad
Desired - Wished For
Variants: Moraad, Morad,
Muraad

Muraffah
Affluent

Muraffal
Respected

Murahiban
Greeter

Muraih
Energetic - Lively

Muraishid
Guide

Murakhas
Authorized - Licensed

Murashih
Mentor - Teacher

Murawwah
Musk-wearer

Murawwih
Perfume-wearer

Murazi
Gainer of Approval -
Satisfier

Murdah
Brave

Murdif
Follower - Succeeder

Murdini
Perpetual

Murfiq
Gentle - Lenient

Murghib
Rich - Wealthy

Murid
Desirous - Seeker

Muridan
Desirous - Seeker

Murih
Gentle - Lenient

Murihan
Gentle - Lenient

Murkhi
Affluent

Murkhis
Gentle - Lenient

Mursali
Message-bearer -
Messenger

Mursalin
Messengers
The name Mursalin is
mentioned in the Quran.
Variants: Morsalin,
Mursaleen

Murshad
Well-guided

Murshadi
Well-guided

Murshid
Guide

Murshidi
Guide

Mursili
Dispatcher

Murtah
Relaxed

Murtahanullah
God's Chosen Servant

Murtahinullah
Dedicated to God

Murtaqa
Bringer of Greatness

Murtaqi
Great

Murtawi
Quenched (not thirsty)

Murtaza
Gainer of God's Approval
Variants: Mortaza,
Mortazaa, Murtada,
Murtadha, Murtadhaa

Murtazi
Satisfied

Muruj
Green Fields

Murzaq
Blessed - Fortunate

Murzi
Pleaser - Satisfier

Murziq
Giver of Provision

Musa
Saved - Saved from Water
- Savior
The name Musa is used in

the Quran and it is the
Arabic name for Moses.
The name is not Arabic
and the meanings were
taken from non-Arabic
scholarly sources.
Variants: Mousa, Mousaa,
Musaa

Musab
Able - Capable - Strong
Variants: Mus'ab

Musabbih
Glorifier of God

Musabi
Capable - Strong

Musabir
Enduring - Patient

Musad
Glad - Happy

Musadan
Glad - Happy

Musaddad
Accomplished - Achieved
- Reached

Musaddaq
Believed - Trusted

Musaddid
Accomplisher - Achiever

Musadiq
Acknowledger -
Confirmer - Faithful
The name Musadiq is
mentioned in the Quran.

Variants: Mosadeq,
Mosadiq, Musaddeq,
Musaddiq

Musaf
Helped - Rescued

Musaghfir
Seeker of God's
Forgiveness

Musahib
Companion

Musaid
Helper

Musairi
Egyptian

Musalim
Peace-lover

Musallat
Powerful - Supreme

Musalli
Performer of Salah

Musallim
Obedient - Submissive

Musan
Guarded - Protected

Musannaf
Book

Musannif
Classifier

Musawi
Equal - Equivalent

Musawwir
Designer - Shaper
The name Musawwir is
mentioned in the Quran.
Variants: *Mosawir*,
Mosawwir, Musawer,
Musawir, Musawwer

Musayeib
Powerful - Strong

Musayyab
Free - Unchained

Musayyib
Freer

Musbih
Kindler - Lighter

Musdi
Bestower - Giver -
Granter

Musef
Helper - Rescuer

Musfir
Glowing - Radiant

Mushahid
Beholder - Observer -
Onlooker

Mushakhis
Differentiator - Discerner

Musharraf
Honorable

Mushawir
Seeker of Advice

Mushaywir
Honeycomb Cell

Mushfiq
Compassionate - Kind -
Sympathetic
Variants: *Moshfeq,*
Moshfiq, Mushfeq

Mushib
Companion - Friend

Mushidi
Fortifier - Strengthener

Mushir
Gesturer - Guide

Mushqari
Fair-skinned

Mushrif
Elevated - Overseer -
Towering

Mushriq
Bright - Well-lit

Mushriqi
Bright - Well-lit

Mushtaq
Desirous - Eager -
Yearning

Mushtaqi
Desirous - Eager -
Yearning

Musjil
Recorder - Registrar

Musli
Consoler

Muslih
Doer of Good Deeds -
Improver - Reformer
The name Muslih is
mentioned in the Quran.

Muslim
Muslim
The name Muslim is
mentioned in the Quran.

Muslimi
Muslim

Muslimin
Muslims
The name Muslimin is
mentioned in the Quran.
Variants: *Moslimin*

Musmih
Forgiving - Lenient

Musnad
Dependable - Reliable

Mustaf
Summer Vacationer

Mustafa
Chosen - Selected
Variants: *Mosftafa,*
Mostafaa, Mustafaa

Mustafid
Benefiter - Earner -
Winner

Mustahaq
Deserved - Earned

Mustahiq
Deserving - Worthy

Mustahsan
Good - Praiseworthy

Mustahsin
Gentle - Lenient

Mustajab
Accepted - Answered

Mustakfi
Needless

Mustala
Exalted - Raised

Mustali
Exalted - High in Status

Mustaltaf
Adorable - Charming

Mustaneer
Enlightened - Illuminated

Mustansir
Seeker of Help
Variants: *Mostansir*

Mustaqil
Independent - Sovereign

Mustaqim
Correct - Straight
The name Mustaqim is
mentioned in the Quran.
Variants: *Mostaqim,*
Mustaqeem

Mustashar
Adviser - Councilor

Mustawi
Even - Flat - Level

Mutaal
Elevated - High in Status -
Sublime
Variants: *Motaal, Muta'al*

Mutahhir
Cleaner - Purifier
The name Mutahhir is
mentioned in the Quran.

Mutahhiran
Cleaner - Purifier

Mutailib
Desired - Sought

Mutair
Rain

Mutairi
Rain-like

Mutalib
Demander - Seeker
Variants: *Mutaalib*

Mutallib
Demander - Seeker

Mutee
Obedient

Muthab
Rewarded

Muthib
Rewarder

Muwaffaq
Prosperous - Successful

Muwaffiq
Successful
Variants: *Mowafeq,*
Mowaffiq, Muwafeq,
Muwafiq

Muwahid
Monotheist
Variants: *Muwahed,*
Muwahhid

Muwaqqa
Brave

Muwaqqit
Time Keeper

Muyassar
Facilitated - Successful

Muyassir
Facilitator - Lenient

Muzaffar
Victor - Winner
Variants: *Mozafar,*
Mozafer, Muzafar,
Muzaffer

Muzain
Rain-Bearing Cloud

Muzaini
Rain-Bearing Cloud

Muzakir
Reminder
The name Muzakir is
mentioned in the Quran
and it means "one who
brings God's
remembrance to people",
a person who speaks

about God to people and
enjoins them to follow His
commandments.
Variants: *Mozaker,
Mozakir, Muzakker,
Muzakkir*

Muzammil
Wrapped in Garments
The name Muzammil is
mentioned in the Quran.
Variants: *Mozammil,
Muzamel, Muzamil*

Muzarib
Attacker - Striker
Variants: *Mozaareb,
Mozarib, Mudharib,
Muzaareb, Muzaarib,
Muzareb*

Muzayyan
Adorned - Beautified

Muzayyin
Adorner - Beautifier

Muzdahir
Flourishing - Prospering

Muzhir
Blooming

Muzn
Rain-Bearing Cloud -
White Cloud
The name Muzn is
mentioned in the Quran.

N

Naaim
Peaceful - Serene - Smooth - Soft

Naba
Announcement - News - Tidings

Nabayil
Aristocratic - Brave - Gallant - Highborn - Noble

Nabeel
Dignified - Gracious - Noble
Variants: *Nabil*

Nabhan
Aware - Vigilant - Wakeful

Nabigh
Brilliant - Outstanding

Nabih
Aware - Vigilant - Wakeful

Nabihi
Aware - Honorable - Vigilant - Wakeful

Nabili
Gallant - Gracious - Highborn

Nabit
Small New Plant - Sprout

Nadeer
Eloquent - Fluent

Nadir
Rare - Unique

Naeem
Bliss
The name Naeem is mentioned in the Quran.

Nafal
Fragrance - Gifts - Presents

Nafees
Desired - Precious
Variants: *Nafis, Nefis*

Nafih
Charitable - Protector

Nafil
Generous

Nafiz
Influential - Powerful

Naghmat
Melody - Tune

Nahad
Honorable - Mighty - Strong

Nahar
Daytime
The name Nahar is mentioned in the Quran.
Variants: *Nahaar, Nehar*

Nahiz
Diligent - Elevated - Energetic - High - Lofty

Nahran
Rivers

Nahshal
Falcon

Nahwan
Intelligent - Wise

Nahyan
Mature - Wise
Variants: *Nahian, Nahyaan*

Nahzan
Advanced - Growing

Nahzat
Advancement - Progress
(Also used in Turkish)

Naif
Elevated - High - Towering

Naimurrahman
God's Bliss

Naizak
Meteor - Shooting Star - Short Spear

Najah
Success

Najat
Rescue - Salvation
The name Najat is used in the Quran.
Variants: *Najaat*

Najd
Highland - Plateau

Najdat
Bravery - Rescue

Najeed
Lion

Najeemuddin
Radiance of the Faith

Naji
Rescued - Survivor

Najib
Excellent - High-born
Variants: Najeeb

Najid
Rescuer - Supporter

Najjad
Rescuer - Savior

Najlan
Beautiful-eyed

Najm
Star
The name Najm is
mentioned in the Quran.
Variants: Nejm

Najmuddin
Star of the Faith

Najud
Intelligent - Sensible -
Wise

Nakheel
Date Palms

Nakhlan
Pure - Purified

Nameer
Fresh Water

Nami
Developing - Growing -
Increasing

Namiq
Adorner - Decorator -
Embellisher

Namir
Leopard

Namran
Leopard-like

Naoum
Blessed

Naqeeb
Leader - Representative
The name Naqeeb is
mentioned in the Quran.
Variants: Nakib, Naqib

Naqeel
Flood - Stranger

Naqi
Pure

Naqil
Copyist - Transporter

Naqqad
Critic - Reviewer
Variants: Naqaad, Naqad

Nasayir
Helper - Supporter

Naseeb
Fitting - Gentlemanly -
Proper
Variants: Nasib, Nesib

Naseef
Secretly Spoken Words
Variants: Naseif, Nasif,
Nesif

Naseel
Pure

Naseem
Gentle Breeze
Variants: Nasim

Naseer
Helper - Supporter
The name Naseer is
mentioned in the Quran.
Variants: Nasir

Nashid
Praiser - Reciter of Poetry

Nashwan
Delirious - Ecstatic
Variants: Nashuan,
Nashwaan

Nasih
Giver of Advice - Guide
The name Nasih is
mentioned in the Quran.

Nasik
Worshiper

Nasikh
Clerk - Copyist - Editor

Nasir
Helper - Supporter
The name Nasir is
mentioned in the Quran.

Nasiruddin
Supporter of the Faith

Nasooh
Faithful - Loyal
The name Nasooh is
mentioned in the Quran.

Nasr
Victory
The name Nasr is
mentioned in the Quran.
Variants: *Nassr*

Nasrat
Help - Support

Nasruddin
Supporter of the Faith
Variants: *Nasraddin*

Nasrullah
God's Help
The name Nasrullah is
mentioned in the Quran.

Nassah
Giver of Good Advice -
Guide

Nassar
Helper - Supporter

Natiq
Articulate - Clear -
Interlocutor - Manifest -
Spokesman

Nattaj
Fruitful - Productive

Nawafil
Gifts - Presents

Nawf
Greatness - Highness

Nawfal
Generous - Gracious -
Handsome - Ocean - Sea

Nawfan
Great - High

Nawhan
Elevated - Exalted - Great

Nawl
Generosity - Nobleness

Nawras
Blossoming - Budding -
Young
(Also used in Persian)

Nawwab
Delegate - Representative

Nawwaf
Elevated - High - Lofty

Nawwar
Glowing - Radiant

Nawyan
Determined - Intending

Nayel
Acquirer - Brave -
Courageous - Finder -
Winner

Variants: *Na'il, Naael,
Naail, Naayel, Naayil,
Nael, Nayil*

Nayem
Calm - Tranquil

Nayir
Brilliant - Radiant

Nazeef
Clean - Virtuous

Nazeem
Orderly - Organized

Nazeer
Cautioner - Harbinger -
Portent - Warner
The name Nazeer is
mentioned in the Quran.
Variants: *Nazeer, Nazir,
Nezir*

Nazhan
Chaste - Virtuous

Nazih
Rain

Nazim
Arranger - Organizer
Variants: *Naazem,
Naazim, Nazem*

Nazir
Beautiful - Radiant

Nazmi
Orderly - Organized -
Systematic

TRADITIONAL AND MODERN ARABIC BABY NAMES

Nazzar
Observer - Spectator

Neem
Affluence

Nehrin
River
(Also used in Turkish)
Variants: *Nehreen*

Neimat
Blessing

Niamullah
God's Blessings - God's
Favors

Nihad
Mighty - Strong

Nimatullah
God's Blessings - God's
Favors

Nisbat
Connection - Harmony -
Relationship

Nisbi
Comparative -
Proportional

Nismat
Soft Breeze
(Also used in Turkish)

Nitaj
Fruit - Product - Profit

Niyazi
Beloved - Desired

Nizal
Strife - Struggle

Nizam
Arrangement - Rule -
System

Nizamuddin
System of the Faith

Nizamul Haq
System of Truth

Nizar
Rare - Unique

Noum
Affluence

Nouman
Blood

Nuaim
Delicate - Soft

Nubugh
Brilliance - Talent

Nudair
Rare - Unique

Nuh
Comfort - Noah - Rest
Nuh is the name of one of
the prophets mentioned
in the Quran, known as
Noah in the Bible.
Variants: *Nooh, Nouh*

Nuhuz
Advancement - Rise -
Rising

Nujaid
Highland

Nujaim
Little Star

Nukhail
Little Palm Tree

Numair
Little Leopard
Numair is an Arabic name
for boys that means "little
leopard", being the
diminutive form of Namir.

Numou
Growth - Increase

Nur
Light - Radiance
The name *Nur* is
mentioned in the Quran.
Variants: *Noor, Nour*

Nuraddeen
Light - Radiance -
Supporter of Islam
Variants: *Nuradeen,
Nuradin, Nuruddin*

Nurahan
Good Tidings - Radiant
King
(Also used in Persian,
Turkish)

Nuri
Brilliant - Good - Radiant

Nurshah
Light of the King

204

Nurulislam
Light of Islam

Nurullah
Light of God

Nusaib
Fitting - Gentlemanly -
Proper
Variants: Nosaib, Nosayb,
Nusayb

Nusaim
Breath - Soft Breeze

Nusair
Triumph - Victory

Nushur
Resurrection
The name Nushur is
mentioned in the Quran.

Nusur
Vultures

Nutou
Elevation - Greatness -
Loftiness

Nuwaib
Chief - Leader

Nuwaidir
Rare - Unique

Nuwair
Light - Radiance

Nuwairan
Light - Radiance

Nuwaisir
Helper - Supporter

Nuzair
Cautioner - Warner

Nuzhat
Chastity - Virtue
(Also used in Turkish)

Nuzhi
Chaste - Virtuous

205

O

Omaijid
Glorious - Noble -
Praiseworthy
Variants: Umayjed

Onays
Consoler - Good Friend
Variants: Onais, Unais

Ons
Gladness
Variants: Uns

Onsi
Bringer of Calm and
Gladness
Variants: Unsi

Oraib
Intelligent - Keen -
Perceptive
Variants: Uraib

Oraibi
Intelligent - Keen -
Perceptive
Variants: Uraibi

Orz
Proximity - Side

Owaib
Repentant
Variants: Uwaibah

Owais
Little Wolf
Variants: Oways, Uwais,
Uways

Owaisi
Brave - Warrior
Variants: Uwaisi

Owaiz
Replacement

TRADITIONAL AND MODERN ARABIC BABY NAMES

Q

Qaaid
Chief - Leader

Qabil
Accepter - Approver -
Endorser
The name Qabil is
mentioned in the Quran.

Qabis
Acquirer of Knowledge -
Educated - Learned -
Wise
Variants: *Kaabes, Kabis,
Qaabes, Qaabis, Qabes*

Qablan
Accepter - Advancer

Qabool
Acceptance - Approval

Qaddar
Arranger - Organizer

Qaddur
Able - Capable - Powerful
Qaddur is an Arabic name
for boys that means
"capable", "powerful",
"able".

Qadeer
Able - Capable - Powerful
The name Qadeer is
mentioned in the Quran.
Variants: *Qadir, Qedir*

Qadim
Advancer - Comer

Qadiman
Age-old - Ancient - Time-
honored
Variants: *Qadeeman*

Qadimi
Advancer - Comer

Qadir
Able - Capable - Powerful
The name Qadir is
mentioned in the Quran.

Qadoom
Bold - Brave

Qadri
Able - Powerful

Qaleeb
Water Well

Qamar
Moon
The name Qamar is
mentioned in the Quran.
Variants: *Qemer*

Qamari
Moon-like

Qamaruddin
Supporter of Islam

Qamarullah
Moon of God

Qamarurrahman
Moon of God

Qamarussalam
Moon of Peace

Qamrani
Moonlit

Qamrun
Moon

Qareen
Companion - Friend
The name Qareen is
mentioned in the Quran.

Qari
Reader - Reciter

Qarib
Near
The name Qarib is
mentioned in the Quran.
Variants: *Kareeb, Qareeb*

Qarni
Bright - Sharp

Qaseet
Fair - Just

Qasheeb
Clean - Fresh

Qasim
Generous - Handsome
Variants: *Qaasem, Qaasim,
Qasem*

Qasimi
Distributor - Divider -
Spreader

Qasmun
Handsome

Qaswar
Lion - Strong

Qaswari
Brave - Lion-like

Qateef
Flower Picker - Fruit
Picker

Qawi
Powerful - Strong
The name Qawi is
mentioned in the Quran.
Variants: *Qawee, Qawiy*

Qayyam
Stander

Qayyim
Good - Proper - Upright

Qiblah
Direction - Direction of
the Kaaba
The name Qiblah is
mentioned in the Quran.

Qindil
Oil Lamp

Qirni
Able - Capable

Qirtas
Paper - Parchment

Qismat
Fortune - Luck

Qiyam
Night-long Worship
The name Qiyam is
mentioned in the Quran.

Qudaiman
Bold - Brave

Qudair
Decree - Reckoning

Qudratullah
God's Power

Qulaib
Conscience - Heart

Qumr
Fair-skinned

Qunbar
Turnstone
A type of bird.

Qurb
Closeness - Nearness

Qurum
Chief - Leader

Qusait
Fair - Just

Qutb
Chief - Leader

Qutbuddin
Leader of the Faith

Qutbullah
Leader in the Service of
God

Quwa
Strength
The name Quwa is
mentioned in the Quran.

Variants: *Qowa, Quah,
Quwwa, Quwwah*

R

Raad
Explorer - Scout

Raafi
Elevated - Exalted - Great
The name Raafi is
mentioned in the Quran
in verse 3:55.
Variants: *Raafei, Raafiy,
Rafi, Rafi'*

Rabeeh
Earner - Winner

Rabih
Earner - Winner

Rabooh
Earner - Winner

Radooh
Bold - Brave

Raed
Guide - Leader - Pioneer
Variants: *Ra'ed, Ra'id,
Raaed, Raaid*

Raees
Chief - Leader
Variants: *Rais, Rayis*

Rafaaq
Affectionate - Gentle

Rafaat
Glory - Greatness -
Highness of Status
Variants: *Rafat, Rafat*

Rafee
Elevated - Exalted - Great
The name Rafee is
mentioned in the Quran
in verse 40:15.
Variants: *Rafee', Rafei,
Rafi, Rafie*

Rafeeq
Companion - Gentle -
Kind
Variants: *Rafeek, Rafiq*

Rafeq
Companion - Gentle -
Kind
Variants: *Raafek, Raafeq,
Raafik, Raafiq, Rafik, Rafiq*

Rafid
Helper - Supporter
Variants: *Raafed, Raafid,
Rafed*

Raghib
Aspiring - Desirous -
Seeking

Raghibun
Aspiring Ones - Seeking
Ones

Rahayim
Compassionate - Merciful
(Also used in Aramaic)

Rahbah
Vast Expanse of Land

Rahbat
Vast Expanse of Land

Rahd
Delicate - Soft

Raheef
Gentle - Tender
Variants: *Rahif*

Raheel
Departure - Journey
Variants: *Rahil*

Raheem
Kind - Merciful -
Tenderhearted
The name Raheem is
mentioned in the Quran
in many places, such as
2:128.
Variants: *Rahim, Rehim*

Rahil
Journeyer - Traveler
Variants: *Raahel, Raahil,
Rahel*

Rahim
Kind - Merciful -
Tenderhearted
Variants: *Raahem, Raahim,
Rahem*

Rahmatullah
God's Mercy
The name Rahmatullah is
mentioned in the Quran.

Raif
Compassion - Kind -
Softhearted
Variants: *Raaef, Raaif,
Raef, Raefe, Rayf, Rayif,
Rayife*

Rajab
7th Month of the Hijri
Calendar
Literally "great",
"tremendous".

Rajhan
Sensible - Wise

Rajih
Predominant - Superior

Rakeed
Tranquil

Rakeen
Composed - Dignified

Rakhs
Delicate - Soft

Rakhwan
Ease of Living - Luxury

Ramlat
Grain of Sand
(Also used in Turkish)

Ramz
Gesture - Mark - Symbol
The name Ramz is
mentioned in the Quran.

Ramzi
Gesture - Sign - Symbl
Variants: *Ramzee, Ramzy*

Ranin
Buzz - Resonance
Variants: *Raneen*

Raqeem
The name Raqeem is

mentioned in the Quran.
Variants: *Rakeem, Rakim,
Raqim*

Raqian
Elevated

Raqqah
Flat Land With Soft Dust

Raseen
Deep-rooted - Stable -
Upstanding
Variants: *Rasin*

Rashad
Right Guidance - Right
Path

Rashdan
Rightly-guided - Wise
Variants: *Rashdaan*

Rashid
Mature - Rightly-guided -
Wise
Variants: *Raashed,
Raashid, Rashed*

Rateeq
Imrpover - Mender

Rauf
Compassionate - Kind -
Lenient - Merciful
Variants: *Ra'uf, Raoof,
Raouf, Reouf*

Rawsan
Light Rain
Variants: *Rausan*

Rayhan
Fragrance
The name Rayhan is
mentioned in the Quran.
Variants: *Raihaan, Raihan,
Rayhaan, Reehan, Reihan,
Reyhan, Rihan*

Rayyan
Quenched - Watered
Name of one of the gates
of Paradise.
Variants: *Raiaan, Raian,
Rayaan, Rayan, Reyan,
Reyyan, Ryan*

Rayyih
Fragrant
Variants: *Rayeh*

Rayyis
Chief - Leader
Variants: *Rayes*

Razaan
Calm - Composed -
Dignified

Razaani
Composed - Dignified

Razeem
Lion's Roar
Razeem is an Arabic name
for boys that means "lion's
roar".

Razeen
Calm - Composed -
Dignified

Razni
Composed - Dignified

Razwan
Chosen - Desired -
Selected

Rehab
Generous - Open-hearted
- Open-minded -
Spacious - Vast
Variants: *Rehaab, Reihaab,
Reihab, Reyhaab, Reyhab,
Rihaab, Rihab, Ryhab*

Reyah
Power - Scents - Victory -
Winds
Variants: *Reyaah, Riah,
Riyaah, Riyah, Ryah*

Riaz
Gardens
Variants: *Riaaz, Riyaadh,
Riyadh, Riyaz, Ryaaz, Ryaz*

Riddees
Strong - Tough

Ridfan
Day and Night Cycle

Rifaah
Greatness - Highness of
Status

Rifaat
Greatness - Highness of
Status

Rifal
Affluence

Rifaq
Companions - Friends

Rifqat
Gentleness - Leniency
Turkish pronunciation of
Rifqah. (Also used in
Turkish)

Rifqi
Gentle - Kind - Lenient

Rinad
Agarwood - Aloeswood
Any tree that has a good
scent.

Riqqah
Gentleness - Kindness -
Leniency

Risl
Gentleness - Leniency

Riza
Contentment - Having
God's Approval
Variants: *Reda, Redaa,
Redha, Redhaa, Reza, Rida,
Ridaa, Ridha, Ridhaa,
Rizaa*

Rizwan
Contentment - Having
God's Approval
The name Rizwan is
mentioned in the Quran
in verse 57:20.
Variants: *Redhwan,
Rezwaan, Rezwan,
Ridhwaan, Ridhwan,
Ridwaan, Ridwan,
Rizwaan*

Rubaih
Earner - Winner

Rufah
Affectionate -
Sympathetic
Variants: *Roofa*

Ruhab
Forbearing - Generous -
Open-minded
Variants: *Rohaab, Rohab,
Ruhaab*

Ruhail
Departer - Journeyer
Variants: *Rohail, Ruhayl*

Ruhan
Kind - Spiritual
Variants: *Rohaan, Rohan,
Rouhaan, Rouhan, Ruhaan*

Rujhan
Intelligent - Wisdom

Rukain
Pillar - Support

Rukn
Pillar - Prop - Support
The name Rukn is
mentioned in the Quran.

Rumaiz
Gesture - Sign - Symbol

Ruqaihan
Earner - Mender

Ruqaim
Mark - Seal

Ruqee
Elevated - Raised

Rushaid
Rightly-guided

Rushd
Maturity - Right Guidance

Rushdan
Right Guidance - Rightly-guided

Rusul
Little Girl - Messengers

Ruwaid
Leniency - Soft Breeze
Variants: *Rowaid*

Ruwaihim
Compassionate - Kind
Variants: *Rowayhim*

Ruwaiq
Pure
Variants: *Rowaiq*

Ruwais
Chief - Leader
Variants: *Rowais*

Ruwaishid
Rightly-guided
Variants: *Rowaishid*

Ruwayfi
Elevated - Exalted - High
Variants: *Ruwaifi, Ruwaifi'*

Ruzm
Lion

S

Saabih
Clear - Handsome

Saad
Blessedness - Hapiness
Variants: Sa'ad, Sa'd

Saadad
Rationality - Sense
Variants: Sa'dad

Saadan
Happy - Successful
Variants: Sa'dan

Saadat
Leaders - Lords

Saadi
Blessed - Successful
Variants: Sa'di, Saady

Saadoon
Happy - Successful
Variants: Sa'dun

Saaeb
Intelligent - Rational - Sensible

Saaed
Great - Majestic
Variants: Sa'ed, Saed

Saaf
Pure

Saafin
Pure Ones

Saaie
Effort - Labor
Variants: Sa'i

Saaigh
Jewelry Maker

Saaih
One Who Fasts
Variants: Saaeh, Saayih, Saih, Sayeh, Sayih

Saair
Avenger - Excited - Revolutionary
Variants: Thair

Saayed
Chief - Dominant
Variants: Saayid, Sayed

Saayed
Hunter

Sabbagh
Dyer

Sabbaq
Racer
Variants: Sabaaq, Sabaq

Sabbar
Enduring - Patient
The name Sabbar is mentioned in the Quran.

Sabeeh
Handsome - Radiant
Variants: Sabih

Sabeel
Path - Road - Way
The name Sabeel is mentioned in the Quran in verse 27:24 and others.
Variants: Sabil, Sabyll, Sebil, Sebill, Sybil

Sabeer
Enduring - Patient

Sabeeri
Enduring - Patient

Sabi
Affectionate

Sabigh
Dyer

Sabihi
Bright - Handsome

Sabiq
Advanced - Ahead
Variants: Saabeq, Saabiq, Sabeq

Sabir
Enduring - Patient
The name Sabir is mentioned in the Quran.

Sabit
Firm - Reliable - Stable
The name Sabit is mentioned in the Quran.
Variants: Saabet, Saabit, Sabet, Thaabit, Thabet, Thabit

Sabr
Enduring - Patience
The name Sabr is mentioned in the Quran.

Sabri
Enduring - Patient

Sabur
Enduring - Patient

Saburi
Enduring - Patient

Sadaad
Rationality - Sense
Variants: *Sadad*

Sadan
Prudent - Reasonable -
Sensible

Sadeeq
Friend

Sadiq
Devoted - Faithful -
Honest - Sincere -
Truehearted
The name Sadiq is
mentioned in the Quran.
Variants: *Saadeq, Saadiq,
Sadeq*

Sadiqin
Truthful Ones
The name Sadiqin is
mentioned in the Quran.
Variants: *Sadiqeen*

Sadqan
Sincere - Truthful

Saeed
Happy - Successful
Variants: *Sa'id*

Saeedan
Happy - Successful
Variants: *Sa'idan*

Safee
Pure
Variants: *Safi, Safy*

Safeen
Ships
Variants: *Safin*

Safeer
Ambassador

Safih
Forgiving

Safiyyaddin
Best of the Faith

Safuh
Forgiving - Lenient

Safwan
Pure - Rock
The name Safwan is
mentioned in the Quran.
Variants: *Safwaan*

Safwat
Best - Finest - Prime

Sahabah
Companions

Sahari
Deserts

Sahbah
Companionship -
Friendship

Sahbal
Brave

Sahban
Companion - Friend

Sahbi
Companion - Friend

Saheer
Caretaker

Sahhah
Flawless - Whole

Sahi
Awake - Sober - Vigilant

Sahib
Companion - Friend
The name Sahib is
mentioned in the Quran.

Sahil
Beach - River Bank -
Shore
The name Sahil is
mentioned in the Quran.
Variants: *Saahel, Sahel*

Sahir
Unsleeping - Wakeful
Variants: *Saaher, Saahir*

Sahl
Easy - Lenient

Sahm
Arrow
Variants: *Sehm*

Sahwan
Awake - Sober - Vigilant

Sahwi
Awake - Sober - Vigilant

Saibal
Heavy Rain - Spike of
Corn

Saif
Summer
The name Saif is
mentioned in the Quran.
Variants: *Sayf, Sayf, Seif*

Saif
Sword

Saifaddin
Sword of the Faith

Saiful Haq
Sword of Truth

Saiful Islam
Sword of Islam

Saim
One Who Fasts
Variants: *Sa'im, Saaem,
Saaim, Saayim, Saem,
Sayem, Sayim*

Sajeed
Prostrator - Worshiper

Sajid
Prostrator - Worshiper of
God
The name Sajid is
mentioned in the Quran.
Variants: *Saajed, Saajid,
Sajed*

Sakheei
Generous - Noble
Variants: *Sakhi*

Sakhr
Boulder - Rock
The name Sakhr is
mentioned in the Quran.

Salaat
Litany - Prayer
The name Salaat is
mentioned in the Quran.

Salah
Faithfulness - Piety -
Purity

Salahaddin
Reformation of the Faith -
Uprightness of the Faith

Salahan
Devoted - Good - Upright

Salam
Peace - Safety - Security
The name Salam is
mentioned in the Quran
in verse 5:16 and others.
Variants: *Salaam, Selaam,
Selam*

Salama
Safety - Security
Variants: *Salaama,
Salaamah, Salamah*

Saleef
Advanced - Preceding

Saleem
Intact - Righteous -

Whole
The name Saleem is
mentioned in the Quran.
Variants: *Salim*

Salees
Flowing - Gentle -
Pleasant - Soft

Saleet
Eloquent

Sali
Amused - Cheerful
Variants: *Saly*

Salif
Preceding
Variants: *Salef*

Salih
Virtuous
The name *Salih* is
mentioned in the Quran.
Variants: *Saaleh, Saalih,
Saleh, Salih, Saulih, Solley,
Soulih*

Salihan
Pious - Virtuous

Salihin
Pious - Virtuous
The name Salihin is
mentioned in the Quran.

Salim
Intact - Righteous -
Whole

Saloof
Advancer

Saloom
Safe - Unharmed

Salsabil
Refreshing and Tasy Drink
Variants: *Salsabeel*

Samaan
Hearer

Samawah
Elevation - Greatness

Samawi
Heavenly

Samd
Composure -
Determination -
Perseverance

Samee
Hearer - Perceptive
The name Samee is
mentioned in the Quran.
Variants: *Samee'*

Sameeh
Forgiving - Gracious -
Lenient

Sameek
Elevated - High in Status -
Majestic
Variants: *Samik*

Sameer
Friend - Night
Conversation Partner
Variants: *Sameir, Samir*

Samer
Friend - Night

Conversation Partner
The name Samer is
mentioned in the Quran.
Variants: *Samir*

Samh
Leniency - Pardon

Samhaan
Forgiving - Gracious -
Lenient

Samhun
Forgiving - Lenient

Sami
Great - Lofty - Sublime
Variants: *Saami, Saamy,
Samee, Samy*

Samid
Firm - Steadfast

Samih
Forgiving - Gracious
Variants: *Sameh*

Samihi
Forgiving - Gracious -
Lenient

Samik
Elevated - High in Status -
Majestic

Samil
Constant - Firmly
Established - Fixed
Variants: *Samel, Thamel,
Thamil*

Samit
Silent - Wise

Variants: *Saamet, Saamit,
Samet*

Saml
Endurance -
Perseverance

Sammad
Determined - Persevering
- Steadfast

Samood
Determined - Persevering
- Steadfast

Samooh
Forgiving - Lenient

Samoor
Night Conversation

Samran
One Who Continues
Conversation Long Into
the Night

Sanaauddin
Supporter of Islam
Literally "greatness of the
faith".

Sanan
Tradition - Way of Life

Sandar
Bold - Brave

Sannee
Exalted - High in Status

Sanubar
Cypress

Saqib
Piercing - Sharp
The name Saqib is
mentioned in the Quran.
Variants: *Thaqib*

Saqqar
Falconer

Saqr
Falcon

Saqri
Falcon-like

Saqrun
Falcon

Saraab
Mirage
The name Saraab is
mentioned in the Quran.
Variants: *Sarab*

Sardee
Like Light Rain
Variants: *Thardi*

Saree
Stream
Variants: *Sari*

Sareem
Firm Decision -
Resolution
Variants: *Sarim*

Sarih
Shepherd - Successful
Variants: *Sareh*

Sarim
Brave - Decisive - Strong

Sarraan
Happy - Pleased
Variants: *Saraan, Saran*

Sarraw
Honorable - Noble
Variants: *Sarau*

Sarwat
Affluence - Fortune -
Wealth
Turkish pronunciation of
Sarwah. (Also used in
Kurdish, Persian, Turkish,
Urdu)
Variants: *Tharwat*

Satal
Type of Bird
An eagle or something
similar to it.

Sattar
Hider
Variants: *Satar*

Saud
Blessed - Fortunate -
Happy
Variants: *Sa'ud, Saood,
Saoud*

Sawab
Repentant - Reward
Variants: *Thawab*

Sawahil
Coasts - River Banks -
Shores

Sawalan
Ascendancy - Domination
- Power

Sawdan
Glorious - Great

Sawin
Guardian - Protector

Sawni
Maintainer - Protector

Sawrat
Revolution - Uprising
Turkish pronunciation of
Sawrah.
Variants: *Thawrat*

Sawwan
Protector - Quartz

Sayalan
Effusion - Flooding - Flow

Saydad
Rationality - Sense

Sayhan
Sayhan is the name of
a river in the Levant and
its meaning may be
"journeyer", "traveler".
Variants: *Saehaan,
Saehaane, Saehan,
Saehane, Saihaan,
Saihaane, Saihan, Saihane,
Sayhaane, Sayhan,
Sayhane, Seehan, Seihan,
Seyhan, Seyhane, Sihan*

Saytar
Hiding

Sayyidah
Chief - Lady

Seef
Coast - Shore

Seid
Lion - Wolf

Sendid
Brave Chief - Forbearing
Master

Seneen
Years

Serir
Bringer of Joy
Variants: *Sirrir*

Siba
Childhood - Emotion -
Enthusiasm -
Youthfulness
Variants: *Seba, Sebaa,
Sibaa, Syba*

Sibagh
Dye - Paint

Siddiq
Devoted - Loyal - True
Friend - Truthful
The name Siddiq is
mentioned in the Quran.
Variants: *Seddiq, Sediq,
Siddeeq, Siddique, Sideeq*

Sidqi
Sincere - Truthful

Sidratul Muntaha
Lote Tree of the Utmost
Boundary
The name Sidratul
Muntaha is mentioned in

the Quran. It is the name
of a tree in or near
Paradise.
Variants: *Sidrat Ul
Muntaha,
Sidratulmuntaha*

Sihab
Deep Water Well

Sihah
Faultless - Healthy

Sihlal
Gentle - Lenient

Sikandar
Defender of Humanity
Variant of Iskandar.

Silaam
Peace-making
Variants: *Selam*

Simar
Night Conversation

Sina
Mountain Sinae

Sinan
Leopard - Spearhead

Sineen
Mountain Sinai
The name Sineen is
mentioned in the Quran.
Variants: *Senin, Sinin*

Sinwan
Multiple Trees Growing
From the Same Root

The name Sinwan is
mentioned in the Quran.

Siraj
Cresset - Lamp - Light
Variants: *Seraa, Seraj,
Siraaj*

Siraj al-Haq
Lamp of Truth
Variants: *Sirajulhaq*

Sirajaddin
Supporter of Islam
Literally "lamp of the
faith".
Variants: *Sirajuddin*

Sirat
Path
The name Sirat is
mentioned in the Quran.
Variants: *Serat, Siraat*

Sirhan
Lion - Wolf
Variants: *Serhan*

Siyadah
Glory - Greatness -
Honor - Leadership

Siyam
The name Siyam is
mentioned in the Quran.
Variants: *Fasting*

Siyaq
Articulation - Context

Sobaan
Repentance
Variants: *Sawbaan,*

Sawban, Sowbaan,
Sowban, Thowban, Thuban

Solwi
Comfort - Consolation

Suaidan
Happy - Successful
Variants: *Su'aidan*

Subah
Flame of a Lamp -
Handsome

Subaih
Handsome - Radiant
Variants: *Sobaih, Sobayh,*
Subayh

Subail
Pouring Rain - Spike of
Corn
Variants: *Sobail*

Subair
Enduring - Patient

Subayyaah
Morning

Subh
Morning
The name Subh is
mentioned in the Quran.

Subhi
Bright

Sudain
Maintainer of the Kaaba
Variants: *Sodain*

Sudaiq
Sincere - Truthful

Sudair
Alder Buckthorn
A type of tree.
Variants: *Sodair*

Sudairi
Alder Buckthorn
A type of tree. The name
is an attribution to said
tree.
Variants: *Sodayri*

Sudais
One Sixth - Sixth
Variants: *Sodais, Sodays,*
Sudays

Sudur
Hearts
The name Sudur is
mentioned in the Quran.
Variants: *Sodur, Sudoor*

Sufan
Amadou

Sufian
Agile - Nimble
Variants: *Sofiaan, Sofian,*
Sufiaan, Sufyaan, Sufyan

Sufyan
Slender - Slim

Suhaib
Red-brown-haired

Suhaibun
Red-brown-haired

Suhaid
Handsome

Suhail
Easy - Lenient
Variants: *Sohail*

Suhaim
Arrow
Variants: *Sohaim, Soheim,*
Suhaym, Suhayme, Suheim

Suhair
Unsleeping - Wakeful
Variants: *Sohair, Suhayr*

Suhbah
Companionship -
Friendship

Suhban
Companion - Friend

Suhbani
Companion - Friend

Sukkar
Sugar
Variants: *Sokar, Sukar*

Sulaaf
Predecessors
Variants: *Solaf*

Sulaif
Advanced - Preceding

Sulaikan
Follower of a Path

Sulaim
Safe - Unharmed

Sulaiman
Peace - Peaceful
Sulaiman is one of the
prophets mentioned in
the Quran, known as
Solomon in the Bible.
(Also used in Hebrew)
Variants: *Solaiman,
Solaymaan, Solayman,
Sulaimaan, Sulayman*

Sulaytan
King - Power - Ruler

Sulh
Ceasfire - Peace
The name Sulh is
mentioned in the Quran.

Suloof
Advancement

Sultan
King - Power - Ruler
Variants: *Soltan*

Sumaih
Forgiving - Gracious -
Lenient

Sumair
Friend - Night
Conversation Partner
Variants: *Somair, Someir,
Sumeir*

Sumama
Rescue - Salvation
Variants: *Sumamah,
Thumama, Thumamah*

Sumood
Composure -

Determination -
Perseverance

Sumou
Elevation - Greatness

Sumran
Tan-skinned

Sunain
Leopard - Spearhead

Sunan
Traditions - Ways of Life
The name Sunan is
mentioned in the Quran.

Sunayyan
Exalted - High in Status -
Radiant

Sunud
Climb - Dependence -
Reliance

Suqaib
Neighbor

Suqair
Little Falcon

Suwaib
Reward
Variants: *Thuwaib*

Suwaibih
Bright - Fresh

Suwaibir
Enduring - Patient

Suwaidan
Great - Noble - Respected

Suwaidin
Maintainer of the Kaaba

Suwaif
Enduring - Patient

Suwaih
One Who Fasts

Suwaihir
One Who Stays Up During
the Night

Suwailih
Good - Pious

Suwailim
Safe - Unharmed - Whole

Suwaim
Bamboo - Gold

Suwar
Fragrance - Musk
Container

Suwayhil
Gentle – Lenient

Sh

Shaalah
Kindler

Shaan
Greatness - Rank - Status
The name Shaan is
mentioned in the Quran.
Variants: *Sha'n, Shan*

Shab
Young Person

Shabab
Young Age - Youth

Shaban
8th Month of the Hijri
Calendar
Literal meaning may be
"branching out".

Shabeeb
Young Age - Youth

Shabir
Handsome

Shaddad
Firm - Severe - Strong

Shaddan
Gazelle

Shadi
Seeker of Knowledge

Shadid
Intense - Severe - Strong
The name Shadid is

mentioned in the Quran.
Variants: *Shadeed*

Shaeef
Strongly in Love

Shafaqatullah
God's Mercy

Shafeef

Translucent -
Transparent

Shafeei
Cured

Shafi
Healer

Shafiq
Compassioante -
Sympathetic
Variants: *Shafeeq*

Shaghaaf
Strongly in Love

Shaghf
Strong Love

Shahab
Meteor - Shooting Star
Non-standard
pronunciation of Shihab.
Variants: *Shahaab*

Shahada
Martyrdom - Testimony
The name Shahada is
mentioned in the Quran.
Variants: *Shahadah*

Shahbaz
Eagle - Eastern Imperial
Eagle
(Also used in Urdu)
Variants: *Shaahbaz,
Shahbaaz*

Shahd
Witness

Shaheeb
Gray-colored

Shaheed
Martyr - Witness
The name Shaheed is
mentioned in the Quran
in verse 28:75 and others.
Variants: *Shaheid, Shahid,
Shehid*

Shaheer
Distinguished - Well-
known
Variants: *Shaher, Shahir*

Shahid
Witness
The name Shahid is
mentioned in the Quran
in verse 33:45 and others.
Variants: *Shaahed,
Shaahid, Shahed*

Shahir
Populizer

Shahm
Intelligent - Rational -
Sensible

Shahr
Month

The name Shahr is mentioned in the Quran.

Shahraan
Famous - Moon-like
Variants: *Shahran, Shehraan, Shehran*

Shaidan
Great - High in Status

Shail
Greatness - Highness of Status

Shajar
Tree
The name Shajar is mentioned in the Quran.

Shakir
Appreciative - Thankful
The name Shakir is used in the Quran.
Variants: *Shaaker, Shaakir, Shaker*

Shakira
Appreciative - Thankful
Variants: *Shaakera, Shaakerah, Shaakira, Shaakirah, Shakera, Shakerah, Shakirah*

Shakirullah
Thankful Toward God

Shakkar
Thankful

Shakur
Appreciative - Thankful
Variants: *Shakoor*

Shalan
Brilliant - Lit - Radiant
Variants: *Sha'lan, Shaalan, Shalaan*

Shaleel
Gorge - Ravine

Shamakh
Great - High in Status

Shamees
Bright - Sunny

Shamikh
Great - High - Lofty - Towering
Variants: *Shaamikh, Shamekh*

Shamis
Bright - Sunlit

Shammam
Muskmelon

Shams
Light and Radiance
The name *Shams* is mentioned in the Quran.

Shamsaddin
Supporter of Islam
Literally "sun of the faith".
Variants: *Shamsadeen, Shamsuddin, Shamsudeen*

Shamsan
Bright - Sunlit

Shannaf
Intelligent

Shaqeer
Fair-skinned

Shaqeeri
Fair-skinned

Shaqir
Fair-skinned

Shaqoor
Fair-skinned
Variants: *Shaqur*

Shaqroon
Fair-skinned

Sharaf
Dignity - Honor

Shareeq
East - Place of Sunrise

Sharfan
High in Status - Honorable

Sharif
Glorious - High in Status - Honored

Shariq
Variants: *Glowing, Radiant*

Sharrah
Explainer - Interpreter

Sharuf
Glorious - Honored - Noble

Shatb
Slim - Tall

Shati
Beach - Coast - Side
The name Shati is
mentioned in the Quran.

Shawal
Great - High in Status

Shawamikh
Great - High in Status

Shawas
Courage

Shaweef
Adornment - Observation

Shaweer
Handsome

Shawqan
Desirous - Longing

Shawqi
Desirous - Longing

Shawr
Honey

Shayif
Observer

Shayraf
Great - Honorable

Shayyir
Handsome

Shayyir Ali
Great - Handsome

Sheaaf
Short Shower of Rain -
Strong Love

Sheeban
Snow - White
Variants: *Shibaan, Shiban*

Shibl
Lion Cub

Shifa
Cure - Healing - Remedy
The name Shifa is
mentioned in the Quran.
Variants: *Shefa, Shefaa,
Shifaa*

Shifaullah
God's Healing

Shihab
Meteor - Shooting Star
Variants: *Shehaab, Shehab,
Shihaab*

Shuaif
Strong Love

Shufaiq
Mercy - Pity

Shuhaib
Little Shooting Star

Shuhaid
Witness

Shuhair
Famous - Month

Shuhud
Witnesses

The name Shuhud is
mentioned in the Quran.

Shujaa
Brave

Shujaat
Bravery - Courage
Variants: *Shojaat, Shuja'at*

Shukr
Thankfulness
Shukr is an Arabic name
for boys and girls that
means "thankfulness",
"appreciation".. The name
Shukr is mentioned in the
Quran.

Shukrullah
Thankfulness Toward God

Shulaykhan
Handsome

Shuqair
Fair-skinned

Shuqairah
Fair-skinned

Shuqairy
Fair-skinned

Shuqur
Blondness - Fairness of
Skin
Variants: *Shoqur*

Shuraa
Consultation - Council -
Honeycomb Cell - View

Shuraif
Glory - Honor

Shuraim
Bay - Gulf - Inlet
Variants: *Shoraim*

Shuraiq
East - Place of Sunrise

Shuruq
Sunrise

Shuwair
Handsome

T

Taal
Ascending - Come
The name can be a
command ("come!") or a
description of the state of
something that ascends.

Taazaz
Honor - Might - Power

Tabarak
Blessed

Tabarruk
Blessedness

Tabseer
Education -
Enlightenment

Tadbir
Contrivance -
Organization -
Procurement

Tadris
Research - Study

Taeb
Repenting - Virtuous
Variants: *Taaeb, Taaib,
Taeib, Taib, Tayeb*

Tafaf
Sundown

Tafali
Sundown - Sunup

Tafheem
Elaboration - Illustration
Variants: *Tafhim, Tefhim*

Tafli
Delicate - Gentle - Soft

Taghlib
The Win - They Defeat
Their Enemies

Taha
Taha is the name of
chapter 20 of the Quran
and is also the word that
the chapter starts with.
The meaning of this word
is not known, some
people think it is another
name for the Prophet
Muhammad (peace and
blessings of Allah upon
him).

Tahani
Congratulations

Tahannud
Friendliness - Gentleness

Tahir
Pure
Variants: *Taaher, Taahir,
Taher*

Tahmeed
Praising of God
Variants: *Tahmid, Tehmid*

Tahrir
Liberation

Tahsin
Beautification -
Improvement
Variants: *Tahseen, Tehsin*

Tahzeeb
Edification - Purification -
Rectification - Refinement

Taif
Circumambulator -
Visitation
The name Taif is used in
the Quran.
Variants: *Taaef, Taaif, Taef*

Taihan
Vast
Variants: *Taihaan,
Tayhaan, Tayhan, Teihan,
Teyhan*

Tajammul
Beautification
Variants: *Tajammol,
Tajamol, Tajamul*

Takleef
Assignment - To Give
Someone a Duty

Takreem
Graciousness - Honor -
Respect
Variants: *Takrim, Tekrim*

Talaab
Desired - Sought After

Talaat
Aspect - Countenance -
Face
Turkish pronunciation of

Talaah. (Also used in Turkish)

Talab
Demand - Desire - Seeker
The name Talab is mentioned in the Quran.

Talal
Coater
One who puts a coat of varnish or dye on something.

Talha
Banana Tree
Variants: *Talhah*

Talib
Pursuer - Seeker - Seeker of Knowledge
The name Talib is mentioned in the Quran.
Variants: *Taaleb, Taalib, Taleb*

Talibullah
Seeker of God

Tamanna
Hope - Wish
Variants: *Tamana, Tamanaa, Tamannaa*

Tamassuk
Adherence

Tamasul
Similarity

Tamheed
Facilitation - Preparation

Tami
Elevated - Exalted - High

Tamir
Date Merchant

Tammam
Complete - Whole

Tammar
Date Merchant

Tamur
Variants: *Tamoor*

Taneem
Blessedness
Variants: *Tan'im, Taneim, Tanim*

Taqadum
Advancement - Progress

Tarashud
Guidance

Tareef
Exquisite - Quaint - Rate

Tareem
Humble Supplicator

Tarheeb
Graciousness -
Spaciousness - Vastness

Tariq
Star
The name Tariq is mentioned in the Quran.
Variants: *Taarek, Taareq, Taarik, Taariq, Tarek, Tareq, Tarik*

Tarkheem
Mellowing - Softening

Tarooq
Star

Tasafi
Loyalty - Sincerity

Tasahir
Vigils

Tasamuh
Forbearance -
Forgiveness - Pardon

Taseen
Unknown
Taseen is a Quranic name for boys. Chapter 27 of the Quran starts with the two Arabic letters Ta and seen, which together are read as Taseen, the meaning of which is not known.
Variants: *Taaseen, Taasin, Tasin*

Taskeen
Tranquility

Tasmir
Blossoming - Flourishing - Producing
Variants: *Tasmir, Tathmir*

Tasneem
Falling Water - Fountain in Paradise
Variants: *Tasnim*

Tasteer
To Author - To Write

Tasweer
To Describe - To Paint -
To Picture

Tatheer
Purification
The name Tatheer is
mentioned in the Quran.
Variants: *Tateheer, Tathir*

Tawab
Repentant
The name Tawab is
mentioned in the Quran.
Variants: *Tawwab*

Tawadud
Affection - Love

Tawaf
Circumambulation
Variants: *Tawaaf, Tewaf*

Tawafiq
Success

Tawakkul
Reliance Upon God
Variants: *Tauakkul,
Tawakkol, Tawakol,
Tawakul*

Tawaqur
Calmness - Composure -
Solemnity

Tawazou
Humility

Taweel
Long - Tall
The name Taweel is
mentioned in the Quran.

Tawfeeq
Success
The name Tawfeeq is used
in the Quran.
Variants: *Taufeeq, Taufiq,
Taufique, Tawfeeque,
Tawfiq*

Tawheed
Belief in God's Oneness
Variants: *Tauheed, Tauhid,
Tawhid*

Tawkeel
Reliance Upon God
Variants: *Taukeel, Taukil,
Tawkil*

Tawl
Might - Power - Strength
The name Tawl is
mentioned in the Quran.

Tawlan
Elevated - Great - Mighty
The name Tawlan is
mentioned in the Quran.

Tawqan
Desirous

Tawus
Beautiful - Peafowl

Tawwad
Affection - Love

Tayil
Great - Powerful

Taymur
Iron - Steel
Originally from Turkic.
(Also used in Persian,
Turkish)

Taysir
Ease - Facilitation

Tayyib
Good - Pure - Virtuous
The name Tayyib is
mentioned in the Quran.
Variants: *Taeib, Taib,
Tayeb, Tayib, Tayyeb*

Tazayyun
Adornment -
Beautification

Tazeen
Adornment -
Beautification
Variants: *Tazieen,
Tazyeen, Tazyin*

Teeb
Perfume

Th

Thaalab
Fox
Variants: *Saalab, Salab*

Thameen
Precious - Valable
Variants: *Sameen*

Thamir
Fruit-bearing -
Productive - Profitable
Variants: *Saamir, Samer, Samir, Thaamir, Thamer*

Thayeb
Repentant
Variants: *Sayeb, Sayib, Thaayeb, Thaib*

Thuailib
Fox
Variants: *SuaylibT*

Tibaq
Equivalent - Similar
The name Tibaq is
mentioned in the Quran.

Tibhaj
Beauty - Radiance

Tibr
Gold Ore

Tilal
Exquisite - Light Rain -
Rare

Tinjal
Beauty of the Eyes

Tireem
Honey - Tall - Thick
Clouds

Tirhab
Graciousness -
Spaciousness - Vastness

Tufan
Cataclysm - Deluge -
Flood
The name Tufan is
mentioned in the Quran.

Tufayl
Beautiful - Gentle - Little
Child - Soft

Tullaab
Seekers - Students

Tumaim
Little Sea

Turas
Inheritance
The name Turas is
mentioned in the Quran.

Tuwaij
Little Crown

Tuwailib
Seeker of Knowledge -
Student

U

Ubad
Worshipers

Ubadah
Worshipers

Ubai
Father
Diminutive form of
Ab ("father").
Variants: *Obay, Obayy,
Ubay, Ubayy*

Ubaid
Servant of God
Variants: *Obaid, Obayd,
Ubayd*

Ubaidullah
Servant of God
Variants: *Ubaydullah*

Udai
Warrior
Variants: *Odai, Oday,
Uday*

Udail
Fair - Just

Ufair
Brave

Uhaid
Covenant - Promise

Uhdawi
Guardian - Protector
Variants: *Ohdawi*

Uhud
Name of a mountain near
Medina where a battle
took place.
Variants: *Ohud*

Ujab
Amazement - Wonder
The name Ujab is
mentioned in the Quran.

Umaijid
Glorious - Majestic
Variants: *Omaijed*

Umair
Life - Long-lived
Variants: *Omayr, Umayr
Omair*

Umairi
Long-lived

Umaizar
Strong
Variants: *Omaizar*

Umar
Life - Long-lived
Variants: *Omar, Omer,
Umer*

Umrah
Minor Pilgrimage -
Overhaul - Restoration -
Revival
The name Umrah is
mentioned in the Quran.

Uraif
Good Scent

Urrab
Eloquent - Fluent

Urwah
Ever-green Tree -
Handhold - Lion
The name Urwah is
mentioned in the Quran
in verse 31:22.
Variants: *Orwa, Orwah,
Urwa*

Usaim
Guardian - Protector -
Refuge
Variants: *Osaim, Osaym,
Usaym*

Usman
Baby Houbara - Baby
Snake

Utaib
Gentleness - Softness

Utaif
Affectionate -
Compassionate

Utaiq
Generosity - Virtue

Utayk
Good - Noble - Pure

Uwaim
Year

Uwain
Helper - Supporter
Variants: *Owain, Uwayn*

Uwaiz
Restitution

Uwaymir
Life - Long-lived
Variants: *Owaimir,*
Owaymir, Uwaimir

Uzaib
Fresh Water

Uzaina
Listener - Obedient
Variants: *Odaina, Odayna,*
Ozaina, Udaina, Uzaina

Uzair
God Helped
The name Uzair is
mentioned in the Quran,
known as Ezra or Azariah
in the Bible.

Uzaiz
Honor - Might - Power

W

Waad
Promise
The name Waad is
mentioned in the Quran.
Variants: *Wa'd, Wad*

Waali
Governor - Prefect -
Ruler
Variants: *Waaly, Walee,
Wali*

Waazi
Distributor - Protector
Variants: *Waazy, Wazi*

Wad
Affection - Love

Waddeen
Loving Ones

Wadeed
Affectionate - Loving
Variants: *Wadid*

Wadi
Valley
The name Wadi is
mentioned in the Quran.
Variants: *Waadi, Wady*

Wadid
Affectionate - Loving

Wadood
Affectionate - Loving
The name Wadood is
mentioned in the Quran.

Wael
Seeker of Refuge - Tribe
Variants: *Waael, Waail,
Wail*

Waf
Faithful - Loyal - Perfect -
Whole

Wafa
Completion - Faithfulness
- Fulfillment - Loyalty

Wafaee
Complete - Faithful -
Loyal

Wafee
Faithful - Loyal
Variants: *Wafi, Wafiy*

Wafeeq
Appropriate - Companion
- Friend - Harmonious

Wafeer
Plenty

Wafi
Faithful - Loyal
Wafi is an indirect
Quranic name for boys
that means "faithful",
"loyal". It is derived from
the Quranic W-F-Y root.
This name is different
from Wafee, they have the
same meaning but
different pronunciations.
Variants: *Faithful*

Wafiq
Waafeq - Waafiq - Wafeq
Wafiq is an indirect

Quranic name for boys
that means "successful". It
is derived from the W-F-
Q root which is used in
the Quran.
Variants: *Successful*

Wahb
Bestowal - Blessing - Gift

Wahban
Generous - Giving

Wahbi
Bestowal - Gift

Wahbullah
Gift from God

Wahdan
Peerless - Unique

Wahdat
Wahdat is the Turkish
pronunciation of Wahdah.

Waheeb
Bestowal - Gift

Waheebullah
Gift from God

Waheed
Alone - Peerless -
Singular - Unique
The name Waheed is
mentioned in the Quran.
Variants: *Wahid, Wehid*

Wahhab
Bestower - Giver
The name Wahhab is
mentioned in the Quran.

Wahib
Bestower - Giver

Wahid
One - Unique
The name Wahid is
mentioned in the Quran.
Variants: *Waahed,*
Waahid, Wahed

Wajeed
Affectionate - Loving

Wajeeh
Honorable - Noble -
Prestigious

Wajeehan
Honorable - Noble -
Prestigious

Wajib
Duty
Variants: *Waajeb, Waajib,*
Wajeb

Wajid
Acquirer - Finder - Loving

Wakib
Gentle Walker

Wakil
Agent - Deputy - Trustee
The name Wakil is
mentioned in the Quran.
Variants: *Wakeel*

Wal
Helper - Master

Walee
Friend - Guardian -

Patron - Protector
The name Walee is
mentioned in the Quran.
Variants: *Walee, Walei,*
Wali

Waleed
Baby - Boy - Infant -
Newborn

Waliyuddin
Supporter of Islam
Variants: *Wali Uddin*

Waqar
Composure - Dignity -
Self-respect
Variants: *Waqaar*

Waqid
Brilliant - Kindled
Variants: *Waaqed, Waaqid,*
Waqed

Waqqas
Breaker - Destroyer

Waqur
Composed - Dignified

Ward
Flower - Rose
Variants: *Werd*

Wardaa
Flower - Rose
Variants: *Warda*

Wardi
Rose-like - Rosy

Wareef
Blooming - Flourishing

Warid
Aware - Experienced -
Learned
Variants: *Waared, Waarid,*
Wared

Warish
Agile - Sprightly

Warith
Inheritor - Long-lived
Variants: *Waares,*
Waareth, Waaris, Waarith,
Wareth, Waris

Warshan
Pigeon

Wasaaf
Describer - Praiser
Variants: *Wasaf, Wassaaf,*
Wassaf

Waseem
Handsome
Variants: *Wasim*

Waseeq
Firm - Strong -
Trustworthy
Variants: *Wasiq, Watheeq,*
Wathiq

Wasfi
Praiseworthy
Variants: *Wasfee, Wasfy*

Washan
Elevated Land - Highland

Wasif
Describer - Praiser

Variants: *Waasef, Waasif, Wasef*

Wasil
Connected – Friend
Variants: *Waasel, Waasil, Wasel*

Wasl
Attachment – Connection
– Juncture – Receipt

Wathaq
Home – Solemn Promsie
Variants: *Wasaaq, Wasaq, Wathaaq*

Wathiq
Certain – Sure
Variants: *Waaseq, Waathiq, Waseq, Wasiq*

Wayel
Clan – Tribe

Wazee
Clean – Handsome

Wazian
Clean – Handsome

Wazin
Collator – Comparer – Weigher

Wazir
Assistant – Helper – Minister
Variants: *Wazeer*

Waziran
Ministers – Viziers

Wazn
Gauge – Measure – Weighing – Weight

Wazzah
Clear – Handsome

Wiam
Concord – Harmony – Peace – Rapport
Variants: *Wi'am, Wiaam*

Wid
Affection – Harmony – Love
Variants: *Widd*

Widad
Affection – Harmony – Love
Variants: *Wedaad, Wedad, Widaad*

Widadi
Affectionate – Loving

Wifaq
Harmony – Sympathy – Unity
Variants: *Wefaaq, Wefaq, Wfaaq*

Wijdan
Affection – Conscience – Fondness – Soul – Tenderness
Variants: *Wejdaan, Wejdan, Wijdaan*

Wildan
Boys
The name Wildan is mentioned in the Quran. It is the plural of

Walad ("boy", "child").
Variants: *Weldaan, Weldan, Wildaan*

Wirad
Flowers – Roses
Variants: *Werad, Wiraad*

Wisal
Communion – Reunion
Variants: *Wesal, Wisaal*

Wisam
Handsome
Variants: *Wesaam, Wesam, Wisaam*

Wuhaib
Bestowal – Gift

Wuraid
Little Flower

Y

Yahya
Alive
The name Yahya is
mentioned in the Quran
in verse 3:39.
Variants: Yahyaa, Yehea,
Yeheaa, Yehia, Yehiaa,
Yehya, Yehyaa

Yamaan
Blessed - Yemeni

Yamam
Dove
Variants: Yamaam

Yamar
Alive - Life - Long-lived
Variants: Ya'mar, Yaamar,
Yaamer, Yamer

Yameen
Blessedness - Power -
Right Hand
The name Yameen is
mentioned in the Quran.
Variants: Yamein, Yamin,
Yemin

Yaqeen
Certainty
The name Yaqeen is
mentioned in the Quran.
Variants: Yaqin

Yaqub
Heir - Successor
The name Yaqub is
mentioned in the Quran.

Variants: Ya'qub, Yaqob,
Yaqoob, Yaqoub

Yasar
Affluence

Yaseer
Blessed - Easy
Variants: Yasir

Yashal
Brilliant - Radiant
Variants: Yash'al

Yasir
Blessed - Lenient

Yazeed
Growing - Increasing -
Prospering
The name Yazeed is
mentioned in the Quran.
Variants: Yazid, Yezid

Yunus
Yunus is the name of a
Prophet mentioned in the
Quran, such as in verse
10:88.
Variants: Yonos, Yoones,
Yoonis, Younes, Younis,
Younos, Younous, Younus,
Yunis

Yusr
Gentleness -
Needlessness

Yusri
Living in Luxury -
Needless - Rich
Variants: Yosree, Yosri,
Yusree, Yusry

Yusrullah
God's Blessing

Yusuf
God Gives
The name Yusuf is
mentioned in the Quran.
Variants: Yoosuf, Yosof,
Yosuf, Yousof, Yousuf,
Yusof

Z

Zaaef
Hospitable

Zaakher
Rich - Wealthy - Wise
Variants: *Zaakher,
Zaakhir, Zakher, Zakhir*

Zaaki
Blessed - Virtuous
Variants: *Zaky*

Zaatar
A type of herb.
Variants: *Zatar*

Zabeer
Handsome - Intelligent -
Witty
Variants: *Zabir*

Zabi
Gazelle

Zaboor
Brave - Lion
Variants: *Dhaboor, Zabur*

Zaeem
Guarantor - Leader -
Resolute
The name Zaeem is
mentioned in the Quran.
Variants: *Za'eem, Za'im,
Zaeim, Zaeym, Zaim*

Zafar
Triumph - Victory - Win
Variants: *Dafar, Dhafar,
Zafer*

Zafaruddin
Triumph of the Faith

Zafeer
Successful
Variants: *Dhafeer, Dhafir,
Zafir, Zefir*

Zafir
Successful

Zaghlul
Baby Pigeon
Variants: *Zaghlool*

Zahaar
Florist
Variants: *Zahhar*

Zahanat
Intelligence - Keeness
Turkish pronunciation of
Zahanah. (Also used in
Turkish)
Variants: *Dahanat,
Zahaanat*

Zahauddin
Supporter of Islam
Literally "radiance of the
faith".
Variants: *Zaha Uddin*

Zaheel
Sure of Heart
Variants: *Zahil, Zahil*

Zaheel
Sure of Heart

Zaheen
Intellectual - Intelligent -
Sagacious

Variants: *Dahin, Zahin,
Zehin*

Zaheer
Blossoming - Flourishing
- Glowing
Variants: *Zahir*

Zahi
Beautiful - Breeze -
Handsome - Radiant
Variants: *Zahee*

Zahian
Bright Day - Brilliant
Variants: *Dhahian,
Zahiaan, Zahyaan, Zahyan*

Zahid
Ascetic
Variants: *Zahed*

Zahir
Bright - Glowing
Variants: *Zaaher, Zaahir,
Zaher*

Zahirulhaq
Visible Truth
Variants: *Zaahirul Haq,
Zaherol Haq*

Zahl
Confidence - Sureness of
Heart

Zahou
Beautiful View - Blooming
Plant
Variants: *Zahu, Zahu*

Zahou
Beautiful View - Blooming
Plant

Zahran
Blossoming - Radiant
Variants: *Zahraan,*
Zehraan, Zehran

Zahri
Flower-like
Variants: *Zahry*

Zahrun
Blossom - Flower
Variants: *Zahroon*

Zahuk
Happy - Laughing

Zahun
Intelligent
Variants: *Zahoon*

Zahur
Radiant
Variants: *Zahoor*

Zahyan
Brilliant - Luminous

Zaifullah
God's Guest - Protected
by God

Zakaa
Intelligence - Keenness
Arabic for "intelligence",
"cleverness".
Variants: *Zaka*

Zakat
Alms - Purification

The name Zakat is
mentioned in the Quran.
Variants: *Zakaat, Zekat*

Zakawat
Intelligence - Keenness
Turkish pronunciation of
Zakawah. (Also used in
Turkish)
Variants: *Zakaawat*

Zaki
Blessed - Pious - Pure -
Righteous
Variants: *Zakee, Zaky*

Zakou
Growth - Increase
Variants: *Zaku*

Zakwan
Brilliant - Intelligent
Variants: *Zakwaan,*
Zekwan

Zaleeq
Eloquent - Fluent
Variants: *Zaliq*

Zaluj
Nimble - Sprightly
Variants: *Zalooj*

Zamaair
Consciences - Hearts -
Minds
Variants: *Zamaaer,*
Zamaer, Zamair

Zamaan
Age - Era - Time
Variants: *Zaman*

Zameel
Colleague - Companion

Zameer
Conscience - Heart -
Mind
Variants: *Dameer, Dhamir,*
Zamir, Zemir

Zamil
Follower

Zamin
Guarantor - Surety
Variants: *Damin,*
Dhaamin, Zaamen,
Zaamin, Zamen

Zamr
Lion's Roar

Zaraafat
Intelligence - Talent
Arabic for "intelligence",
"cleverness", "talent".
Variants: *Zarafat, Zerafat*

Zarar
Experienced - Intelligent
Variants: *Zaraar*

Zareeb
Attacker - Likeness -
Similarity
Variants: *Dharib, Zarib*

Zareef
Charming - Intelligent -
Witty
Variants: *Dharif, Zarif*

Zargham
Brave - Lion - Warrior

Can be pronounced with a long or short second "a" sound. (Zarghum or Zarghaam)

Zarib
Attacker - Striker

Zariyan
Dispersed

Zarnab
Fragrant Plant
Scientific name: Taxus baccata. (Also used in Persian)
Variants: *Zarnaab*

Zaufishan
Radiant - Spreader of Light
(Also used in Persian)
Variants: *Zaufeshan, Zaufishaan, Zofishan, Zowfishan*

Zauq
Enthusiasm - Joyfuless
Variants: *Dhawq, Zawq*

Zawal
Sundown
Variants: *Zawaal*

Zaweel
Motion - Movement
Variants: *Zawil*

Zawqi
Enthusiastic - Joyful
Variants: *Zawqee, Zawqy, Zowqi*

Zawri
Intelligent
Variants: *Zauri*

Zayd
Growth - Increase - Progress
The name *Zayd* is mentioned in the Quran.
Variants: *Zaed, Zaid, Zaide, Zeid, Zeyd*

Zayed
Increasing - Progressing - Prospering
Variants: *Zaayed, Zaayid, Zaied, Zayid*

Zayef
Hospitable
Variants: *Dayef, Dayif, Dhaye, Dhayif, Zaayef, Zaayif, Zayif*

Zayir
Roaring Lion
Variants: *Zayer*

Zayn
Adornment - Beauty - Excellence - Grace - Virtue
Variants: *Zain, Zaine, Zane, Zayne, Zein, Zeine, Zeyn, Zeyne*

Zaynul Abidin
Supporter of Islam
Literally meaning "adornment of the worshipers".
Variants: *Zaynulabidin*

Zayyan
Adorner - Beautifier - Decorator
Variants: *Zaiaan, Zaian, Zaiane, Zayaan, Zayan, Zayyaan, Zayyaane, Zayyane, Zeyan, Zeyyan*

Zeeshan
Dignified - Respected
Variants: *Zishan*

Zehn
Intellect - Psyche - Reason
Variants: *Zihn*

Ziauddin
Radiance of the Faith

Zidan
Growth - Increase - Progress
Variants: *Zidane, Ziedaan, Ziedan, Ziedane, Ziydaan, Ziydan, Ziydane, Zydaan, Zydaane, Zydan, Zydane*

Zihni
Intellectual - Reasonable - Understanding
Arabic for "intellectual", "understanding", "reasonable", "deep thinker".
Variants: *Dhehni, Zehni, Zihnee, Zihny*

Zikr
Mention - Remembrance
The name *Zikr* is mentioned in the Quran.
Variants: *Dhekr, Dhikr, Dikr, Zekr*

Zil Allah
God's Mercy - God's
Protection
Literally meaning "shade
of God".
Variants: *Zell Allah,*
Zilallah

Zil Elahi
God's Mercy - God's
Protection
Literally meaning "shade
of God". (Also used in
Urdu)
Variants: *Zill Elahi*

Zil Yazdan
God's Mercy - God's
Protection
Literally meaning "shade
of God". (Also used in
Persian, Urdu)
Variants: *Zil Yazdaan*

Zilal
Shade
The name Zilal is
mentioned in the Quran.
Variants: *Zelaal, Zelal,*
Zilaa, Zylal

Zill
Shade - Shadow
Variants: *Zel, Zell, Zil*

Zimr
Brave

Zirar
Warrior
The name of a Sahabi,
whose full name is Zirar
bin al-Azwar.
Variants: *Zerar, Ziraar*

Ziyad
Growth - Increase -
Progress
Ziyad is an indirect
Quranic name with the
same meaning as Zayd
and Zidan: growth,
progress, increase, and
being blessed by Allah.
Ziyad is derived from the
Z-Y-D Quranic root
which is used in a number
of places in the Quran,
such as in 10:26: "Those
who do good works shall
have a good reward and a
surplus. No darkness and
no ignominy shall cover
their faces. They are
destined for Paradise
wherein they shall dwell
forever."
Variants: *Zeyaad, Zeyad,*
Ziaad, Ziad, Ziyaad, Zyaad,
Zyad, Zyead

Zoomeer
Radiant
Literally "kind of light".
(Also used in Persian,
Urdu)
Variants: *Zoumeer, Zumir*

Zoraiz
Enlightener - Spreader of
Light
(Also used in Persian)
Variants: *Dhuraiz, Zoreez,*
Zoriz, Zouraiz, Zuriz

Zuaib
Guide
Variants: *Zoaib*

Zubaid
Gift from God
Variants: *Zobaid, Zubayd*

Zubair
Firm - Intelligent -
Powerful - Wise
Variants: *Zobair, Zobayr,*
Zubayr

Zufar
Brave
Variants: *Dhufar, Zofar,*
Zofer, Zufer

Zufunoon
Skilled - Talented
Literally "possessor of
many arts".
Variants: *Dhufunoon,*
Zufunun

Zuhain
Intelligent
Variants: *Zohain*

Zuhair
Blossom - Flower
Variants: *Zohair, Zohayr,*
Zuhayr

Zuhdi
Ascetic
Variants: *Zohdi*

Zuhni
Intelligent - Wise

Zulfateh
Guided

Zulfiqar
Name of the sword that

was given to Ali bin Abi Talib by Prophet Muhammad ﷺ. The word literally means "that which has vertebrae". Variants: *Zulfeqar, Zulfiqaar*

Zulghaffar
Forgiving

Zulghina
Wealthy

Zulhijjah
12th Month of the Hijri Calendar

Zulhimmah
Resolute - Resolved

Zulikram
Gracious - Honored
Variants: *Zolikram*

Zuljalal
Majestic - Mighty
The name Zuljalal is mentioned in the Quran.
Variants: *Zul Jalal, Zuljalaal*

Zulkifl
One of the prophets mentioned in the Quran (peace be upon him). He is the same as the Biblical Ezekiel.
Variants: *Dhulkifl, Zul Kifl, Zulkefl*

Zulnoon
Literally "possessor of the whale", a nickname for

prophet Yunus. The name Zulnoon is mentioned in the Quran.

Zulnoorain
Radiant
Zulnoorain was the nickname of Uthman ibn Affan, may Allah be pleased with him, literally meaning "possessor of two lights".
Variants: *Dhulnurain, Zul Nurain*

Zulqadr
Composed - Dignified

Zulqarnain
Two-horned
The name Zulqarnain is mentioned in the Quran.

Zultan
King - Leader
Urdu variant of Arabic Sultan. (Also used in Urdu)
Variants: *Zultaan*

Zumail
Companion - Friend
Ancient Arabic name without a clearly defined meaning, may be pet form of Zameel, meaning "colleague", "friend", "companion".

Zumar
Groups - Throngs
The name Zumar is mentioned in the Quran.

Variants: *Zomar, Zomer, Zumer*

Zuraib
Eloquent
Variants: *Dhuraib, Zoraib, Zorayb, Zurayb*

Zuraib
Attacker - Striker

Zuwail
Motion - Movement
Variants: *Zowail, Zowayl, Zuwayl*

Zuwayhir
Radiant
Variants: *Zowaihir*

Zyan
Adornment - Beautification - Decoration
Variants: *Zeyan, Ziyaan, Ziyan, Zyaan*

Zyaud Deen
Supporter of Islam
Literally "radiance of the faith".
Variants: *Zya Uddin, Zyaauddin, Zyauddin*

Zyauddeen
Supporter of Isam
Literally "brilliance of the faith".
Variants: *Diaudin, Dyauddin, Zya Uddin, Zyaaudin*

TRADITIONAL AND MODERN ARABIC BABY NAMES

Printed in Great Britain
by Amazon

23177779R00142